Dear Reader:

The book you are about to read is the latest bestseller from the St. Martin's True Crime Library, the imprint the New York Times calls "the leader in true crime!" Each month, we offer you a fascinating account of the latest, most sensational crime that has captured the national attention. St. Martin's is the publisher of bestselling true crime author and crime journalist Kieran Crowley, who explores the dark, deadly links between a prominent Manhattan surgeon and the disappearance of his wife fifteen years earlier in THE SURGEON'S WIFE. Suzy Spencer's BREAKING POINT guides readers through the tortuous twists and turns in the case of Andrea Yates, the Houston mother who drowned her five young children in the family's bathtub. In Edgar Award-nominated DARK DREAMS, legendary FBI profiler Roy Hazelwood and bestselling crime author Stephen G. Michaud shine light on the inner workings of America's most violent and depraved murderers. In the book you now hold, WHILE SHE SLEPT, Marion Collins details a troubled marriage that ended with a husband found guilty of his wife's murder.

St. Martin's True Crime Library gives you the stories behind the headlines. Our authors take you right to the scene of the crime and into the minds of the most notorious murderers to show you what really makes them tick. St. Martin's True Crime Library paperbacks are better than the most terrifying thriller, because it's all true! The next time you want a crackling good read, make sure it's got the St. Martin's True Crime Library logo on the spine—you'll be up all night!

Charles E. Spicer, Jr.
Executive Editor, St. Martin's True Crime Library

While She Slept

MARION COLLINS

St. Martin's Paperbacks

NOTE: If you purchased this book without a cover you should be aware that this book is stolen property. It was reported as "unsold and destroyed" to the publisher, and neither the author nor the publisher has received any payment for this "stripped book."

WHILE SHE SLEPT

Copyright © 2005 by Marion Collins.

Cover photo of Jill Cahill courtesy Russell family.
Photo of Jeff Cahill courtesy *Post-Standard*.
Photo of house © Stephen D. Cannerell / *The Post-Standard*.

All rights reserved. No part of this book may be used or reproduced in any manner whatsoever without written permission except in the case of brief quotations embodied in critical articles or reviews. For information address St. Martin's Press, 175 Fifth Avenue, New York, NY 10010.

ISBN: 0-312-93396-7
EAN: 80312-93396-8

Printed in the United States of America

St. Martin's Paperbacks edition / July 2005

St. Martin's Paperbacks are published by St. Martin's Press, 175 Fifth Avenue, New York, NY 10010.

10 9 8 7 6 5 4 3 2 1

Acknowledgments

Thanks to all of the friends who generously shared their memories of Jillian Catherine Russell Cahill and especially to her family, in whose hearts she lives on.

While She Slept

1

A Painful Death

Clinical technician Tyrone Hunter was on 2 North, the second-floor rehabilitation unit at the State University of New York Health Science Center in Syracuse, that Tuesday night of October 27, 1998, working the 3:00-to-11:30 P.M. shift. He was wheeling a patient back from a trip to the radiology unit on the third floor when he saw the man coming down the corridor.

A housekeeper, Tyrone thought at first—but his hospital uniform was all wrong. He was white, aged 35 to 40 and roughly 5'8". Instead of the dark blue Dickies work pants and the regulation shirt with the hospital logo on the left breast, he was wearing light-colored chinos and a blue polo shirt banded with thin horizontal white stripes. On his feet were brown Timberland boots, instead of the sneakers employees customarily wore to keep the noise down. Tyrone wondered if the guy was new–maybe he hadn't had time to get properly kitted out, and then he noticed the mop; hospital-issue dust-covers were white, this one was a pale blue.

He looked for the hospital I.D. that would have a name

and photograph with *Environmental Services* printed at the bottom, and as he drew level he saw a plastic tag—but where his picture should have been there was a blank piece of paper. When he noticed Tyrone staring, the man put his head down and took off down the wall, noisily banging the mop against the baseboards.

Licensed Practical Nurse Vicki Dunning was at the nurses' station in the middle of the unit just before 10:00 P.M. She was measuring out doses for the medication cart she took around to her patients every night when she noticed the man coming towards her. As he passed by, she gave him a friendly "Hi." He glanced at her from behind horn-rimmed glasses and for a few seconds, their eyes locked. My God, she thought, what an oddball, what's with the weird hair? It was an unnatural sandy color and somehow it didn't quite fit his head. He disappeared towards the coma unit at the end of the floor. Vicki returned to checking her meds.

Suddenly Tyrone was at her side. "Did you see that guy with the white pants and blue shirt who just came through here pushing a broom?" he asked. "I got a gut feeling, I don't think he belongs here." Vicki was suddenly filled with alarm. She pointed to her right. "You go that way and I'll go the other," she told him. She ran along to the end of the floor, but the man had vanished. Doubling back, she met Tyrone at the middle. "Did you find him?" He shook his head and her unease gave way to foreboding. "Come to Jill Cahill's room with me," she said.

With Vicki at his heels, Tyrone ran into room 2206, to where Jill had been moved just the day before. The room was darkened, lit only by a sliver of light from the bathroom. She lay motionless. He got down on his knees and peered under her bed.

Cleaner John George had also spotted the intruder in the hallway and noticed that his I.D. tag lacked a photo; Nurse Marie Morley saw him sweeping near the nursing station.

She said hello, he nodded in reply and before he dipped his head, she got a good look at his face. Cynthia Jones had also seen him. The mother of nine had been working as a clinical technician at the hospital for less than a year and it was her first day on the late afternoon shift, a change in schedule that tied in nicely with her early morning job as a manager at Wendy's. She was looking for a housekeeper to clean up a spill when she spotted him, but when she signaled that she needed help, he had just walked right by, heading towards room 2206. Uneasy, she went hunting for a supervisor. He had also noticed the stranger. Together they hurried towards the coma unit.

Back at the nurses' station Vicki called security, then ran to find Julie Labayewski, the registered nurse in charge. She was sitting doing paperwork when Nurse Lynne Penny came to tell her that a suspicious-looking character had been seen on the floor and everyone was looking for him. Julie jumped up and flew over to the emergency door across from the nurses' station to make sure it was locked, then followed Vicki into Jill's room. She knew that Vicki had put her to bed and had checked on her just minutes before; she had been sleeping peacefully.

Snapping on the light, Julie saw instantly that something was terribly wrong. Jill's face was blue. "I could see she was not breathing normally, she was taking very deep breaths, gasping for air," said Julie. "I wasn't even thinking that something had happened to her then. I called for extra help. Other nurses came, but her condition changed very rapidly, she went from gasping to having periods where she just wasn't breathing at all."

Tyrone was struck by the look of sheer panic on her face, and the pungent odor of bitter almonds. Even though he was coming down with a head cold, the acrid aroma hit him loud and clear.

Julie turned off Jill's feeding tube and laid her down flat.

She checked Jill's vital signs, her heart and lungs. She shined her flashlight into Jill's eyes looking for some sort of reaction. She called her name and shook her, willing her to give some sort of response. "When I went into the room she was awake, she opened her eyes and looked at me. Within a minute, I was no longer getting anything. She never managed to speak."

Then she saw the white substance on the neckline of Jill's hospital gown. Small lumps of it were scattered on her chest and caught in the hollow groove of her clavicle. When Julie touched it, the sticky mix rubbed off on her hands. Beside Jill's head, she found what looked like a small white bottle cap. "Something's been given to her. We have to get her out of here," she told Vicki. "We don't know what we are breathing here." They hauled the bed out of the room and into the staff dining area next to the nurses' station. In the few seconds it took them to get her there, Jill had stopped breathing altogether. Her pulse was gone. "Hit code blue!" Julie yelled.

She started CPR. Seconds later the organized chaos of a hospital emergency sprung into top gear. The crash team, which included the duty nursing supervisor, an anesthesiologist, a respiratory therapist and the house doctor, raced along the corridor. "I started the chest compressions, then a few minutes later the respiratory therapist changed places with me. At that point they did regain a pulse and moved Jill to the E.R. about a thousand feet down the hall. It was hectic," said Julie. "There were at least ten people around her bed."

The staff that worked feverishly to resuscitate her had cared for Jill since April when she was brought into the emergency room just before dawn, having been beaten into a coma by her husband, who had whacked her repeatedly with a baseball bat until half of her head was totally caved in and her beautiful face was barely recognizable.

For the next six months, she had clung to life. She had

endured fifteen surgeries, had become emaciated, her body able to cope with only small amounts of intravenous feeding. She'd battled brain damage, insufferable pain, deadly infections, and repeated bouts of meningitis. There had been numerous scares when they thought they'd lost her and just as often, she had fought back. She was making such progress that she didn't need constant supervision anymore. And although she was still in the coma unit, barring any unforeseen setbacks, the next step was a move to a rehabilitation facility.

That day had been one of the good ones. Her family was at the hospital as they had been practically every waking minute since neurosurgeon Gerard Rodziewicz and his skilled team removed the massive blood clot on her brain. They had watched her weather every setback, struggle to relearn the most basic functions and to simply speak the names of her children, Tim and Mary. Months after the awful night they were told she would not survive, Jill could move her left leg and arm, wanted to wash her own face and swallow. It was nothing short of a miracle.

Her father and brother had gone with her to her therapy session. One of the exercises that morning had her lying face down on the floor, in front of a large mirror. Beside it were Styrofoam blocks painted with stars and moons and crescents. When she was told to pick up a star, she'd pick up a star. When she was asked for a moon, she'd reach for a moon. When she was told to hand them to David, she'd hand them to David. Everyone was delighted.

Later, back in her room, propped up on her pillow, she'd downed a few mouthfuls of ice cream and in a halting whisper, managed to say a few words to them. Jill's sister Debbie had brought her a Bloomingdale's catalog, and she had pointed to all the clothes she liked. Now, just a few hours later, they were all back in the E.R. There were tubes, wires and monitors attached to her everywhere, the doctors and nurses that hovered over her were garbed in white hooded hazmat suits and cops were swarming over the building. For the rest of the night, and throughout the next day, she lay unconscious, her heart beating, kept alive by a respirator, her brain showing no sign of activity. As soon as doctors realized they were dealing with cyanide, they had pumped her full of antidote. But this time, the lionhearted Jill had no defenses left. The deadly poison had shut down her organs. Her distraught family and friends gathered at her bedside to say goodbye.

At 6.45 P.M. on Wednesday, October 28, with all hope of a recovery dashed forever, Jill Cahill was taken off life support. She was 41 years old. Her 38-year-old Ivy League–educated husband, whose vicious assault had put her in the hospital back on April 21, was the prime suspect.

2

The Cahill Boys

Nobody saw it coming. Jeremiah himself would not have prophesied such a future for James Francis Cahill III, who was born on July 28, 1960, the same day that the Republican National Convention chose Richard Nixon as their presidential candidate. James was the third of six kids, including two sets of twins, born to James (Jim) Cahill II and his wife, Patty, the former Patricia Morrissey. First to arrive in 1958 were Brian and Kevin, then James, known to everyone as Jeff; Mark and John came along a year later and were followed by the youngest, Tim, in 1962.

When John was born on July 22, 1961, he made history, according to an article that appeared in the next day's Syracuse *Post-Standard*, his mother being the only local woman to have given birth to five boys in three years. They all had nicknames: Mark was Nipper, Kevin became Howdy, John answered to Weasel and Jeff was known by a clutch of handles—at one time or another he'd been Jack, Bouncer and Spot.

The Cahills were like a small tribe, raised to believe that family came first. John described their steadfast bond at his brother's murder trial: "It was like having built-in friends," he said. "We didn't fight, we weren't allowed to. It wasn't tolerated by my father and mother and, quite honestly, it just wasn't something we did. I don't recall us ever wanting to get into down-and-out, drag-out fights. We were friends as well as brothers."

Because of Jim Cahill's work, the family relocated frequently. There were at least four or five moves while Jeff was a child, from Syracuse to Wellesley and Framingham in Massachusetts, to Pittsford, New York, and back to Syracuse where Jim took a job at the financial behemoth Merrill Lynch. During a six-month-long trial period, he commuted between Syracuse and Rochester, staying with the kids' grandmother in Syracuse and returning to his wife and children on weekends. With six little mouths to feed, Patty worked part-time as a substitute teacher to help make ends meet.

As the boys grew, their parents continued to urge them to stay close. "One night we were at the dinner table—I might have been in the eighth or ninth grade—and we were discussing who our best men would be when we got married," said John. "We all brought up our basketball buddies. My mother was listening patiently to this and she said, 'Well, that's all fine and dandy, but your brothers are your best friends and they will be the best men in your weddings or maybe I just won't come.' She made it clear that as a family we need to stick together, especially in something sacramental like a marriage."

In the early seventies, the family moved to Skaneateles, a pretty village on the shores of Skaneateles Lake, about eighteen miles from downtown Syracuse. Their spacious old wooden house at 10 Onondaga Street dated back to the Civil War era and had five bedrooms and an old cellar. It also was in dire need of some repair, but as Patty and young Jeff were the only ones handy with a hammer and nails, the quick makeover dragged on to become "a little thirty-year project," according to John.

The neighborhood was teeming with kids, large families being the norm in a small town; just down the street from the Cahills were ten Morrissey kids and eight little Majors. Jim and Patty enrolled the boys in the local school, sending them off in the morning with strict instructions to walk together until they got there. All were average students and they were all sports-mad; John played basketball, Jeff and Tim preferred soccer. Kevin also played soccer and, along with Brian and Mark, he took up tennis. Football wasn't an option—none of them were big enough. Jeff, who emerged as a bit of a loner, became a fisherman who liked getting up at the crack of dawn to go out on the lake and snag some rainbow trout.

Nothing was more important to Patty than her Catholic faith. She saw to it that the boys went to religious instruction classes at St. Mary's of the Lake Church through eighth grade. In high school she sent them to the neighboring town of Marcellus, where one of the priests, Father Nicholson, was especially skilled at communicating with teenagers. Unlike most youngsters who'd rather be outside kicking a ball than on their knees, none of the young Cahills seemed to have griped about having to attend either the classes or daily Mass.

Not that any of them dared disobey their martinet mother, who insisted on total obedience and chores taken care of at once. If any of her brood forgot to make his bed before he left the house, she would march into the school, find the culprit and take him home, where she'd stand over him as he smoothed the sheets and tucked in the blankets, before sending him back. One story that became embedded in local lore has Patty finding a *Playboy* magazine under one of their beds, hauling the alleged sinner out of class and making him sit in the living room for the rest of the day.

When the kids turned 16, they were looking for summer jobs. "My father made it quite clear that staying around the house in the summer was unacceptable. Whether it was [as] a dishwasher, a paper route—actually it had to be more than a paper route, we had to go out and get full-time employment to keep us busy," recalled John. But summers weren't all work and no fun. Every year, on the day after school finished, Patty piled them into the family station wagon—the kids dubbed it the Paddy Wagon—with a stack of comic books and warnings to behave for the seven-hour drive to Cape Cod where her doctor father had bought a vacation home in the 1950s. She had spent blissful summers there and was determined her gang would come to love it as much as she did.

The house was far from luxurious, not much more than a cabin, and habitable for only three or four months of the year, since it wasn't winterized. The place had no television and a radio that rarely worked, so the kids learned to entertain themselves. They were joined by Patty's brother John Morrissey and their four girl cousins from New York, and for week after glorious week, school was forgotten as they threw themselves wholeheartedly into games of kick-the-can and crab apple fights.

"One time Uncle John had your basic ten o'clock crab apple fight, and it was winding down, and we had a bag of apples left and my uncle said, 'Oh, what the hell,' and he threw them all up in the air and it was just like slow motion, they were just cascading through and landed on Jeff's head. The whole damn bag—great shot," said John. "While the others were at the beach, Jeff would disappear into the old toolshed where he'd spend hours knocking together pieces of wood and teaching himself how to make things. When the others broke their fishing rods they would bring them to him to fix.

"It's a small place, but it's quite comfortable," said

Morrissey, who would regale his awestruck young nephews with stories about New York's subways and ball teams. "We shared the property mutually and very congenially. It was a little tight on occasions, but it was never a problem. The kids got on deliriously well. I guess you would liken it to the Kennedy family, how tight that bond was. Everyone looked forward to the summers," he would later tell the court at Jeff's trial. As they grew up, the cousins drifted apart and saw less and less of each other. When the old man died, Patty and her three brothers inherited the house, though it was she who assumed responsibility for opening it each spring and closing it in early fall, and for maintaining it.

Jim Cahill joined his rambunctious clan for two of those weeks, and his arrival caused a great stir. "He would leave work from Syracuse and drive the seven hours, so we would wait up for him outside in the road or in the driveway until his headlights would appear. It was kind of exciting when he showed up, especially if he brought a new car," said John.

But not everyone thought the Cahill kids' life was idyllic. Their Skaneateles neighbors were aware of Patty's religious devotion and at least some of them thought it bordered on fanaticism. "I was friendly with Timothy, the youngest of the boys," said Tom Tulloch, whose father Donald was a doctor in the town. "They were a very odd family. They had all these weird names, Howdy, Nipper, Weasel; they were like the Seven Dwarfs. The mother was a very difficult, right-wing Catholic. She ruled the boys. If they didn't go to church every day, that was a sin. I remember she would sit in church always with gloves on and always in the same spot in the same pew facing the altar with the crucifix above it. I used to wonder about it, and then it dawned on me—she always sat at the right hand of God."

Michelle Morris also grew up with them. "Jeff was the year behind me in school," she said. "The twins, Brian and

Kevin, were in my grade. They were very different from each other. Brian—I don't remember him having a nickname—he was studious, but Howdy [Kevin], was just a jerk, obnoxious and arrogant. Jeff wasn't like that at all, he was very quiet, very studious and sports-minded. I didn't really get to know him until he and Jill were together." Suzanne (Zaney) Haux remembered Jeff as cute and popular, especially with the girls. "All of my friends had crushes on him," she said. But if Jeff knew he was the object of teenage passion, he didn't take advantage of it. No one can remember him dating or being involved with anyone.

With everything they needed within walking distance, and with college tuition bills looming, the boys knew cars were not going to be an option. In fact, the prospect of putting six kids through school was a daunting one for their parents. In 1978, Jim held a family meeting in which he leveled with them. They were men now and they needed to make choices. "I can't afford to put you all through college. You can put yourselves through college, you can pay for yourself, you can take years off and work or you can go into the military." Another alternative was to attend community college, and four of the boys, Jeff, John, Kevin and Tim, opted for that.

Since they had no wheels, Patty transformed herself into a shuttle service. She ferried them back and forth in the Paddy Wagon to Cayuga Community College after stopping off at the church for the mandatory early morning Mass. Jim took care of applying for financial aid and requisitioned anything they earned during the summer to help defray expenses. Their stockbroker father's careful planning paid off: all six boys achieved degrees from four-year schools. Jeff 's was in economics and was from the prestigious Cornell University in Ithaca, NY, an Ivy League school. His older brothers, Brian and Kevin, joined the CIA.

After graduating, Jeff followed his dad into the investment business and joined him at Merrill Lynch in Syracuse. By 1984, he had moved into an apartment in the city. His roommate was his childhood friend Mike Morrissey, who had graduated from the State University of New York at Buffalo and returned to Skaneateles after living for a spell in Rhode Island. He had just started working for Catholic Charities. He moved into the Syracuse digs after the pal Jeff had been sharing with found a job in Rochester and moved away.

At Merrill Lynch, Jeff was paid $578 every two weeks (around $15,000 a year) during the first few months while he was training. Once he was considered to be a fully fledged financial consultant, he made another $38 a week on top of that, with the promise of earning commissions on sales. Zaney Haux joined the company shortly after.

It was not an easy job. The company, which boasted a billion-dollar annual turnover, was a hard-nosed player in a cutthroat business. It had prospered by snapping up the brightest and most ambitious college grads and, after their initial rookie stint, throwing them into the deep end of the shark-filled stock trading pool, where they would either sink or swim. Most of them sunk: 70 to 90 percent of those confident young recruits fell by the wayside, according to Jeff's immediate boss at Merrill Lynch, Stanley Lis.

"It's a difficult position trying to manage people's money," he admitted in court. "There really isn't any secret degree or secret classes or courses that you can take that will make you successful. Back in the eighties the job was more of a sales position than a financial adviser and if you didn't sell, you didn't make any money. You have to be really thick-skinned in that business, because there is a lot of rejection from calling clients and trying to get them to talk to you. Most people have a hard time with that."

And the pace was unrelenting. "The first two years you literally live in the office, almost seven days a week, every night until eight or nine o'clock, compiling lists of people to contact, sending out letters to introduce yourselves and making numerous phone calls. They literally live on the phone trying to contact individuals." Mike Morrissey remembered Jeff leaving the apartment at 7 in the morning and returning around 5:00 P.M., when he'd bolt down a quick dinner and go straight back to work making cold calls to prospective clients until 9 or 10 at night. It was especially hard for anyone who was not really motivated by money.

Everything changed when Jeff was run over by romance. Mike had known Jill Russell, a pretty USAir flight attendant, for a couple of years before he moved in with Jeff, having bumped into her in the bars where the local kids hung out. One Friday night in the summer of 1986, he and Jeff decided to stop off for a few beers at a place on Geddes Street in Syracuse after a game of softball. That same night, Zaney, who shared a little house in Skaneateles with Jill and another friend, Martha Williams, had arranged to meet Jill after work at the same watering hole to kick the weekend off with several glasses of champagne. As happens when any bunch of healthy, attractive and available young people fueled by alcohol get together, they began scanning the room for potential romance.

"We were scoping the place out when Jill spotted Jeff and made a remark about him being cute," said Zaney. "I said, 'Him, Jeff Cahill? I know him and his friend. I grew up with them and I work at Merrill Lynch with Jeff.' And then I walked over to introduce them." She later said she hadn't much hope for her friend's chances with Jeff. "He didn't date much that I was aware of. He seemed to be a guys' kind of guy, always playing sports or watching sports and drinking with his buddies."

The few brews stretched into a fun-filled evening out and,

according to Mike, the attraction was instant between Jeff, then 26, and the three-years-older Jill. For his part, he enjoyed the company of the stunning 5'10", also blonde, Zaney. "We had a great time, we danced, had fun and went back to their house for like an after-hours party and stayed there most of the night."

Martha remembered Jill bursting into the house full of the new guy she had met. "She and Zaney had gone out for Happy Hour to a bar in Syracuse and when she came home she said, 'Oh, Martha, I just met this very cute boy, I just wanted to kiss him.' That was Jill's way of saying he was so adorable, she wanted to go out with him. I knew he was a hometown boy—I grew up in Syracuse, but I had lived in Skaneateles since 1974. At the time I was working at the Sherwood Inn alongside John Cahill—we called him Weasel—and I knew one of his other brothers from the bars around town. I remember when I met Kevin, a friend brought him up to my apartment and afterwards I said 'I don't ever want that guy in my house again.' He was just squirrelly-looking, I didn't like him at all. But I just loved Weasel. And when I met Jeff, he was adorable, so shy, so humble, he would do anything for you."

While many people found Jeff likeable, they found his brother Howdy off-putting and argumentative, according to Zaney. "Whatever the topic is, he knows everything there is to know about it and he likes to make others feel stupid. I suppose his friends unconditionally accept this behavior because they have known him his whole life and this is a part of who he is," said Zaney. "He has never had a girlfriend. I am sure that Howdy has suppressed emotions and feelings and this is part of the reason he argues. It is the only place he can feel superior, even though nobody really gives a hoot." She felt that he seemed to particularly resent her when she became engaged for a time to his best friend, Kevin Morrisscy.

From then on, Jeff spent very little time with his room-mate. "He was definitely in love," said Mike. "I'd only see him early in the morning or when he would stop after work to change his clothes and then he'd go right out to Skaneate-les where Jill was living. She was his first love, definitely." Michelle Morris wasn't surprised that the handsome, affable Jeff had never had a serious romance before he met Jill. "She was his first girlfriend. I think it's odd, but knowing him the way I do, I understand that. Girls weren't really a priority with him. I think that was the religious impact of the mother."

Although most of his belongings were still at the Syra-cuse apartment, Jeff and Jill had rented a small place on West Lake Road in Mandana. "Jill had her own furniture and things, so Jeff kind of left his stuff for me. Then I moved in with someone else and he never came back for it," Mike said at the trial.

Not everyone was thrilled that Jeff had found love; her son's new domestic arrangements deeply offended Patty, who viewed the relationship as the work of the Devil. "When they were dating and Jeff would sleep over at Jill's, [Patty] would leave notes on Jeff's car warning him, 'You are giving in to the biggest temptation that there is. You are going to go to Hell,'" recalled Debbie Jaeger, Jill's sister.

John also remembered the effect his brother's relationship with Jill had on the devout Patty. "There was some problem with my mother," he admitted. "They [Jeff and Jill] were spending a lot of time together, spending nights together, and that's something my mother wasn't particularly in favor of. She woke me one morning, around three in the morning, and said, 'I'm going out and I'll be back.' It's unusual for my mother to leave at three in the morning. And she went to his house, said hello to Jeff and said, 'I kind of disagree with you being here at this particular hour. If you want to marry this girl, that's a fine thing to do, but it would be appropriate for you to go back to your apartment and court her in the appropriate way.' "

But if his mother thought he was bound for Hell, Jeff was in Heaven. Not only had he discovered the joy of sex, but Jill, a beautiful blonde with a stunning figure, was a fun-loving free spirit who seized every new day as if it was an adventure. She was artistic, athletic and surrounded by equally attractive and entertaining friends. She didn't care how much money he made. In short, the love of his life turned out to be the very opposite of his controlling mother, who seemed at a loss on how to cope with her son's belated sexual awakening and emotional dependency on another woman. Her middle-of-the-night sermons stemmed from something deeper than the usual parental outrage that is often little more than a symptom of a generation gap.

"Patty Cahill is a person who uses religion as a shield instead of something that [you] would embrace to enhance your spirituality. She has a rather dysfunctional view of God and how [religion] should affect a person's life," contends Onondaga County District Attorney Bill Fitzpatrick.

But Jeff wasn't paying attention to his mother's entreaties, and to the sympathetic Jill he poured out his delight at having found love and his loathing of his job. Hawking financial services over the phone was not anything he enjoyed or was even good at. In fact, he was so spectacularly bad at it, his commissions were not enough to cover his salary, and he may have actually ended up owing Merrill Lynch money. In July 1986 he quit.

"I don't remember him working too long as a stockbroker, I remember him in a suit and tie when they first met. Both he and Zaney worked as stockbrokers and neither of them liked it," said Martha Williams. "So when he complained to Jill, she'd be like, 'If you hate it, what are you doing it for, then?'

She was one of those people who was never looking for anyone to pay her way. She was from a blue-collar, but very proud, family. She had wonderful parents who loved her very much and raised three wonderful kids in this little teeny house and you just knew that Joan was keeping those kids spotless and proud and happy. And Jill was such a happy person, so that when she met Jeff, I'm sure she was the one who said, 'Well, don't do it if you don't want to.' "

What he did want to do was to turn his natural talent for fixing things into a home renovation business. He began by taking a job with the Richard Meyer Window and Door Company replacing clapped-out windows. "Meyer did quality work," said John Cahill. "He was known around town as a quality workman and Jeff trained well and learned a lot and did things the right way. We all worked for Richey on and off through our high school years, but Jeff mastered the craft. For us it was more labor. He really enjoyed doing it and did it well."

After a few months, Jeff left, saying he wanted to be his own boss or—depending on who is telling the story—after an argument with Meyer, and launched his own construction outfit, naming it Common Structures. "He wasn't motivated by money. Starting out, he went out and knocked on doors, made telephone calls. It's the kind of business where you basically make cold calls, to call up and say, 'How are your windows and roof?' " said John.

"Back then Jeff was a totally different person. He was sweet and kind," said Zaney Haux. "He and Jill loved to do outdoor things together, make gifts for people, and be cozy alone together. They were both very artistic and creative. They loved their dogs—Snoofy and Nick."

Life was good that first year together. Yet, although they were obviously a couple, Jeff didn't always join in with Jill and her party-loving pals, who celebrated every holiday with enthusiasm. Her friend Katy Price later remembered looking for him at a Halloween party Jill threw before they were married. "She had a tape recorder rigged up in a tree outside playing all these scary sounds, and we sat around carving pumpkins, drinking and eating goodies, but Jeff wasn't there. Although they were deeply in love, It seemed to me he was never there."

By early next summer Jill was pregnant and talking about a wedding. "There never was a [formal] proposal," Zaney said. "They talked about getting married and finally decided it was time. They went to our friend, Georgia, who was a jeweler in town, and Jill picked out a dainty wedding band with diamond chips wrapped around her finger. It was barely noticeable it was so small, but she liked her jewelry to be understated and classic."

She made the announcement with her usual singular style. "She had told us, 'I've met someone,'" said Joan. "Then she sent Fred a Father's Day card with a picture of the five of us skiing, and inside she wrote, 'Well I'm pregnant and getting married—in that order. Tell Mallory she's going to have a cousin.' But she didn't tell us the date until two days before and we couldn't get off work to go."

"How can you get married in a Catholic church?" Joan wanted to know. Jill explained that since her first marriage in Fort Lauderdale was a civil wedding, it was not sanctioned by the clergy. Joan knew all about that. When she'd married Fred they had been wed in his church—she was Catholic, but Fred wasn't. "After we had the kids, we had nuns knocking on our door drumming up business," she says. "We went through another Catholic ceremony. The priest asked, 'Are you happily married?' By this time, we had three children and like all marriages, it had its ups and downs, so I said, 'Why do you ask?' and I was told, 'Well, the first doesn't count.'"

The Russells met their new son-in-law when Jill finally brought him home a few weeks after the wedding. "He was such a handsome boy, he looked like a young Robert Redford then," remembered Joan, who was convinced he had come along just at the right time. Jill called him The Prince, a nickname that cheerfully caught on with the rest of her family, who were charmed by her easy-going, sweet-natured husband.

Although delighted in her daughter's joy, she did have a beef with the newlyweds. "Getting pregnant and having to get married, that's what twenty-year-olds do. You two should know better," she told them. "Well, Jeff didn't want me on the pill," Jill replied

But if Jeff and Jill were delighted about the impending birth, Patty was not. Jill had been married before, though not in a Catholic church and therefore, "not in the eyes of God." And while Jill was undoubtedly enchanting and lovely, she was not what Patty had in mind for her son. She was more convinced than ever they were both on the road to eternal damnation and set about trying to save their souls. Martha Williams recalled being astounded when Jill described a bizarre scene that apparently unfolded: "They were going to get married and had taken a little house on the other side of the lake. [Jill] told me, 'Jeff's mother comes to our house and lets herself in. I wake up at six-thirty A.M. and there she is sitting on the edge of our bed, reading the Bible to us.'

"I don't know why I didn't protest more at the time. Patty was so against Jeff being with Jill, and now that Jill was pregnant, this was just the worst: I was a little more cynical and skeptical—being seven years older than Jill, I'd been around the block—and I should have pressed more. But I did ask her, 'How come Jeff lets his mother come in the house? Why don't you lock your house, number one, and why don't you put a bolt on your bedroom door besides? I can't imagine why he puts up with this.' And I told her, 'Jill, that is very strange. I'd be very nervous about getting into a family like that. You're going to have to live with your mother-in-law all your life.' But she was in love, they were in love, and when you looked at Jeff, he didn't seem like the rest of his family.

"Then when they did the right thing, [Patty] didn't go to the wedding. Mr. Cahill went. It was a very small group, eight or ten people," said Martha. "We all just went to the ceremony and then we went to dinner at this quiet little place down the other end of Skaneateles Lake. Nobody said anything about Patty, Jeff's mother, not being there."

Zaney was also at the wedding. "Jill looked so lovely. She wore a flowered dress, yellow with pink and blue flowers and it came from a store a friend of ours had in Syracuse. Patty didn't approve of the marriage at first, that was a well-known fact. They exchanged their vows at St. Ann's, a tiny church in Owasco, and then we went to the Glen Haven [at the south side of the lake, nestled in the foothills]. We sat around and talked, and it was very nice, very informal. Jim, Jeff's dad, was more supportive, but it seemed to me he wouldn't go that extra mile to get involved, because Patty wore the pants. She was very opinionated. We always knew what she thought about things, or she showed it by her body language. But Jill had this very easy-going manner and she was madly in love with Jeff, and to her, love conquered all."

Mike Morrissey also turned up to see his friend married and John Cahill stood up for his brother at the July 9 ceremony. "I was working at Cohen Textile Services at the time. And my wife, she was my fiancée at the time, or my girlfriend, was the office manager. Jeff called me on a Tuesday afternoon. He said, 'What are you doing on Thursday?' I said, 'I'm playing golf at Bellevue and I've got . . . 'I'm We chitchatted for four or five more minutes and . . . said, pened to say, 'What's going on Thursday?' A. I can break going to get married to Jill.' And I said . . . my golf game for that.'"

Everyone was very excited abo . . . e baby, who was to be

the first grandchild in the Cahill family. Even Patty had let her grudge drop and seemed to have lulled herself into denial over how the baby was actually procreated, prompting her daughter-in-law to remark to her mother, "She is so damned Catholic that I bet she hasn't had sex since she had her last kid."

3

The Golden Girl

The girl Jeff was so enamored of had grown up at 349 Morgan Street, Tonawanda, a small upstate New York town near Buffalo, ten miles from Niagara Falls. Jillian Catherine Russell arrived on March 9, 1957, two years after her older sister Debra Joan and two years before her brother David. Her dad, Fred, had been a U.S. Navy flier during the Korean War and her mother, Joan, would joke that every time Fred walked off the plane, she became pregnant. After leaving the service, he went to work for Spalding Fibre and became a foreman in the paper mill.

Jill thought she was an ugly duckling, despite the overwhelming evidence to the contrary. "She hated her crooked teeth, her long neck, there was something wrong with her nose and she thought she was going to be 6'3" like Fred," remembered Joan. "His mother had these deep wrinkles that ran down her cheeks, and he looks just like her. One day Jill came home, looked at me and announced, 'I'm going to kill myself when I am twenty-one. I look just like Fred, Fred looks just like Grandma Russell and I don't want these things on my face.'" Of course no one took her threat seriously and an aunt sent her a sympathy card on her 21st birthday. "She used to sit with an Ace bandage wrapped around her head so she wouldn't get a double chin," said Debbie. "She was always funny."

Money was scarce, but if the Russell kids were deprived of anything, they never knew it. To help stretch the family budget, Joan did odd jobs. One summer she worked at Helf 's, a hot dog and ice cream stand down the street. The children thought that was wonderful because she doled out free treats whenever they dropped by.

"Jill would play house and she'd be the dog. She could bark like a dog. She used to say she was going on the Letterman show to bark like a dog," said Debbie. Childhood friend Diane Russert also remembered Jill skipping around the yard imitating a horse.

"She loved animals," said Joan. "We had dogs when she was growing up. We had a hunting dog that Fred brought home, we called him Herman, the German. There was another mutt called Spot, and then we had Grace." The vet said she was part Irish setter, part greyhound, and she was entirely devoted to Jill, who'd found her wandering emaciated and trailed her home. "Can we keep her?" Jill had pleaded. "We'll give her a six-week trial," her parents agreed.

The young Russells attended local schools and in the summer the family went camping in Allegheny State Park for the last two weeks in July. "It was an itty bitty tent, 8' by 10' and there was no TV—the kids made their own amusement because there was nothing else to do," said Joan. "One year they spent a whole week covering a big rock with moss. I guess they thought it made it look prettier."

"The huge elephant rocks there date back to the Ice Age and the kids scampered all over them, especially Jill. She was fearless," said Fred. Joan remembered watching her with her heart in her mouth and she'd be yelling down, "Hi Mom."

"It was a lot of fun," said Debbie. "Our aunts, uncles and grandparents would visit and we'd sit around the campfire baking potatoes and singing songs. And Grandma would go pee behind a tree. We'd all do that." Diane tagged along with the Russells most summers. "The Park was a two-hour drive from Tonawanda. We slept in tents at first and then eventually we moved up to having a cabin, just a one-roomed thing. We were all crammed in there. I loved it because my family never took vacations and Jill's parents just treated me as one of their own kids." In winter, Fred and Joan would take the children back to the hills to teach them how to ski. Jill became an accomplished downhill skier.

Holidays were family affairs with aunts, uncles and cousins at Grandma's house. "She would give us a quarter to Pledge her furniture, so we were always asking, 'Grandma, can we wax the table for you?' She made us kiddy cocktails with maraschino cherries in them and at Christmas she'd add a little crème de menthe and wine," said Debbie.

Jill was a tomboy. She'd tag along with her dad, who coached David's Little League team. The youngsters affectionately called him Derf (Fred spelled backwards), and the nickname stuck—the family still often calls him by the moniker. "David was a good ballplayer and at that time girls didn't play. She would come to his games with me and get mad. She'd want to know, 'Why can't I go out there and play?'" said Fred. "She was also very independent. She wouldn't take anything from anybody, and she fiercely protected David. 'Don't pick on my little brother,' she would say."

During high school she worked as a lifeguard in the summer. "She'd leave the house, hit the porch and run the whole way. Jill never walked. She was go, go, go. Or she'd be on roller skates. She skated everywhere. She ran track one summer when she was in junior high. When she was eleven her coach put her in a race with thirteen-year-olds and she pissed everyone off by coming in first. And he couldn't give her anything because she wasn't in the right category."

She gave it up at fourteen when she got interested in boys—and one in particular, Steve Solomon. They'd meet at the little park near Niagara River and at the Riviera Theater, home of the Mighty Wurlitzer Pipe Organ in North Tonawanda where Wurlitzer had its factory and exported its world-renowned instruments as far away as New Zealand. "The balcony was the smoking and necking lounge," remembered Debbie. "Everyone went there. Then there were street parties. We'd go to each other's houses to play Ping-Pong and hide beer in the rafters." Diane Russert remembered hours spent singing along to Beatles records and hanging out at what was then a pretty lively downtown.

Debbie's boyfriend, Bill Jaeger, was especially fond of her younger sister, with whom he bantered good-naturedly. "When she was about fourteen, Jill disappeared on us one night. I dropped her off at Murphy's and she said she'd be back by nine, but by eleven she wasn't home and we couldn't find her. David was crying on the couch, 'I want my sister,' and she's walking around town with Bill. They had gone to the Woodshed Bar where you could sneak in the back if you were underage. She always looked older than she was. The night she went to Debbie's prom with Mark Smith she was the youngest one there and the only one who didn't get carded," said Joan.

Mark's father was the superintendent of schools and the Russells' small brown house was on what used to be known as the wrong side of the tracks, an accident of birth that didn't daunt Jill for a minute. "I will never forget when he rang up and asked her for a date," said Joan. "She hung up and looked at me and said, 'Oh, my God, Mom, you are not going to believe this. The upper-class just asked the lower-class for a date.'" She wore a gown made by her Aunt Ruth and didn't go to her own prom because by that time, Mark was in college.

After graduating Jill began studying art history at the State of New York Agricultural and Technical College in Canton with the idea of becoming a teacher. She had chosen the school to be near her boyfriend, who was going into his junior year at nearby St. Lawrence University. She went up to visit him and fell in love with the area. Two weeks after beginning her first semester, she fell out of love with Mark.

"Mister Pfister came along," said her mom. Steve Pfister, who is now a Washington lobbyist, was also a student at Canton. "He was so thrilled to be dating the prettiest girl in school. He wanted to marry her, but she said no. When she broke up with him he told me: 'Mrs. Russell, when I grow up, I am going to marry Jill.' We used to tease her that she should have."

With Steve consigned to history, and an associate degree in art in her pocket, Jill transferred to SUNY–Plattsburgh, in 1976 and met Rick Thomson, whose wealthy family operated several businesses, including Thomson Tours and the Pine Tree Point Resort on the St. Lawrence River, where Jill spent summers working at different restaurants. In the winter they'd fly up to Montreal where his parents had a chalet and fend off the Canadian cold wrapped in his mother's fur coats. But the romance was short-lived. The next Valentine's Day he sent her a diamond ring inside a Valentine's card. He wrote, "This is for you, Chipper—just in case you change your mind." Jill was not impressed.

In Plattsburgh Jill shared a house with a bunch of girls. One of them, Rosie Rausseux, had a brother who played in a band in Florida. Life was one big party. When Jill was more than halfway through her junior year she called home and told her parents that she and Rosie had decided not to finish school; they were off to Fort Lauderdale, "where the action is."

"There they got waitressing jobs at a local dive. It was named at the O. J. Simpson trial, there was some cocaine connection down there," said Debbie. "It was a party bar, a beach hangout with wet shirt contests. During that first year down there she met Greg Owens; she and Rosie were in a hospitality suite at Buttons with the band, and Greg was working for the bar that was running the drinks up to the room. She thought he was kinda cute."

"He *was* cute," said Joan, who went down to Fort Lauderdale to check him out for herself. On Memorial Day, 1979, Jill called her mom. "You'll never guess what I did today," she said excitedly. "Well, the way you are saying it, you either got engaged or got married," guessed Joan. "The second one is right," she said.

Nobody was surprised. Her family knew Jill would never follow the conventional path down the aisle, as Debbie had done two years earlier when she married Bill, her high school sweetheart. The traditional wedding had been such a blast that Debbie called from her honeymoon to ask, "Mom, were you at the reception? I don't remember seeing you there."

Back then, Jill did have some wedding plans of her own, according to Joan. "The day after Debbie got married we put [Jill] on the plane [the] next day to go to Texas to marry the [then] man in her life, Micky Maynard. She came back three weeks later. It didn't work out. It was hot and ugly and there were these little armadillo things. 'Mom, I got off the plane and hated Texas,' she said."

Greg had grown up in Skaneateles and was related to the people who owned the Owens Corning glass manufacturing empire, but wanted nothing to do with the family business. When Jill flipped for him he was tending bar and was an excellent water-skier. "He gave lessons," said Fred. "In fact, the year we were down there, he was training with the Olympic water-ski team. He had his own water-ski boat and everything." Jill quit the job and did some modeling. On one of her trips back home, she collected Grace the Wonder Dog.

"She got into that little car and drove back down to Florida with Grace sitting in the front seat just like a person," said Fred. "That dog was reincarnated. It knew what she was doing. At first it was falling off the seat when Jill would turn the corner, so it began to watch Jill, figure out when she was going left or right and lean into the turn."

One night she had called her mother and told her they nearly lost Grace when a firecracker had gone off and the dog bolted. They had searched the neighborhood for hours before giving up and going home, where they got a call from Buttons telling them she was there. When they went to retrieve her, she was sitting up on a stool at the bar. Another time they found her playing with a six-foot-long alligator.

At Jill's urging, David had also moved to Fort Lauderdale. "After I graduated from high school," he said, "I was looking around for something to do and Greg said, 'Why don't you come down to Florida? We'll get you a job tending bar.' So I talked to my buddy Kevin [Killian] and said, 'Let's do it.' The first three years we were down there we would go down after Thanksgiving and work right through Spring Break and then go back up north. We all lived about thirty miles north of Fort Lauderdale and had a boat on the lake there. Mom and Dad came down a lot."

Debbie recalled visiting her brother and sister in 1980. "It was our first vacation since we got married. Jill had told me they had an apartment with a golf course view and we went down there thinking we would be living in this fancy situation. She picked us up at the airport in this little white Triumph convertible, and she had on a little white outfit to match. We kept driving past all the nice places till we got to this little box house. You walked into the living/dining/kitchen room, there was a bedroom and a bathroom in the back and that was it. Jill and Greg, Kevin and David were all living in this place with

Grace and a brown dwarf rabbit named Barrington who left little pellets all over the place. Bill and I walked in and thought, 'What the hell are we doing here?' It was just a pit. Bill said, 'Jill, I can't believe you live like this,' and she replied, 'I know, isn't it awful?'"

Their summers were spent in Skaneateles where they bunked with Greg's mom and slept on a mattress propped up by cement blocks. Jill fell in love with the pretty little town and Greg promised her they would settle there. She took a job as a waitress on a dinner boat that ferried fifty people around the lake and met the then 20-year-old, equally fun-loving Zaney, who describes how they got the boats ship-shape before the passengers boarded. "We had to do the sanding, painting, and we had to do it by hand. But we had a riot, we'd sit up top and drink champagne, we'd get the dinners, and with five minutes left, we'd be passing out desserts."

Katy Price was 22 when she met Jill in 1980. "She and Greg were living at his mom's apartment on Genesee Street which was about five doors down from me—there was a beauty salon in the basement and a boutique where Jill later worked was on the main floor. I lived with my now ex-husband above Hahn's Pharmacy, it is now a health food store, and Martha lived above Fleur-De-Lis florist, three doors down. One day Al was talking to Greg and this woman is just tooling around on roller skates. We got chatting, realized our men were friends and hit it off instantly. We were always doing stuff together. She'd come over with her bunny and Grace and the two of us would go out on the lake on her Hobie Cat. Sometimes a bunch of us would go out on the water and tie all the boats together. We called them flotillas, there'd be about thirty boats tied together about a mile out of town. We'd drink beer and play Frisbee—they were really fun, fun times.

"I can still picture Grace on the boat, I had a dog too and

they'd sit together in the back. Everyone used to laugh at us. Grace looked like a greyhound, but she was red and neurotic as hell. She always had a little change purse in her mouth and she wouldn't go anywhere unless she had it. Jill would say to her, 'OK, I've got my purse, you've got your purse, let's go.' And Jill went everywhere on skates. She was the only person I knew who could go up and down stairs on roller skates. I lived two flights up and she'd hop in the door and roll around my house."

"She always seemed to have a Jeep—I remember a red one and an off-white one—and one day we were right outside the village when we ran out of gas on the hill just outside town. So we're stuck and we're like, 'For crying out loud, we're only two blocks from home and we're out of gas.' The top's off and everyone could see us and we just start rocking and rocking until the thing finally started rolling, and we rolled right down the hill and into a parking place.

"Greg was the nicest guy. You couldn't help but like him," said Katy. "He was doted upon by his mother, just the golden boy of Skaneateles. Everybody knew him and everybody loved him; he dressed cool, he looked cool and he was in Florida every winter, which, of course, made everyone jealous. She wrote me some letters from Florida that were absolutely hysterical."

According to Debbie, the marriage began to falter when Greg made some acquaintances that her sister did not approve of and she made it clear to him that she didn't want to get involved with them. Dave recalled Jill deciding to tell her husband it was over. "The thing with Greg started going on the rocks, and I wanted to break off my own engagement and right after the holidays, we were sitting at a bar in Skaneateles talking about it, we had a couple of drinks and Jill said: 'To heck with this. We should just go down there and take care of this.' And that's what we did," he said. "I got out of Tonawanda, went to Jill's, packed the Jeep, attached the U-Haul and drove down to Florida. And Grace the Wonder Dog came too."

A year later, in 1983, the couple found themselves in divorce court. Yet despite the split, Jill still cared for him and remained close to his mother and sister, Lisa. Her parents were saddened by this turn of events since they had been genuinely fond of Greg. "Jill was just 22 when she met him," said Joan. "He was a poor little rich boy and he screwed up. The thing is, he was a really nice guy. We all could see why she fell in love with him."

Although her marriage was over, Jill stayed on in Skaneateles still living for a while with her former mother-in-law before moving in with Martha, whose neighbors were Katy's friend Michelle Morris and her husband, John Eppolito. Jill took a job at Morris's bar and grill on W. Genesee Street where she spilled the drinks and no one cared because she dazzled the customers. "She was a lovely girl, just wanted to talk to everybody, she had an absolutely gorgeous face and a drop-dead figure, but she was wholesome," said Martha. "There was nothing seedy about Jill, she was not like a Britney Spears. Guys would ask her out and she was too naive to think anything but that they were just being wonderful and friendly. Even after people told her, 'Jill, these men want a date,' she would just laugh it off. But she would never go out with them."

Not only was she noticeable because she was so gorgeous and sociable, but she'd walk around town with her hand in Grace's mouth. It looked for all the world like the dog was holding her hand, and she'd sing to her, making up little songs off the top of her head. In summer she'd wear a straw hat with fresh flowers around the brim, a sundress and flip-flops. Walking with her mutt by her side or gliding along on skates, with her blonde hair flying behind her and her megawatt smile, the ex–Mrs. Owens turned heads wherever she went.

None of this escaped Larry Van Olstein, a renowned local artist who created the posters for the 1980 Olympic Games in Lake Placid. He was in his late forties when they became an item. "They had a lot in common," said Fred. "They were both artists and he was really a handsome man. She was like a sponge, she just absorbed everything. They went to all these art shows all over New England. I think she viewed it as just another experience. He kept showing up years later and Jill would explain his fascination with her as, 'I'm the one who got away.' " Debbie says he really cared for Jill. "I think that would have ended up being something permanent if there hadn't been such an age difference."

But Jill had other plans. What she wanted was a career. She decided she had found the perfect one when one of her friends from the St. Lawrence River resorts, Chris Tormey, who had just started work as a flight attendant at Empire Air, persuaded her to give it a try. The day before her interview she bought a white wool suit and when she walked in the door, the recruiter told her, "You've got the job." For the next eight weeks, she and Chris commuted to the flight school in Utica, NY, where the airline was based. In her uniform, Jill was a knockout. During one flight, Buffalo-born rocker Rick James became so smitten with her that he badgered her for a date. He didn't get anywhere either.

One admirer who did break down her resistance was Sal Piamonte, who was then the youngest district attorney in Syracuse and blessed with a gift of gab that could silence an Irishman. "Sal swept her off her feet," said Debbie. "They actually ended up getting engaged, and even bought a house together. Then he took her home to meet the folks. She burst out laughing and told me, 'Just sitting around the table with that Italian family I just knew, that is *not* going to work.' Sal had also become abusive. One night he went to meet an old girlfriend and Jill couldn't find him. She told me he showed up late and the ensuing confrontation turned nasty. That ended the relationship." Zaney Haux remembered being in their house when he erupted at Jill and threw a large jug full of coins at her.

Onondaga County District Attorney William Fitzpatrick recalled meeting Jill a few times when she was dating Sal. "The last time I saw her alive was when my wife and I were traveling to Florida and she happened to be in the crew. She was strikingly beautiful and I am stammering and trying to explain [to my wife] just who this gorgeous flight attendant was. She had broken up with Sal by then."

Jill loved flying, but it played havoc with her sinuses and killed her social life. She was required to carry a beeper at all times and when it buzzed, she had to be at the airport ready to fly in two hours. She was just about to be assigned a regular schedule when Empire was bought by Allegheny Airlines and in turn incorporated into US Airways. She found herself back on constant call.

Being Jill, she made the best of it. "One time while stationed at Cortland, she called up Zaney in the middle of a snowstorm saying, 'Come on down, I got this hotel room and we'll party down here.' I can't believe that we drove through that weather and we partied until four in the morning," said Katy. "We were literally jumping up and down on the bed and doing everything you're just not supposed to do and we're laughing and laughing. And when we tried to go to sleep in these two king-sized beds, we got the giggles like little kids and giggled until six. If you said something dumb she'd smack you in the forehead with the palm of her hand. And you never knew when that was coming."

"Every Christmas we would rent a limo, get dressed up and drink champagne in the back while driving around town," said Zaney. "It sounds extravagant, but it wasn't, not at Skaneateles prices. We did it sometimes in the city too. One time when Jill had just started seeing Jeff we went to a place at the bottom of the Plaza Hotel and they wanted forty dollars each to get in. Jill talked to the guys at the door and got us in for twenty dollars apiece."

In 1985 Jill moved with Martha and Zaney to a little 1800s house on East Lake Road. "Flying meant she had strange hours, she'd be gone for a few days, then back." said Martha. "I worked evenings as a waitress at the Sherwood Inn and then at [the now defunct] Possibilities, so she would wait for me to get home from work and then we'd go out roller skating like around midnight. We'd go grocery shopping and roll around the aisles. I can still picture her making apple crisps at two o'clock in the morning in her big bunny slippers. During the day we'd do a lot of swimming and sun bathing; she was an incredible water-skier, she was one of those trick–water-skiers, in fact, she could water-ski without skis."

"She just loved life," said Zaney. "She loved sunny days, loved the snow. She had this big furry rabbit hat that was just awesome and we would have snow fights, make snow angels, go cross-country skiing or ice skating. Every day was a jolly holiday when I lived with Jill. Amber Calloway, Katy, Jill and I, we were The Four Musketeers. We were always highlighting our hair. Jill just loved to highlight our hair. We'd have champagne and do our hair and find out about the men in our lives. We'd go out every Wednesday in Syracuse—they used to have something called Jazz in the Plaza there—and we'd meet to catch up."

But still, there was something missing. When she turned 29, Jill looked hard at her life and it came up short. She envied Debbie, happily married to a good man and now the mother of two sweet little kids. "Just before she met Jeff we got a letter from her that showed she had reached a point where she was assessing her situation," said Joan. "In it she wrote, 'Mom, you've got Dad, Debbie has Bill, Mark and Mallory. I've got no husband and no family.'"

And so when she glanced around that crowded Syracuse

bar and lit on Jeff Cahill, it seemed to her and her friends that this was an ideal match. "Jill had been through these relationships, Greg, then Sal and the artist she dated, but they weren't the kind of people you'd want to settle down and have a family with," said Zaney. "And here's Jeff, who came from this nice Irish Catholic family, who everybody loves and he works at Merrill Lynch and has a brother working on Wall Street, another in the CIA; he's an athlete and a nice guy who liked to keep to himself. It was perfect."

4

The Married Life

After the wedding, Jeff and Jill moved into a rented house down the street from Jeff's parents' home at 10 Onondaga Street. Jill worked for the airline until her advancing pregnancy made squeezing into her flight attendant's uniform impossible. She walked away with no regrets. Her ex-stockbroker husband had taken to his new career like a duck to water and, like most expectant young couples, they were deliriously happy and filled with optimism for the future.

"They were like soul mates," said Debbie's sister-in-law, Rita Winkowski. "They did things together. He would build the furniture and she would paint it, he would build a bird-house and she would paint it." Jeff was amiable and obliging. "I remember the winter after they were married, I was living in Syracuse and it snowed so much," recalled Martha Williams. "I had asthma at the time. I couldn't even get out to clear it and Jill said, 'Oh, don't worry, I'll send Jeff over.' Next morning I'd look out my window and there was Jeff out shoveling my driveway and not even knocking at my door to tell me he was there. He'd just stop off on his way to work, shovel my driveway and be gone."

Despite Martha's earlier warnings to Jill about marrying into the Cahill clan, by the time their new daughter-in-law presented them with little Timothy Egan Cahill on February 2, 1988, even Patty had come around, although she did have an odd way of trumpeting her joy at the birth of her first grandson. "I got a call from Jeff's mother," said Joan. "I picked up the phone and this great booming voice rang out: 'Mrs. Russell? This is Patty Cahill. That's a very nice specimen my son and your daughter have come up with.'" Joan was temporarily struck dumb as, without missing a beat, Patty thundered on: "I have a very large house with five bedrooms. When Jill comes home from the hospital, you can stay with me and go and do whatever it is the mothers of girls do."

"When I next spoke to Jill I asked her, 'What does your mother-in-law look like? She sounds like a sergeant major.' Jill said, 'Oh, no, she's just a little thing.' The next weekend was when I was supposed to be going to stay with Patty, but we had this huge storm and I couldn't get out of town. It ended up that Debbie and Mallory and I went down the following weekend and by that time she didn't want me to stay." With the arrival of Tim, Patty got a nickname all her own. To differentiate between the two grandmothers, she became Nano. Grandma Joan was called Mame by little Mallory Jaeger.

"We never really knew Jill's in-laws," said Joan. "I was only ever in her home once and that was when Tim made his first communion. I always thought that we weren't good enough for them. We are just ordinary working people while Jeff's grandfather and Patty's father were doctors."

Although Joan is convinced that Patty never approved of Jill because she had been married before, the two women got along well at first. Jill made an effort to fit in. While she was pregnant she had started going to church, which she hadn't done for years, and Sunday mornings she and Jeff joined his folks for Mass at St. Mary's. Jill had stopped working to become a full-time mom. She told her mother that in the Cahill family, the women stayed home with the kids and the husband took care of the money and worked. Patty had raised six boys and knew pretty much everything there was to know about looking after babies. Besides, she was nearby to help out and Jill's own parents were a three-hour drive away.

Apart from both loving Jeff, they had something else in common. "Jill was a total clothes horse and she had great taste. She was into Laura Ashley and also had this kind of medieval clothing, like jackets that the men would wear back then, like with ruffles sticking out the sleeves. She was always on the cutting edge, wearing things that everyone else wanted to have as soon as they saw them," said Katy Price. "Patty had a quite wealthy and privileged upbringing and she had some amazing clothes from the fifties, really formal, kind of Jackie Kennedy stuff with long, slim skirts. She gave some of them to Jill and Jill wore them a lot."

Although the birth of their son had been extremely difficult for the petite Jill, Jeff wanted to have another baby right away. The doctors told her she should wait for a while, she needed to heal completely after Tim. She was very, very thin and the pregnancy and labor had taken a toll on her tiny body. Despite their warnings, shortly after, she was expecting again. Mary Catherine arrived on July 15, 1990, three months premature and weighing just over two pounds. Jill pumped her own milk and spent every day in the hospital with her baby daughter until she could come home, while Jeff and her in-laws looked after Tim.

But though she was minute, little Mary was tough—she thrived enough to be discharged in September. Although in looks she took after her dad, she picked up all Jill's quirky habits like standing on one leg and bending the other one to rest the sole of her foot against the inside of her knee. Tim turned out to be the spitting image of his mom.

Jill and Jeff had a good-natured rivalry going on with his younger brother John and his wife, Darlene. Both women were pregnant at the same time and Darlene had her heart set on producing the first Cahill granddaughter. "We were looking forward to having a girl, and Jill beat us by three weeks," said John. "It wasn't fair."

During Jeff's trial for Jill's murder, John described how the two couples swapped notes whenever they got together. "We'd talk about parenting, just the natural stuff, diapers, how to stop the kids' crying." Jeff had been particularly good at teaching the kids hand/eye coordination. John recalled him doing drills with Tim when the tot was just two. His children enjoyed visiting and his daughters thought Jill was wonderful because she'd let them play dress up. "She was fun and my girls just loved being around her, they liked being around her kids. It was kind of like going to a camp up there. Jeff would take [my son] Joe and Tim and go out and do guy things, and my three girls and Jill would do girl things." Elizabeth was especially close to her aunt. "They both had beautiful blonde hair," he said.

With two kids growing rapidly, Jeff and Jill had been looking for a home to buy and found the perfect place at 2444 East Lake Road in Spafford, just outside Skaneateles and about fifteen miles southwest of Syracuse. The single-story pale green farmhouse, built in 1890 by a farmer named Karlic, sat on a good-sized piece of land on a gentle hill and had an unobstructed view of Skaneateles Lake. They could afford it because it was in desperate need of attention.

It became their pride and joy. Gene Beckeman, a friend of Jeff's, who had also been a friend of Greg Owens, described the house as pretty much a shambles when they bought it. "I helped them move in," he said at the trial. "The previous owner had started renovating it and it hadn't been completed, so Jeff finished it. It was basically somewhat of a fixer-upper. I worked on the floors and helped him pour his basement floor. Several years later, Jeff added the second floor himself."

"It was an adorable little house," remembered Martha, "and Jeff was always working on it. At the time, he was making a living selling windows, Jill was always stenciling things, hand-painting the furniture, and they seemed very happy for a while."

It was a storybook life, at least on the outside. "Her kitchen was the cutest little place you ever saw in your life," says Katy. "She made curtains from this really cool cotton material that had an unusual print and came from France. Amber used to sell really good fabric and she would give Jill all her samples.

"She sewed little pink pom-poms on the bottom of everything, on the bottom of the lampshades. She painted everything all different colors; the hutch would have trim that would be like the vines painted down the legs of the kitchen table, every detail was tied into the next detail. She had little fairy lights above her cupboards and she had two big birdcages for her cockatiels, Cozy and Powderpuff. Cozy was real smart, you'd walk in and start singing "A Spoonful of Sugar," and it would finish the song for you. It was just a silly place, all chaos between the dogs and the birds and the kids, a great place to sit and hang out. I think it must have been her favorite room, it's where she always was."

Jill loved making things to delight her youngsters. One winter Tim and Mary stepped off the school bus to find a life-size snow sculpture of a unicorn underneath the old 1800s street lamp in front of their house. "Here's this unicorn laying in the snow. She used an icicle for its horn and it was the most beautiful, magical thing I ever saw," remembered Katy. "Who has a unicorn waiting for you when you come home from school?"

Although the old farmhouse fairly oozed whimsical charm, it was cramped, said Debbie. "From the front door, there was the living room and a little alcove area where they would put their Christmas tree. The kitchen was on the right and then there was the mudroom and to the right of the mudroom there was a pantry. At the top of the stairs was Tim's bedroom, to the right was the bathroom, Mary's room and Jill and Jeff's room. The stairs were treacherous, you had to walk down them sideways. The Cahills fixed them, when they cleaned up the house."

Every fall they'd pile into the car and drive to Tonawanda for Thanksgiving at Fred and Joan's. Jill stayed close to her family; she had promised her parents after the children were born that she would bring them home often and made the trip north once a month, depending on the winter weather, and Debbie and Bill and their kids drove down to Skaneateles from their home outside Buffalo especially during the warm summer months. "The first three or four years of their marriage was very happy," said Joan. "I thought Jeff was great. When I called and Jill was out, he would chat on the phone for half an hour. Even towards the end, we all thought, 'Good old Jeff.' "

Jill kept up with her old party-going pals, Zaney, Katy and Amber. Jeff was a homebody and was perfectly happy for his wife to enjoy her "girls' nights out" with her buddies. "He knew we all liked to go out and he could join us or not and he didn't care. When she was with us 'downtowns' he'd stay home because he didn't like going out much," said Zaney. When they dropped by the house, he'd stick around for a little while sipping a beer, and then disappear, leaving the women to quaff their favorite champagne and talk.

Those friendships sustained all four women. Whenever one of them had a problem, the other three would be steadfastly in their corner. "I would say, 'I hate my job,' I hated working for Merrill Lynch. And when I decided to go back to school and be a teacher and they were so supportive, they all kept saying, 'Do it, Zaney, you'll make such a great teacher.'

Jill especially had a way of making you feel really great. Here's this gorgeous girl who was very smart and funny and very good at pulling prank jokes and she was brilliant at not sweating the small stuff and enjoyed every moment."

The only sour note was their fractured relationship with the King family, who lived up the hill from them; Jill told her friends that they were always doing strange things. After she died, it emerged that it was Jeff who was doing the antagonizing. But he made Jill wary of them, claiming the Kings were messing with their mutual utility and water lines while they were in the process of installing a pond on their [the Kings'] property. And since the blameless Kings were not locals, they were easy to pick on.

When she had moved to East Lake Road, Jill had drawn up an ambitious plan to transform her yard. "She got into gardening because of my mother," said Katy. "We went up to her house, this was about fifteen years ago, it was a beautiful summer's day and everything was in bloom. Mom is Mother Nature, and she had this huge garden with perennials and trees and a pool—she does it all herself—and Jill was like, 'Oh, my God, this is so beautiful. What's this and this and this?' She started really getting into it. I think she realized she could connect her artistic side through this living stuff."

Around this time, Katy moved to Pennsylvania and Jill grew closer to Katy's friend, Michelle Morris. They would talk every day on the phone about their kids and their flowers. They'd trade cuttings and fantasize about making money fixing up gardens for their neighbors. Dr. John Eppolito remembered his wife planning out their yard one shimmering May morning when Jill waved her arms around like a maestro conducting an orchestra: "The roses need to go here, and I see this all lined with lavender, poppies over here with delphiniums and foxgloves," then pointing to the lake side of the house, she looked at Michelle and they chimed in unison, "And the white garden should go there."

Zaney knew that Jill, unlike her more comfortably off friends, was looking for a way to supplement the family budget, because Jeff's income barely covered their expenses. She began to notice that he seemed different, somehow less comfortable in his own skin. "His whole look started to change. I would come by and talk to him and I thought he didn't look good, I thought it was the stress [over their dwindling finances]. I thought people took advantage of his niceness and I would tell him, 'You have to be harder.' I used to give him advice, I'd asked Jill, 'What can I do to help out?' and that's when she said she was thinking about getting the business with the flowers going."

In 1990, Jill and Michelle took a course at Syracuse University along with Cathy McDonald, who was married to a local realtor and lived farther down East Lake Road. The classes motivated them to strike out on their own; Jill would dream up the ideas and draft the plans, Michelle would keep the books and Cathy's connections would have commissions rolling in. After shelling out for a few basic supplies, they rolled up their sleeves and went to work.

Jill came up with the company name, Flower Fairies. "We can't call ourselves that," Michelle had protested. "I remember when we went to the courthouse to get our business certificate, writing that down on official documents was mind-boggling to me. I couldn't believe I was actually doing this, I was the scientist, after all, I was a nurse by trade," she said. But word quickly spread that there was a new ground force in the local garden renovation business and commissions came flooding in. "We did no advertising whatsoever, we had to work a schedule that worked for us because our children were priority number one. I did the scientific part of it and Jill was the artist. We taught each other as we went along and got to the point where we knew exactly what the other was thinking."

They started on a small scale and soon progressed to landscaping the lavish new homes springing up all around the affluent little town. They had few overheads; in the new developments, construction crews cleared away boulders and other obstacles to let them turn what had been piles of rocks and clay into virtual Gardens of Eden. "Her gardens were phenomenal. Everything she touched turned beautiful," said Zaney. "Their own houses were beautiful, even the little cottage she rented with Jeff before they were married was beautiful." In her yard she created a rockery and pond that one contractor estimated would have cost $15,000 if she'd hired a builder.

It helped too that Patty took the children to Cape Cod for the first two weeks every summer after school was out and Jill could throw herself wholeheartedly into her job. For the first year, the business teetered along. After initial outlays, it netted her just $300, but their customer list was growing, they had learned quickly from their early mistakes and the partners thought that they could realistically expect to earn around $20,000 each in their second year of operation.

Jill and Michelle grew even closer outside business hours. "We have a place down on Hilton Head, and she and I would go on vacation together with the kids and it was great fun," said Michelle. "We'd drive down there over the Easter break and the husbands stayed home. The first time we went we took a baby-sitter with us, but Tim ended up with chicken pox and she had to turn around and go right back. We did that for a couple of years and then she couldn't afford it anymore."

While Flower Fairies was taking off, Common Structures was struggling. Jeff couldn't bring himself to charge his friends and neighbors as much as he should have for repairs and he was hopeless at billing for what he was owed. "I knew that they were having money problems," said Michelle.

At his trial details of how feckless he was about money emerged when invoices he had submitted to an elderly lady

were read aloud in court. One satisfied customer, George
(Woody) Malone traveled from his home in South Carolina
to be a character witness for him. The eight-year Air Force
vet, who'd served in Japan, had a sheaf of bills Jeff had submitted to elderly Maria Crouse, whose house he'd refur-
bished a couple of years before: "Fix down spout, no charge,
five minutes' work, repair of a hole in the soffit, rear corner
of house, primed areas ready to paint, thirty-five dollars, repair of front light, brick molding, both old, looks like both
outside and top, replace lower windows, lower window stop
was rotten, repair rotten area of the garage door, remove rotten wood and filled with, forty dollars.

"It says, just send this [to] me whenever," read Malone
and went on to list repairing broken tiles and regrouting the
bathroom and vanity, removing tar from gutters, sealing
joints, resetting corner tiles and countertop. The entire bill
amounted to just over $150.

"We didn't have any secrets, Jill was very honest about
the financial strain she was under. There was one job he took
on which went very bad. He ended up working for a very
long time on a project and then he never got paid, and that
really put them behind the eight ball. He didn't have a contract and the guy said it wasn't done in the time allotted or
something. But I really don't know if that's what happened."
She did notice a change in Jeff's behavior after that and said
it seemed to be the beginning of the end of financial stability
for the couple. After that he would lie about money and began bouncing checks. Jill blamed him for taking on the job
without a contract.

Whether Jeff's version, the one that trickled down to
Michelle, was fact or fiction, it was just part of the problem.
It was obvious that Jeff had lost interest in going to work. Jill
used to say she had three kids, Mary, Tim and Jeff, and to get
anything done around the place, she had to tell him what to
do. He had struck out on his own because he wanted to be his

own boss, but was unwilling or unable to put in the hours any new venture requires before it becomes viable.

One of his clients, Edward Mazur, who shared Jill's love of gardening and would ask her advice about flowers and plants, described a typical day for the court: "I couldn't get him up to the house on time because he was putting the kids on the school bus or he had to leave early because he had to pick them up. Sometimes it was quite late when he showed up, nine-thirty or nine-forty-five A.M. He'd get the kids on the bus, make sure they were all right, then he had to go pick up supplies. I didn't care because I knew the work was good."

Bill Jaeger wondered how Jeff made any money at all. "Debbie would come home from visiting Jill and say Jeff was fooling around with the kids. It would be a weekday and I'd say, 'I know guys who work for themselves and they are working seven days a week.' I talked to Jeff one time about his business and it didn't seem to me like he knew what he was doing. People who work for themselves can only take on so much, then they have to hire people. He never wanted to hire anyone. When you went to his house it didn't look like much was happening. If someone is working as a contractor you would expect to see a pickup truck, equipment, supplies, around the yard. I never saw any of that."

Joan remembered calling Jill one morning and Jeff picked up. "It kinda shocked me, I hadn't expected him to answer," she said. "When Jill got on the phone I could hear him asking, 'What the heck is she so surprised about?' She told him, 'She thought you'd be working.' Jeff grew angry, 'Fuck your mother,' he shouted and stormed out of the room."

By now the only time the couple would go out together was to attend Tim's baseball games and go to church. Jill kept up her friendships with her girlfriends, but Jeff had given up a social life. He had also lost interest in their home. "She used to complain, 'I can't even have people over. I have all these friends and nowhere to entertain them.' He would always talk big, he was going to put this big extension on, but it was never done. Jill made it look good. She had fresh flowers everywhere," said Rita, who remembered walking away from the house thinking, "I don't know how she lives in this." "What you did see was a cosmetic fix. When you looked closely you could see Jill's artistic cover-up."

"That's what made the house attractive, but it needed a lot of work," said Debbie. "For instance, they had an old toilet with a handle high up that you have to pull. That broke and he would never fix it. The kids could never flush the toilet because they couldn't reach it. There was no money to do anything. She was trying to get him to take a regular nine-to-five job with full-time benefits." Around the summer of 1995 Debbie thought that Jill didn't seem as happy as she had been. It wasn't anything she said in particular, it was just a feeling Debbie had.

Dave Russell met his brother-in-law only once, and didn't like him at all. "There was a five-year period when I had gotten married, and between work and marriage and everything, I didn't go back up north for almost five years. Jill came down a couple of times, but without him. I had been up a couple of times prior to that and went to see her, but he was never around, out on a job or something.

"About two years before it happened, Debbie met me at Buffalo airport and we drove down to Skaneateles. Jill was defensive about him then. I had been a tiny kid growing up and all of a sudden I got big. Jill was very petite and she had explained to Jeff that I was a big guy. The first thing that came out of his mouth was, 'Huh, Jill told me you were fat.' I thought, 'Well, that's a nice way to start off.' Minutes later we are all in the back yard playing baseball. Jeff never bothered to really talk to me, he was too involved playing ball with Tim, who was about nine then. He would never look you in the face when he did talk to you. It was just very weird."

"As time went on she started dropping hints that Jeff was avoiding responsibility and not holding up his end of the deal," said Katy. "She had to be the adult, and I think that's ultimately what started them falling apart—she needed a man and she had another little boy to take care of, then she started seeing him quite differently.

"He was so irresponsible. Jill would say, 'Look at this, this has got to be fixed and this has got to be moved, and he'd just be out there day after day playing with the kids. And I know people weren't too happy with the jobs he did. He had this reputation that he knew what he was doing, but he really didn't. I think it was something he just thought up one day where he could have his own hours and not really work. Jill was the only one making money and then he'd get in an argument because she'd buy plants, she bought the pool, bought everything she had. He just didn't understand.

"I noticed that they didn't seem to do anything together the last couple of years—Jill would do things with her friends, Jeff with his family, but they never seemed to go anywhere as a couple. He rarely went to Buffalo with her to visit her folks, which I thought was nuts since they're so fun! Come to think of it, it was almost like he was pulling away from her and giving her all this freedom to kind of set her up.

"Then she'd go buy clothes—she did have a weakness for clothes. She was a terrible person to go shopping with, because she'd sit there and say, 'You have to have it, you know you are not going to stop thinking about it. Just buy it!' To this day I'll see something—the other day I bought a pair of black shantung silk capri pants with little cocktail glasses embroidered on them, they're hysterical and they were, like, ten dollars on sale from seventy dollars, and I'm going, 'Where am I going to wear these things?' And I can hear Jill: 'You gotta get these, where else are you going to see something like this?' He got mad at her for being extravagant, but she earned it. She worked her butt off."

The more Jill earned and plowed into the family budget, the less support she got from her husband, and when she tried to expand her business and solve their cash flow problem, he pulled the rug out from under her. Flower Fairies was doing so well that in 1996 when a Skaneateles nursery went up for sale, Cathy, Michelle and Jill decided to buy it. At first Jill wasn't keen on the idea, but the others talked her into it. Cathy's husband, Tom, was going to finance it. She called Debbie to say it was a done deal. Then in one of their increasingly frequent squabbles over money, Jill had told Jeff, "If this goes through, I am going to work as hard as I can, and I'm leaving you."

Her threat didn't motivate him to take his job more seriously, as she'd hoped. Instead it prompted him to sabotage the whole scheme. He called Tom McDonald and told him, "Don't go ahead with this, Jill has no work ethic and she's not going to follow through." Understandably, McDonald pulled out. And while Jill had initially been ambivalent about the purchase, concerned that it wouldn't leave her enough time for Tim and Mary, she had to be humiliated by having her husband undermine her.

He reacted to her success by doing even less as the family breadwinner and spending hours with Tim's Little League and soccer teams. The parents and kids loved him—and no wonder: he seemed to have all the time in the world for practices and games. "I've heard people describe him, and the reason he was popular as a soccer coach was that he was on the same mental level as the kids. I don't think this was a particularly mature individual," said Bill Fitzpatrick.

Jill stopped asking Jeff for help, relying on friends and family instead. Even her mother-in-law rolled up her sleeves and pitched in, although the experience wasn't always joyful, said Katy. "Patty was very masculine. One time I helped Jill put in one of her gardens—this was probably about a year or so before he killed her. Her mother-in-law came over to help. She was just all business. We would sit there and joke and were having fun, we were just planting plants and shoveling manure and stuff, and she was, 'Get this done, get this in.' She talked real tough and rough, and I'm thinking, 'What is your problem, lady? Lighten up.'"

Jill longed to have a swimming pool for the kids. Michelle told her go ahead, build one, she would lend her the money and Jill could pay her back from the jobs they worked together. Fred drove down from Tonawanda to help and remembered that Jeff didn't lift a finger. "Jill did most of the work," he says. "I helped her dig the trench to put in the electricity. He wasn't even around. All he did for the pool was to take the deck down."

When Jeff later rebuilt the deck, Fred discovered another side to his son-in-law that shocked him. "He stole the timber, he went to the lumber company, loaded his truck and took it home. Never paid for it. When the pool was put in he was in Cape Cod with the kids doing something to his mother's house. Jill wanted it in before the children came home as a surprise for them. When Jeff pulled into the driveway and saw it, he acted like a complete jerk. We were trying to get him to go in the pool and he would have nothing to do with it."

Joan put down his petulance to her belief that when all was said and done, Jeff was a mommy's boy. And to the Russells, the devout Patty seemed to be increasingly prone to impromptu bursts of religious fervor. During family gatherings, Joan and Fred were nonplussed by her party trick of spouting excerpts from the Bible at the drop of a hat. Joan recalls one particularly odd incident. "We were all there for Mary's birthday, and as Jill was cutting the cake, Patty stood up and started preaching. I couldn't deal with it; I excused myself and went to the bathroom. Later, I asked Jill, 'How do you stand it?' 'Oh, she doesn't come around much,' she said."

For a time Jill had been happy to let Patty take over the kids' religious education. "I thought Patty was a religious fanatic, but Jill had a lot of respect for her in the beginning. She wanted the children to learn the more traditional Catholic tenets," said Michelle.

"She tried to buy into the whole religion thing," said Debbie. "When she'd come home to Tonawanda she'd be trying to find out the time of the Masses to take the children to church. But that was for a very short period of time. Jeff went to church every day. She began to think there was something wrong here. There was one Thanksgiving and Christmas when Jill had had enough and refused to go to the Cahills'. Patty came up to the house and said to her, 'Who do you think you are? Do you think you are better than us?' Jill told her, 'No, I am just not going to put up with the bullshit. I think you people are nuts.' " Fred had a simpler take on Patty: "She is overly religious. In my estimation, she could run a cult."

5

Along Came Tom

On the Fourth of July, 1996, the cops arrived at the door in the middle of a family cookout. Jill thought it was a joke. But it was far from funny. They were there to arrest Jeff for bouncing some checks. She hurriedly tried to shoo the kids inside, but not before they saw their father handcuffed and stuffed into a police car. Jill took money out of her own account to buy money orders to cover whatever bills were owed.

That same summer the feud Jeff had engineered with the neighbors threatened to get out of hand. One morning Jill took her husband's truck to the nursery to pick up some plants and supplies, with Michelle following in her car. "We were coming into Syracuse to do a gardening job, I looked in my rearview mirror and the tire was falling off the truck. Someone had loosened all the bolts," she said. Jeff immediately blamed Dale King.

While their marriage was quietly unraveling, Jill kept her family in the dark. Loyal to a fault, she believed their problems would diminish if she could only get Jeff out from under his family's clutches, and she pleaded with him to look for work elsewhere. She would have done anything to keep her marriage going, according to her mother, who says Jill told her she would move anywhere, she'd move to Europe, to get him away from them. All she wanted was for him to get a regular job with benefits and normal hours; she would work at her business and they'd have a little place to stay.

Zaney thinks that by this time, Jill must have felt isolated. Although she had Michelle and Cathy to confide in, three of the Musketeers were no longer around: Amber was in Bedford, NY, Katy in Pennsylvania and Zaney was living in New Jersey. "When we moved away it was a different place," she said. "When Michelle, Cathy and Jill decided to go into business, it was really beneficial to all of them and they created beautiful, beautiful gardens. I've never seen anything like it. Jill had the most talent and she did it because she enjoyed it, but she also needed the money and that made all the difference. When Amber and I and Katy left, she got close to other people, but it wasn't the same. It was hard on her. She thought, 'Why am I here?' She knew what Florida was like, the New York winters were hard and she was on a tight budget and the people she was hanging out with didn't have those concerns."

"When I look back on it, there were clues," said Debbie. "They'd arrive for Thanksgiving and then Jeff would take the kids back home. She'd stay for the whole weekend, we would go Christmas shopping and her credit card was always being refused. And she'd say, 'Jeff must have transferred funds for the business,' and she'd try a different card." I didn't suspect, I didn't know anyone who ran their own business to know if that was typical, I just thought he was juggling things around, that's all. She had always told us that everything was fine, but she'd go home in the middle of winter and call, saying, 'The furnace is broken but we got a fire going and it's OK,' or 'The lights are out, something is wrong with the electric here.' But the truth was that Jeff was not paying the bills and they'd been cut off. And Jill didn't know because he'd been intercepting the mail to stop her finding out. She also didn't know they had no insurance."

What nobody knew then was that the endless money troubles were only deepening cracks that already existed in the marriage. Their sex life was nonexistent, she and Jeff hadn't made love for years. They had wanted more children, but after Mary, Jill was advised against another pregnancy. With hindsight, they should have seen the signs that situation was bleaker than Jill let on, said Joan. "She kept things to herself. After the fact it's so easy to say, 'Gosh, we should have picked up on that.' But she said nothing until six months before the end."

But Katy Price was beginning to get the picture. She knew her friend's life was in turmoil. She had returned to live in Skaneateles and was struck by the change in Jeff Cahill. He was no longer the amiable, laid back guy who'd pour a drink for his wife and her pals in the pretty kitchen where Jill always had music playing. "He had gotten more cynical and snotty. He would laugh to cover up, but you still got the drift of his comment not being very nice," she said. "When I was at their house Jeff became more stilted with me, whereas it had previously been easy to talk with him— we both like to read a lot—now he would just kind of stay outside or go somewhere when I visited."

The two women met several days a week to walk in the park near Skaneateles Lake, and during those hikes, Jill began to unburden herself. "As we were going around the track she would tell me all the stuff she was finding out and all the petty stuff he would pick on her about—the gall of him saying, 'Jeez, you're spending money on this and we just don't have it,' " says Katy. "And she had just fallen in love with Tom."

Tom Tulloch was tall, dark and handsome, and at 33, seven years younger than Jill. They met one night late in the summer of 1997 at the Skaneateles Country Club when Jill arrived with Amber Calloway and Tom was having dinner with Amber's fiancé, John Ginley. "She ended up down by the water with a bunch of people, Frank Sinatra was on the sound system and [Tom] danced with her and kissed her. Then she was like, 'Oh, my God, this is amazing,'" said Katy. It was instant attraction. It didn't hurt either that Tom admitted to harboring a longtime crush on her.

"We knew right away," he said. "I knew that it was an unhappy marriage. By the time we got involved she had been married for ten or eleven years. She told me that the marriage had ceased to be a marriage for years and that they barely tolerated each other for the sake of the children." At the time, Tom was living in Charlotte, North Carolina, where he was vice president of sales at National Processing, a company that facilitated the flow of payments between car rental firms and travel agencies. He had developed a software program to improve the system and was earning a comfortable salary.

The romance blossomed long distance and they spent hours on the phone, running up a $500 bill in one month alone. Tom set up an 800 number for her to call him any time. But physically getting together wasn't easy, even after the phone chats escalated into a full-blown affair. Amber and John's house in Bedford became a safe haven. Katy recalls going to a party there not long after Tom and Jill had become an item. "It was just an absolutely beautiful weekend, the leaves were peaking and Jill wanted to bring a bunch of flowers. I go to pick up Jill and she has buckets and buckets full of flowers. The whole car was full of them and we are going around every corner admiring the colors of the trees and going, 'Wow! Look how beautiful that is.'

"Someone at the party had infrared glasses. They were scary. You could see anything anyone is doing. At this point Jill had disappeared with Tom for a while and I was getting worried because it could end up getting back to Jeff. I think she ended up sleeping with him that night, probably for the first time, and then she was all sick about it, sick about being hungover and sick about being in love and maybe being caught. I think there must have been something more going on with Jeff because she seemed really worried about it."

Now everything had changed. Jill, who had been prepared to put up with a sexually unsatisfactory marriage, was dealing with a whole new set of emotions. "I don't think Jeff and Jill ever had a normal passionate relationship. I don't think Jill ever did until she met Tom. I don't think she ever really knew what that was like," said Katy. "I remember a couple of bizarre conversations with her when a bunch of us were out having drinks downtown and we were all like, 'You've never done that? Oh come oo-on, girl, get out there and do some of this stuff.'"

"We met very much on the fly for the most part and we didn't get to see a great deal of each other very often," said Tom. "Sometimes she would make an excuse to go out of town to meet a girlfriend and we would rendezvous somewhere. I would fly her to New York City or I would fly up to Syracuse and meet her at a bed and breakfast—that sort of thing." They tried to be very discreet, mingling in a group where their mutual attraction wouldn't be so obvious, meeting at Amber and John's home, at hotels in Manhattan when Tom had business in the city, at the Brae Loch Inn in Cazenovia near Syracuse, and in Buffalo, when Jill was visiting Debbie.

Since Halloween 1997 fell on a Friday, Rita and Tom Winkowski decided to throw a party the day after, on Saturday. Jill and Jeff and the kids drove up from Skaneateles and headed straight to Debbie's house where they were staying the night. As Debbie was helping her unload the luggage, Jill suddenly burst out, "I don't know if I am going to be married this time next year." Astonished, Debbie stared at her and asked, "What's going on?" Jill told her, "I'll explain it to you later," before clamming up.

When they arrived at the party, Jeff ran up to one of the bedrooms to change into the costume he had been keeping under wraps all day. When he reappeared, everyone was dumbstruck. He was dressed up as O. J. Simpson, and slung around his neck was a blonde Barbie doll. "He had wanted Jill to come as Nicole, but she wouldn't," said Joan.

"That Halloween was the most amount of time we spent with him," said Debbie. "He started drinking as soon as he got there. He seemed to be having fun and I thought, 'Isn't it great that Jeff is so relaxed, laughing and having a good time?' At one point he pinched Rita on the butt. I'd never seen him this way."

"It was out of character for Jeff, and I think it repulsed Jill," said Rita. As the evening wore down, Jill and the kids went home with Bill and Debbie, leaving Jeff to hang out with his new drinking buddies. "Tom, Jeff and a friend of ours named Steve, who was dressed as the Devil, decided to hit the local bars," said Rita. "They stayed out late and Jill called and reamed me out. She wanted to know where Jeff was and was upset they were out drinking. I thought she was worried he would drive drunk and I told her, 'No, it's OK, Steve is driving.' I called the bar they were at and told Steve, 'Get Jeff home.'" Bill admits thinking "Hey, he's in trouble, this is going to be good. I'm going to wait up and listen to this." But when he was dropped off there was no row, no argument. They found out later that they were living on handouts from his family and Jeff had arranged to meet his father to borrow money the next day. Jill was afraid he would turn up drunk.

With her marriage in ruins Jill turned to Michelle for support. "My husband was the one who actually saw this coming," she says. "I would say, 'No, no, no.' She was down here day after day. Whatever happened at home, she was safe here. From the fall of 1997, that whole winter right through until March, she would leave the house in the morning and she was here every day, and she was distraught, she wanted out, she didn't know the right thing to do. She would say, 'All I want to do is to be able to take my kids to Disneyland and not have my power cut off.'

"Jeff wrote checks that bounced everywhere, the fuel oil supplier wouldn't take their checks, he demanded cash. It was just so bad that they had to go to his parents to borrow thousands of dollars and they just kind of bailed him out. Things had gotten very bad and they were fighting. By the time Mary was two they stopped having intimate relations. Jill loved him, but not as a husband. She couldn't be sexual with him anymore. She said, 'I felt like I was having sex with my brother.'

"When I started hearing all these things, I was shocked. Like everyone else, I had thought Jeff and her were a match made in Heaven. I didn't think that much of it at the time, as I thought that maybe just the passion was gone from the marriage. I didn't take her literally as I should have. They always seemed to be kind to each other and loving."

But although she was hiding out at Michelle's, Jill never told her, or even Tom, what had really gone wrong between her and Jeff. "She was an intensely loyal person. I know there was a catalyst that ended their relationship as man and wife, but she never talked about it," said Tom. "She said it was all in the past, something had happened at summer camp or at a relative's wedding, I'm not sure, but she didn't want to share what it was. She said he'd always been a bit of a strange bird from the start. He was never much of a smoker or drinker, but he had started coming home and drinking a six pack of beer and lighting up a cigar, which was sort of out of character for him."

"The whole winter was very bad," said Michelle. "I was very fearful of him, not that I ever thought he'd hurt her like that, but he was driving around without any registration or insurance and I would say to her, 'Let's just call the cops and they will arrest him, then at least he'll be out of the house.'

She wouldn't do it. She would say, 'Michelle, he will not touch me because of the kids.'" But she did try to get help. That Christmas, one of their customers who was aware that she was having a horrible time gave her some money. In January 1998, Jill found a therapist and dragged Michelle along with her. The first words out of her mouth were, "My marriage is over, I just want help for the children and getting out of it." She pleaded with Jeff to go with her to marriage counseling, but he refused.

"Is there anyone else?" Debbie had wanted to know when they finally talked after the holidays. "No. Well, there could be," Jill had replied, then told her about Tom Tulloch. Her sister was upset: "I didn't want to hear any more," said Debbie. "Jill was meeting Tom. Jeff called my house and she told me, 'Tell him I am out with a girlfriend.' I thought, 'I can't get involved in this.' 'Don't put me in this position,' I told her. 'If you are going do this, you have got to take time to be yourself. What about your kids?'"

Jill said that Tom was in love with her and she had fallen for him. She wanted a divorce but she didn't have the money. She said they hung out with Amber and her husband, but they weren't dating. "I think she just needed someone to get through this," said Debbie. "He promised to love and cherish her and give her a great life, and she was stuck in a sexless marriage. She really believed he was her knight in shining armor, and I really believe if they'd met earlier it would have been wonderful for her. He loved her."

There is no doubt that Tom opened the escape hatch for Jill. Michelle says Jill would not have left Jeff if Tom had not come into her life. "She would have just gone on and occasionally gone out with her friends for fun, and flirt with guys as she loved to do. [Something] I recall her saying quite often was, all that she wanted was to be provided for and that shouldn't be too much to expect. She didn't have extravagant wants, she just wanted Jeff to provide for her and the kids."

In the next few weeks Debbie and Rita got Jill to admit what was going on. They were broke, Jeff wouldn't take a job and their health insurance had been cut off. She told them that she had come in late one night and parked her car in its usual place near the septic tank. She stepped out in the dark and fell into a hole. Jeff was supposedly doing something with the tank and had dug a pit, then left it uncovered.

She'd call Debbie and say, "My lights have been turned off, my heat has been turned off, I'm getting threatening voice mails from people saying he owes money . . . and if I don't get five hundred dollars by this time tomorrow I am going to do this or do that." Jeff also forged her signature on her checks and cashed them. He'd sent out checks to pay the bills and then put a stop on them.

He had started doing freaky things. "He would write to celebrities, sports heroes and politicians to get autographed pictures or souvenirs," said Debbie. "He would make up a story about his dad or uncle or someone was on their deathbed and the person was his favorite, and they'd send him stuff. I thought it was quite clever at the time and it didn't bother Jill at first. She truly was blinded to him for a long time. Now it is just another example of his sneaky, lying behavior."

"She said she'd find his pants stained with semen and when she asked him about it he would tell her, 'I have my needs,'" said Rita. "When she would come to Tonawanda and we would talk as girls and talk about sex, she would say, 'I just don't do it.' And we'd all laugh and say, 'Oh that's funny,' and then we found out that was absolutely true. She told us that she would try to initiate sex with him, but it would never happen. He had shut her out."

"Then his truck was impounded, he had no insurance, he hadn't paid the registration. He said he was taking care of all the financial stuff, he'd been a stockbroker, after all. When he was supposed to be working, he was at the library and having lunch with his mother. But Jill had been too private to tell her family, even Debbie, this before. I think she finally told us this stuff to try and explain what was going on."

"She was really at the point she needed to reach out," said Debbie. "In the spring before she died she called me at work and said, 'We are trying to get Jeff a different job. Is there any way we can get him a job in Buffalo?' She said one of her garden clients worked for Welch Allyn, a medical supplies business that was a really big deal, and she was trying to get him a job as a salesperson or something like that. She said, 'I am willing to move to the Midwest, I am willing to move anywhere to get him away from his family and his mother. We just have to start over again away from this influence here. Is there anything in Buffalo you know about?'

"I circulated his résumé around. Of course, he didn't have any qualifications for anything except stockbroking and being self-employed, and that never panned out, but he did go on several interviews that I know about and he turned jobs down because he didn't want to work for anybody. He'd come home and say, 'What if I don't like it?' 'Well, then you quit and look for something else,' she would tell him.

"About the same time he called me to tell me he was worried about Jill's mental state. He said she was depressed and crying all the time and saying things like she'd be better off dead." Alarmed, Debbie got on the phone immediately and Jill was fine. "I'm sure she may have been unhappy, but definitely not suicidal. He was quite the conniver."

She says Jill told her of another time when she was puttering around the house and reached into a cubbyhole and pulled out a box that was full of condoms and makeup. Jeff told her the makeup was for his job interviews. D.A. Fitzpatrick recounts what he was told: "She was in the kitchen, which had a recessed ceiling with track lighting above it, and as she was looking up, she noticed the outline or shadow of some object and so she removed a ceiling panel and found a box of condoms. She confronted Jeff with this and he came up with an explanation that he was holding them for his brother. Fitzpatrick went on to say that the explanation didn't make any sense to him because Jeff's brother was single and he assumed in this day and age he would be able to purchase his own prophylactics without embarrassment. "My thought was that Jeff was still engaged in some sort of sexual activity, but not with women and not with Jill."

Once they heard how dire her situation had become, her family urged Jill to get away from Jeff. All her friends and especially Tom Tulloch, had been egging her on to leave for months. Knowing she didn't have the money to pay for legal help, he made out a check to Michelle to hide the fact that the money had come from him. Michelle went with her when Jill hired divorce attorney Anthony DiCaprio to start formal separation proceedings on February 11.

Despite DiCaprio's repeated advice to get legal representation, Jeff did not retain a lawyer. According to Tom, Jill was very anxious that Jeff would not be blamed for the breakup, or that anyone would think it was caused by something he had done. She was very concerned about him, mentally and in every other way, and wanted the divorce to be amicable.

Two days later, he was arrested for shoplifting steak, lobster and shrimp from Wegmans supermarket in Auburn. The arresting officer noticed that the insurance on his truck had lapsed and took the vehicle off the road. Jill found out about it when she was rummaging through a drawer looking for something else and found the charge papers.

The incident was devastating for everyone. In his own defense, Jeff wrote to the Cayuga County District Attorney and laid the blame for his pilfering on his wife:

> *"This incident is unquestionably the most embarrassing and humiliating ever to happen to me. While sitting at Wegmans and waiting for Officer Cornell to come, my thoughts centered around the*

*disbelief that I had put myself in this position and
the events of the previous weeks had now culmi-
nated to this event.*

*About four weeks ago prior to the week of the
13th. Feb., my wife had given me three credit cards
that totaled approximately $3,000 in charges. I
certainly knew she had these cards but I didn't know
the debt was so enormous and that she now couldn't
make the payments. A week and a half later, I found
that she had been unfaithful to me and our two children (8 & 10 years old). She presented me with the
fact that she had an attorney and was given a statement of worth to fill out.*

*The dazed and despaired state that I was in
came from the crumbling state of my marriage, the
impending disruption of my children's lives, and
the financial pressures that were now becoming
overpowering with this added bad debt load.*

*The difficulties that this past month have brought
on me do not justify or explain what I did and yet I
do realize that I shouldn't have let those difficulties
be an excuse for what I did because it was wrong
and will NEVER happen again.*

He added that he had already contacted the store to
arrange for restitution "because that is the right thing to do."
He had learned his lesson and accepted that, despite his
problems, robbery was not a solution.

"When Jill confronted him about it, he got down on his
knees, then rolled into the fetal position and begged her not
to tell his mother," said Joan. "When she found out he'd told
the cops that she had run up thousands of dollars of debt on
her credit card and she was having an affair, she really went
off the deep end at that." Jill made a copy of the report and
left it at Michelle's house. "Anything she had of value, she

would bring it here. It was just very sad and heart-wrenching to go through all that," said her friend.

In March, Tom packed up his belongings and drove back to Skaneateles through a blinding snowstorm. Even though he was now living just a few miles away, they were careful not to flaunt their relationship. "I saw her on very rare occasions after returning from Charlotte," he said. "Occasionally we'd just walk by each other in town and just smile, not even stop to talk, it was just a chance to see each other. Jill and my sister Laurie attended the same aerobics class in a church in downtown Skaneateles and sometimes Jill would pass a note to her and Laurie would drop by my office and hand it in. One time she gave Laurie a beautiful bouquet of yellow tulips to give to me."

When they did get together, Katy said she provided cover. "They'd meet every now and then near where I was living and we'd have breakfast so she could say, 'I was at Katy's house, I met Katy,' it gave it the patina of truth. But she was so in love with Tom and it was all she could think of. It was like, 'Why can't Jeff be nice about this and let me go? Why does it have to be a problem?' I don't think she realized how obsessed he was."

Katy was wrong, Jill was very aware of how unhealthy the atmosphere had become. Midway through April, she called her mother. "This is so hard, Mom," she told her and started to cry. Joan's stomach lurched and she wanted to get there as fast as she could. "Do you want me to come?" she asked. But Jill had gotten control of herself and said, "No, Mom, I'll be all right."

A couple of weeks before her husband erupted into a murderous rage, Dave got a call from his sister. "Tom was meeting some business clients down in Fort Lauderdale and she was going to meet him. She wanted me to call the house and leave a message that I'd pick her up or something—obviously she didn't want Jeff to find out. That never developed because he assaulted her," he said. "I had no idea what she was dealing with, she kept it to herself. She didn't want anyone to know or burden them with it. That was Jill, she'd deal with whatever she had to deal with."

While her home life was falling apart, Flower Fairies was raking in orders. The McDonalds had them landscaping and building gardens all around town. "It was a good-going business—better than anything Jeff did. Here's a guy with an Ivy League education, who got a job as a stockbroker and threw it all up to become a jack-of-all-trades. I think he had real trouble with authority. People were beginning to say, 'What did she ever see in him? He's a ne'er-do-well.' She was moving on and he couldn't handle it," said Tom.

6

The Ticking Bomb

What finally pushed Jill to the edge was the discovery of a cable protruding from the telephone. She followed it down into the basement where she saw it was attached to a voice-activated recorder. She was furious and confronted Jeff about it. They argued and as the row turned nasty, Jeff knocked her to the floor, twisted her arm behind her back and ripped the telephone cord out of the jack. She told Michelle that he had shoved her against the wall and she'd grabbed a knife.

Next day she had handed over the tape machine and the cassette to the Eppolitos for safekeeping and poured out the ominous story. "She was terribly upset because she had said things on the phone to Katy, incriminating things that he could use, and that's when she pulled a knife on him. That's when things were getting really bad. "I was like, 'Oh, my God, I can't believe this,' " said Michelle. "I just wanted her out of there. I told her, 'Do what you want to do, but get out. Come over here, I have a room, go to Buffalo, go back with your family.' I tried, but she was very headstrong. She said, 'Nothing will happen to me, because of the children,' and I told her, 'OK, but take care of it.' Michelle drew some comfort from the fact that Jill was adamant she was in no danger.

Over the last few years his family, who were fully aware that there was something wrong between Jeff and his wife far beyond having to bankroll their work-shy son, had given up any pretense of liking Jill. "They didn't treat her nicely, they didn't support her and she would get really sad about it," said Zaney. "She'd get the children ready to go to church and they excluded her. They'd go out and invite Jeff and the kids along and not invite her. Patty would say very edgy and crass things to Jill. Some spiritual thing like Easter, they'd be all ready to visit and they'd call and say, 'Jeff, bring the kids over.' They'd do things within their family and not ask her to join them. And that hurt her."

Michelle may have believed Jill when she said she was on top of the worsening situation at home, but she wasn't. It was fast spinning out of control. A few days later, Jill was heading over to the Eppolitos' house on a Friday morning when she caught sight of Jeff on her tail. He followed her down the one-lane road and when she turned into a driveway in front of Michelle's neighbor's house, he pulled in right behind her. When the neighbor heard angry voices, he went to his window and saw them yelling at each other before Jeff backed out and took off.

"When she arrived she said, 'Michelle, lock your doors and windows, don't let Jeff in the house.' This was new, I'd never heard her say anything like this before. Skaneateles is the kind of place you never lock your doors, I leave my keys in the car. After that incident, my husband told me, 'She can't come here anymore. We can't take the risk, we don't know what he's going to do.' I was very upset about it, she needed someplace to go and I felt I was letting her down. We met on Monday morning and I had to tell her. I said, 'Jill, you just have to take care of this. He's still out there driving around with no registration or insurance, call the cops and have him arrested.' I had the phone in my hand and I was pleading with her, 'Call, please call, right now.' "

Even though Jill had assured the Eppolitos over and over that Jeff would never do anything violent, John and Michelle had an alarm system installed in their house. "I was afraid, he knew she was here all the time. And he didn't like me because for some reason, he got it into his head that I always got exactly what I wanted," said Michelle. "They would make me stuff for Christmas and one year I wanted this pretty little birdhouse and he wouldn't make it for me. He told Jill, 'She gets everything she wants, I'm not making it for her.' I never knew why he thought that."

On April 9, with a settlement hammered out, Jeff and Jill signed separation papers at Anthony DiCaprio's office. They agreed to share custody of the children, who would live with their mother one week and their father the next, and both could visit with them a couple of times on the weeks they didn't have them. They were to equally split birthdays and holidays, Jeff was to pay $400 a month in child support. Jill didn't ask for and would receive no alimony; instead she agreed to take $75 a week to give up any claim to the home where she'd lived for nearly ten years. Jeff got the house and had to pay off the balance of the $86,000 mortgage. Jill was given "a reasonable time" to move out, and for the next five years, she could raid her treasured garden of any of the trees, shrubs or flowers she had planted. They also promised not to harass each other.

In fact, the separation agreement showed just how little there was to divvy up and revealed the depth of the financial hole they were in. Common Structures, Jeff's flailing business, made just $35,765 in the year used to calculate their earnings; Jill's fledgling landscaping enterprise netted just $300. She had to pay credit card bills amounting to $1,380 and her outstanding $2,000 student loan. Jeff was liable for a further $10,501 in credit card charges and took sole responsibility for repaying the $17,000 he owed his brother Mark, and for $12,000 he had borrowed from his father.

Although on the surface the decision was mutual and the split amicable, the tension between them was building. Broke and in debt, there was no way Jill could afford to move out without help. Again, Tom Tulloch told her not to worry about money, he'd been trying to get her away from Jeff for months and said he would put down the deposit on new digs. Despite her repeated protests that she wasn't afraid, he was desperately unhappy she was still living under the same roof as her estranged husband, especially since Jeff's threatening behavior had forced the Eppolitos to roll up the welcome mat.

"She knew it wasn't good. But what could she do? She had her children. By this time something was not right. So what do you do? You spend as little time as you can at home. She was busy being places, that's why she went to Michelle's, but she was trying to keep some normalcy for the children and she never felt that he was going to harm her. She always said Jeff couldn't hurt a flea. I look back at her saying that—I think she believed it for a while, but in the end it became a blanket statement to protect everyone else, all her loved ones," said Zaney, who had barely survived a terrifying encounter with a stalker three years before and understood what Jill was dealing with.

"He had started working out in the basement. That was unusual, he'd never done that. She should have been out of there sooner, but it's hard when you don't have the cash, and knowing that Jeff has already manipulated certain situations, he's already lied to people and created stories. Jill knew he was doing that, Tom knew that. She just wanted to keep the peace until she was completely out. She almost made it. He was freakish for a while and she knew she had to get away. You see it, you know there's danger. When someone has decided to do something to you, they are very sneaky, very clever and have a different mind-set. They can manipulate you because they know you are afraid and they know when to be sweet to get what they want. And you don't know what to do. Jill was aware of all this and I have no doubt she was doing everything she could.

"You don't want to burden anyone. When I was going through my thing, Jill helped me every step of the way. And this is happening to her three years later. She had been experiencing some stuff, you think it's just dumb things when it starts and then it gets stranger and it's difficult to get out. She had two kids in the school system, they loved the school, this was where her family and her business were. And Jeff had us all fooled."

Jill went house hunting. Although she was planning a new start, she had no desire to cut Jeff out of Tim and Mary's lives or even out of her own, says Joan. Nor had she any plans to move away from Skaneateles—she would never do that to Jeff, he loves his kids too much, she told her mom. In the same conversation just before her world imploded, she admitted that she was heartbroken about the disintegration of her marriage. She didn't hate Jeff. "He's one of the nicest people I've ever met," she'd said.

Tom found her a small place in Skaneateles Falls on the outskirts of the village and they arranged to have lunch on Tuesday, April 21, when he would give her a check for the deposit. It was to be their first meeting since he moved back into the area the month before. The next weekend Jill and the children were driving to Tonawanda to spend a week with her family. She said that the trip would give them both some badly needed space. Before she left, she called the Eppolitos. "John took the phone and she told him that Jeff had signed the separation papers and that he seemed fine with everything, he was OK with it. And that's the last I heard from her," said Michelle.

Jill arrived at Debbie and Bill's at the wheel of a black Jeep Ranger borrowed from Jeff's brother Mark. It was no surprise to Zaney that, despite the deteriorating situation between his brother and Jill, Mark let her run about in his car. "He was always friendly with Jill," she said. "He lived in New York and when I moved to Paramus, New Jersey, and John and Amber were just outside the city, it was a great opportunity for us all to get together. When Jill would come into the city we'd try to do something together because Mark was so much fun, he was really cool. At one time I had a kind of crush on him, but there was another part of me that said if there was going to be anything between us, it would have happened by then. Jill and I used to say, 'Wouldn't it be great? We could be sisters-in-law,' but it never went that direction for Mark and me."

And so when Jeff's truck was impounded and he started using Jill's white Ford Taurus station wagon for his business, she drove the Jeep that Mark kept at his parents' home. By the time she reached Buffalo, she felt as if a cloud had lifted. "She had made a decision, she was moving on and she was excited about it," said Debbie. "She convinced me that all her bases were covered," agreed Rita. "She kept saying she was ready to move on, she seemed very strong, the kids would be fine, Jeff was fine with it. There was no going back. She did it all herself, the separation. She went to counseling. She pleaded with Patty to get Jeff to go too, but was told that all he had to do was to go to church and say his prayers.

Back in Skaneateles, her friends brooded over what had gone wrong. "I think Jeff just couldn't take the idea he couldn't have her. She was a trophy to him. In retrospect I think he's always been gay and was just always in denial about it," said Katy. "They loved each other as friends really, but I don't think either one of them had that spark and didn't really know they were missing it, and then of course, she gets to kind of resent it because you are really holding back half of what you are about and it just started eating away at him. It was like, 'You're my wife and we're together and we never tell anyone anything.' That was another thing. I think he realized she was talking to people. When I would drop in, he'd hover around me. At the time I thought he liked me too, but he was listening. He was so private, he didn't want anyone to know the details of his life, he was embarrassed by it."

Jill described her father-in-law, Jim Cahill, as a man who had never done a day's manual labor in his life. Tom figured that Jeff had been raised and continued to live in a male universe even though his mother was plainly the dominant parent. "He didn't really get women, didn't get that Mary was more sensitive, and didn't have time for her. But Tim was like his best friend. His father had a poor relationship with his wife. There was clearly emotional confusion. Who knows where these feelings come from?"

As the warmer spring days of 1998 enticed people back into their gardens, Flower Fairies was so inundated with offers the women had to turn work away. "Jill could pick and choose who she wanted to build a garden for. Her friends, the McDonalds, were her biggest clients," Tom added. "She was so smart, so quick on her feet. She was the first one in her family to go to college. She didn't like the area she grew up in and got out of Tonawanda. She was a free spirit and she was very determined to carve out a life she was happy with."

On the day Jill and the kids headed north, Jeff called Dr. William Allyn, whom he had known since they were in second grade. At the trial Dr. Allyn recalled picking up the phone early on Saturday, April 18. It was about 7:30 or 8:00 A.M. and Jeff said he needed to speak to him about a health-related problem. Even though he wasn't Jeff's usual doctor, Allyn told him to go downtown to his office, and although he didn't work Saturdays, one of the other physicians in the practice would see him. When Jeff said he didn't want to do that, Allyn told him to come to his house.

When he arrived, he complained of having problems sleeping; he was under great stress, his marriage was breaking up and he was worried about his children. He said that Jill and the children were in Buffalo and he was worried about that. He also told his friend that Jill had been seeing another man for the last two and a half months and he claimed to have stumbled on the affair while checking out their phone company bill.

Dr. Allyn said Jeff revealed a whole pattern of behavior that no one, apart from him, ever seems to have witnessed. According to him, Jill admitted to flirting with and kissing another man or men. He said there were times when she would become irrational, drink too much. He talked of her anger and rage. At one point he maintained she had become so overwrought that he felt he needed to remove the children from the house. He had driven them over to his parents' place and when he returned home, he described her as being irrational and extremely upset.

"He then told me that she had threatened to kill herself with a knife and then he said she had threatened him with a knife. According to Jeff, she said, 'If I stab myself, they'll think that you did it,' and he admitted that on several occasions, quarrels between him and Jill had erupted into violence."

Despite Jill's optimism that she was on the brink of a new life, there was some unfinished business that followed her to Tonawanda. During her visit, Amber Calloway called. At first Jill thought she was calling about her upcoming wedding to John Ginley that was to take place on the Fourth of July. She was to be in the wedding party and there were a thousand details to discuss, but Amber had something darker to talk about: Mark Cahill had bumped into her brother-in-law in the village and allegedly told him that Jill was having an affair and that she and Amber were the sluts of Skaneateles. Furious, Jill got on the phone with Jeff and read him the riot act. "So she was here thinking everything was fine, and the pot was being stirred in Skaneateles," said Debbie.

The night before Jill and the children were due to go home, Jeff called and Debbie again heard them exchange angry words. Troubled, she asked Jill if she was sure she wanted to go back, given what appeared to be her husband's foul mood. Her sister had shrugged the question off, but when she was packing up the Jeep, her mother sensed that she seemed loath to go. Usually, after spending a weekend with them she left early, around 1:00 or 2:00 P.M. so she didn't have to drive in the dark. But on this Sunday, she seemed to be dragging her feet. Quietly, she took Jill aside and asked her if she was afraid of going home. Were things okay with Jeff? Had he ever struck her, was she concerned that he would harm her? Jill had shaken her head. "Nah, Jeff loved his kids too much to ever lay a finger on me," she reassured Joan.

Nobody was happy to see her go. Bill and Debbie wanted her to reconsider. "If you need to stay, stay," they urged her. "If you think you are in any danger at all you have to stay." She told them the same thing: "Absolutely not. Jeff would never do anything to me, he loves those kids so much." Then she turned around, grinned at Debbie and said: "If Jeff tries to kill me, you get all my stuff."

Before she climbed in behind the wheel, Bill hugged her and told her, "I love you and I'll protect you." He couldn't get the picture of Jeff in his sick Halloween costume out of his head. He remembered being haunted by what his brother-in-law had told him at Rita's party. Patting the doll strung around his neck, Jeff hid leered, "People think it's Nicole, but it's actually Jill."

When she got home Jill called Debbie to tell her they had arrived safely and that everything between Jeff and her was fine, he had cleaned up the house and even had dinner ready and waiting for them. The next day she phoned again and this time she sounded nervous. Jeff was acting weird again: "He's been at Austin Park with the kids three times today." Then she said one last time, "But it's fine."

But things were far from fine. In the early hours of Tuesday morning, with their sleepy-eyed children, who had wakened to a living nightmare, watching in horror, Jeff Cahill took a baseball bat to his wife's head and hit her. He hit her again and again, and when she tried to escape, he dragged her back into the house and hit her again, and again and again and again.

7

The Assault

New York State Trooper Thomas Haumann was first on the scene. He was on night patrol and had just reached the intersection of Howlett Hill and Onondaga Roads when his radio piped up. "We've had a call for a response to a domestic altercation dispute over in Spafford, both parties are hurt and we're being told there is a knife and a baseball bat at the scene," the Skaneateles Police Department dispatcher informed him. "Can you get over there and take a look?" As Haumann turned the car, he glanced at his watch; it was 5:34 A.M.

He switched on his emergency lights and siren and sped to the location the dispatcher had given him, 2444 East Lake Road. When he pulled onto East Lake/Route 41, he could see the green two-story clapboard farmhouse about sixty-five feet up a hill from the road. There were two figures on the front porch silhouetted in the lighted doorway; one was fully dressed and waving to him; despite the cool night, the man standing behind him was wearing only dark blue shorts. When Haumann got out of the car, he could see that the half-naked guy was bleeding from some superficial cuts on his left hand and arm, and from his bare chest.

"She's in the kitchen," Kevin Cahill told him. Nothing in the dispatcher's dispassionate briefing of a dispute between a husband and wife could have prepared Trooper Haumann for the carnage that met his eyes. The place was literally awash with blood. Lying, faceup, on the carpeted floor, her pink flannel pajama–covered leg sticking out from under the pile of blood-sodden bedclothes that covered her, was the crumpled body of a woman. Hovering behind him were three older people, two men and a woman. Haumann crouched down to see if the victim was alive. "What's her name?" he asked. A voice from behind him said it was Jill.

Haumann took a deep breath as he took in the damage. "She was lying on the floor kind of wrapped in blankets and sheets off her bed. There was a pool of blood about three feet wide around her head soaking into the carpet. Her hair was all matted with blood, I couldn't even tell what color her hair was, there was so much blood. Her eyes were swollen shut and you could tell that a whole part of her skull, right above her temple, was caved in and she was just kind of convulsing on the floor."

She was barely alive, moving slightly and her eyes were open, but he didn't think she was conscious. "Jill, can you talk to me? Can you hear me?" he asked. She writhed in pain and mumbled something he couldn't make out. Haumann immediately ordered everyone away from her, telling them to go into the living room. "Has anyone tried to get this woman help?" he wanted to know. One of the men, who said he was a doctor, nodded, stony-faced. The trooper got on his radio to the ambulance and rescue crew staged down the road waiting for him to say it was safe to approach, and gave them the all clear. Realizing that this was a major crime, he asked for his supervisor to come over. Looking at his watch, he clocked the time. It was 5:50 A.M.

A minute later, the Syracuse Area Voluntary Emergency Services (S.A.V.E.S.) was the first of four ambulance crews and the Borodino Fire Department to answer the call. As two of the crew went to work on Jill and the other EMT took a look at Jeff's wounds, Haumann asked for everyone's names. Patricia Cahill made the introductions; she and her husband James were the parents of both younger men, and the guy who had been waiting for him on the porch was Kevin, Jeff's older brother. The doctor was John Kelly, a family friend.

Haumann turned to Jeff. "You her husband? Do you want to tell me what happened here?" Jeff told him he'd clobbered his wife in self-defense. "He claimed she had attacked him in an upstairs bedroom during an argument and the argument went downstairs and she had grabbed a knife and gone at him and he had grabbed a baseball bat to defend himself. 'I hit her in the mudroom at the back of the house to defend myself, the fight moved back into the kitchen where I hit her hard,' he said."

"Are there any other injured persons in this house?" the trooper asked.

"My kids are upstairs," Jeff replied.

"Are they hurt?"

"No."

"Where are they?" asked Haumann.

"In their rooms."

Haumann bounded upstairs and found 10-year-old Tim and 8-year-old Mary huddled together in their parents' room, numb with shock. After checking that they were at least physically OK, he came back down.

After the crime specialists and the investigators began showing up, he took a walk through the house to try to figure out where everything had gone on. "There was blood on the kitchen ceiling, blood had bounced off the floor to the underside of the countertops and in the sink were a bucket and washrag—it looked like someone had tried to clean up in the mudroom and there was a three- or four-foot spray of blood at the back entrance out by the lawn." The sheer amount of the stuff and the obvious force Cahill had used against Jill took Haumann's breath away. It was as if he had stumbled onto the set of a gory horror movie.

"Everything about it told me [Jeff's excuse] was not right. He was claiming that she had attacked him with a knife, but everything was so lopsided, I could tell that even if he was telling the truth, his response was beyond anything that could reasonably be expected."

He talked to Patricia Cahill a couple of times and each time she gave up less information. She told him her son had called the house and she could overhear her husband talking to him and he'd repeated "baseball bat," "knife" and "serious." She and Kevin had gone to the house after he called the senior citizen emergency line. "She arrived with a bottle of holy water which made me think she had more than an inkling of how badly Jill was hurt," said Haumann.

Patricia told him that there was a baseball bat and a knife in the kitchen and sure enough, he found a knife and aluminum bat lying on the right side of Jill's body at her feet. The bat was dented and the business end was saturated with blood. He went out to retrieve evidence bags from the trunk of his car, then put the knife in one plastic bag and the bat in another.

He walked through the rear door of the kitchen into a small mudroom that was also splattered with blood. He followed the trail outside. There was more blood on the patio's slate tiles. At the top of the basement stairs, one of the detectives had picked up a jacket that had started the day yellow and was now stained a reddish brown. He went outside and saw two cars parked in the driveway, a white Ford Taurus station wagon and a black 1988 Jeep Ranger. As he shined his flashlight on the Ford, he could see a nozzle taped to the tailpipe and a piece of red-and-white garden hose lying beside the car. "I didn't make the connection at first—his brother at some point had moved it—but the window was open a little bit and the hose was supposed to go through it into the car," said the trooper. "It made me wonder about the time line. If Jeff Cahill had attacked his wife just forty-five minutes or so before, how would he have had time to call his parents and do this." Haumann wrote down the registration and license tag; it had a New York plate: C20 8WS.

When he went back inside, the S.A.V.E.S. 1 crew, Patrick Gannon and paramedic Norman Carroll, were ready to load Jill into their ambulance at 6:06 A.M. Dr. Kelly told driver Charles Knickerbocker, "Don't give her anything, don't take her to Community, take her to University and don't stop for anything." He knew that the standard procedure was to take her to the nearest hospital in Auburn, but it had no brain trauma unit and she would need to be airlifted to Syracuse later. Given the condition this woman was in, she probably wouldn't survive the journey. Then Kelly called the hospital to say she was on the way and to ensure there was a surgical team scrubbed in and units of her blood type waiting for her when she arrived.

As soon as their mother was gone, Haumann went back upstairs where Kevin was talking to Tim and Mary. "I started asking them about the time. It was all supposed to have occurred between 4:30 and 5:00 A.M. The little boy was hazy on details—he reminded me of a typical little boy, he said they were arguing and when I asked him when this was happening he said, 'Oh around midnight.' He woke up in the dark and thought, 'It's midnight.' The little girl told me, 'I woke up and I looked at my clock and it was two-thirty.' Cahill's story was coming apart right there. He asked, "Did you go downstairs to see what was happening?" "No," they told him.

It was arranged that Jim Cahill would take the children to his home. "When we were getting them out of the house, there were two entrances to the kitchen and the deputy stood in the door of one and the kids' jackets were at the other. We just didn't want them to see how bad it was, so when Mary said, 'I need my jacket,' I went and got it. And we got their clothes on so they could leave with the grandfather and when they walked out, for all the attention that that room was getting, they never looked in it. That struck me as odd, it still does. Kids always want to know what was going on. It gave me the impression that they knew what had gone on because they had seen it."

Haumann went back down into the living room, where Jeff was sitting with a pillowcase wrapped around his left hand, and pieced together more of the story. They were in bed—they still slept together although they were legally separated—when Jill had attacked Jeff out of the blue. He had gone downstairs to get away from her, but she had followed, yelling at him. They had fought all the way downstairs and into the kitchen where she had grabbed a knife and started slashing him. "She cut me," he said, holding out his arm as proof. The fight had tumbled into the mudroom and it was there he had picked up the bat and lashed out, cracking open Jill's head. His mother, who was holding his hand as he gave his account, offered, "She threatened Jeff with a knife three weeks ago." She also claimed Jill had threatened suicide and she had the documentation to prove it. Haumann logged the interview at 6:15 A.M.

Next he talked to 40-year-old Kevin, who said he lived with his parents. He'd been awakened by the phone ringing at 5:30 A.M. He heard his father answer it and could tell that he was talking to Jeff. His father then told him that Jill had pulled a knife on Jeff and he'd had to stop her, and needed help. Kevin said he had called an emergency number before driving his mother out to Spafford. His father had gone to collect Dr. Kelly, his old friend since they were students at the University of Notre Dame together, and they had reached East Lake Road shortly after.

A couple of minutes later Haumann's supervisor Sergeant June Worden arrived and was followed at 6:19 A.M. by Sergeant James O'Brien and Trooper Richard Dix. While Haumann continued talking to the family, they secured the house as a crime scene and began taking photographs.

By the time S.A.V.E.S. 2, Carl DeSalvo, Carol Korcz and Robert Feldman, arrived at the house, Jill had already been removed. Accompanied by Sergeant Dix, they took Jeff to Syracuse Community Hospital, logging their arrival at 6:49 A.M. As they left, Patty said to Jeff: "She started it. You'll be OK."

She couldn't have been more wrong; nothing would be OK for Jeff or her daughter-in-law again. Jill was fighting for her life on an ambulance gurney, her lovely head distorted and swollen, her eyes reduced to slits in her bloodied face, moaning and twitching and babbling incoherently, incapable of responding to anything but pain. As Charles Knickerbocker gunned the accelerator, knowing that she had lost so much blood that every second was critical, the crew in the back of the bus were desperately trying to keep Jill's airways clear and willing her to hold on; she was literally gasping for every breath when they pulled up to the emergency room. Opening the doors of the ambulance, Patrick Gannon and Norman Carroll gingerly handed her over to the medics, who raced her into the emergency room.

When they called in, Dr. Kelly and the E.M.T. crew had not minimized Jill's condition, but the experienced E.R. staff were still unprepared for what they saw. The neurosurgeon in charge was Gerard Rodziewicz, who had been called at home by Dr. Patty Galnar, the resident working emergency that shift. When he got there, Galnar and his team had put a breathing tube in Jill's lungs, hooked her up to a blood transfusion drip and were inserting IV lines to pump in fluid to raise her blood pressure. She had been barely responsive when she was first admitted but now she was totally unconscious.

A check of her eyes showed that the right pupil was enlarged. When she stirred, she moved the right side of her
body much better than the left. Put together, this told
Rodziewicz that there was a problem on the right side of her
brain since the right side of the body is controlled by the left
portion of the brain. Whatever it was, he had no doubts it was
life-threatening. When a CT scan confirmed his suspicions
and revealed a blood clot on her brain, Jill was rushed into
emergency surgery. But before he could begin, he and his
team had to spend nearly an hour closing the gashes on her
head.

"In the operating room we got some clippers and removed her hair so we could see the cuts that were bleeding.
They were bleeding so vigorously that we were afraid that
had we not sewn them up, that she would simply bleed out
and die while we were trying to remove the blood clot," Dr.
Rodziewicz said at the trial.

He told the court that he had made an incision along the
entire right side of Jill's head and removed her scalp. Then
he drilled some holes in her skull, and with a surgical saw,
cut between these holes and lifted out a sizable chunk of
bone to let him see the extent of the damage. A large blood
clot was pressing on her brain and when it was removed, it
spouted like a fountain. It was clear to him that Jill had been
hit so hard, the blood vessels connecting her brain to her
skull had been torn and her brain had been virtually knocked
loose. The blow—or blows—had damaged the brain tissue
and caused it to swell. What remained of her skull was fractured in several places.

Most of those cracks were at the base of the skull underneath the brain. "She had a fracture at the outside part of
her eye socket, she had ragged torn cuts right and left, at the
front and back of her head. The biggest of them was a sort
of burst laceration at the back of her head, the pieces of
skin there came out in a star-shaped fashion. Actually, the

skin on the entire back of her head had been lifted off her skull. You could stick your finger in through the cut on the left side and have it come out on the right side in the back," he said.

The Jaegers were wakened by the phone ringing at 5:30 A.M. Debbie groped for the handset and jammed it to her ear. Patty Cahill was on the other end. She told Debbie that there had been an incident at Jeff and Jill's house. Patty claimed she had tried to call Fred and Joan, but had gotten no answer, then said: "Jill is on her way to the hospital with what seems like stab wounds to her head, and Jeff has been injured too. Are you going to work? I have that number."

Still half asleep and stunned by what she was hearing, Debbie processed the information. Her sister has been stabbed in the head by her husband, is she going to work? "What's going on?" she asked. "I'll call if I have any more information," said Patty. Then she added, "Jim and I were afraid that something like this would happen."

"We were in a panic, didn't know what to do," said Debbie. She called her parents and repeated the gist of Patty's call. She called her sister-in-law and told her, "I have to go to Syracuse, can you take care of the kids? Something's happened at Jill and Jeff's house."

"Do you want me to go with you?" asked Rita.

"No," said Debbie. "I have no idea of what is really going on."

They decided that Bill would go to work and call the New York State Police immediately when he arrived. He was put on to Detective Doug Gilmore, who filled him in with what he knew, then added, "Tell her family to get there fast." Debbie called Jill's divorce lawyer, Anthony DiCaprio, and told him the news. She threw enough clothes for a couple of days into a bag and picked up her parents. As they pulled onto the highway, they had no idea of what they were driving into. During the three-hour-long trip they hardly spoke, each afraid to put voice to coherent thoughts. At worst, they thought Jill's face had been slashed.

When they arrived at the hospital around 1:30 P.M. they were met by Martha Williams. "A friend of mine heard it on a police scanner radio that she kept at her job in Skaneateles and called me at work and said, 'My God, I am hearing that something terrible is happening down the road at Jill's house,' and now I'm thinking, 'Of course, it must be that neighbor [that Jeff was always complaining about].' I was told that she was at Upstate [the local name for University Hospital] and I ran.

"I got there about twenty minutes before Joan, Fred and Debbie—Jill was in surgery at that point—and the state police met us and ushered us into this room where they told us the grim story. We didn't know what to expect, but we certainly knew it was a very real possibility that she wouldn't make it."

"We waited around for what seemed like forever," remembered Fred. "Then the doctor came out of surgery and proceeded to tell us what they did. He said she was in very bad shape." The Russells listened incredulously as Rodziewicz described the operation. He explained that Jill's skull had multiple fractures, her cheekbones and her arms were broken. He said they had actually carved out a large portion of her head, which they would "warehouse" until she healed; they had to do that to relieve the pressure that was crushing her brain, and take away a blood clot that had been as big as the palm of his hand. The next forty-eight hours would be crucial, he warned them and then held out the faintest shred of hope: "It's a minute-by-minute thing with Jill, but I think I have accomplished what I wanted to do. With luck, she should be coming along."

They knew he was trying to make them feel better, but there were no words that could make them feel anything. They were in a daze, hardly comprehending the enormity of the injuries inflicted on her by the husband she insisted, only the day before, would never lay a finger on her. Joan later recalled trying to move, but her legs felt like lead. A hospital worker brought them something to eat and they couldn't look at it.

An hour later, having undergone nearly half a day of surgery, Jill emerged from the operating room and was taken to the Neurology Intensive Care Unit. "You can come in and see her now," they were told. Fred describes the horror of that first glimpse of his battered daughter: "It was devastating. We couldn't see any of her [face] and her head was twice the size it should have been, she had things over her eyes, her head was totally covered in bandages. Her arm was broken and it was strapped down and there were tubes coming out of her everywhere. It didn't look like her. She was almost completely drained of blood. I thought, 'What happened? Oh my God, what happened here?' "

The doctor explained that she be would be kept in an artificially induced coma. Her injuries were so severe that she had to be kept totally still, they could not take the chance she would move her head. "You couldn't even cry, you were just so overwhelmed," said Debbie. "This wasn't even a person that I knew. How could anyone do this to another human being? This was the woman I was with just the day before? It was the most horrible sight I've ever seen."

Martha stayed with them for the rest of that endless day. "I was stunned. By then I had heard that it was Jeff who had beaten her, and Debbie was starting to fill me in on all this awful stuff that had been going on and I am saying, 'What do you mean, Jeff beat her; it wasn't the neighbor?' " Tom Tulloch arrived. He told Joan that he and Jill were supposed to be having lunch that day to arrange her move the following weekend into her new digs. Instead, two detectives had knocked on his door. He said that he had been crazy about Jill for twenty years, from when she first came to live in

Skaneateles with Greg Owens, and that they had planned to get married as soon as her divorce was final.

While they were trying to console each other in the little room off the I.C.U. waiting area, Jill's old boyfriend Sal Piamonte showed up. Through their shock and grief they tried to take in what he was saying about the many legal issues they would now be facing. He offered his help and told them there was a bail hearing for Jeff scheduled for 9:00 A.M. on Tuesday morning. They should be there, he advised. Anthony DiCaprio arrived too.

By this time the Russells and Debbie were emotionally spent and physically exhausted. Hospital social workers had booked them in the Sheraton University Hotel, two blocks away at the special rate of $30 a night. The staff had been instructed to do whatever they could for the family, who found out later that John Ginley's father had built the place. Before they left to check in, Detective Gilmore spoke to them again. He was very concerned about Jill and told them that when he'd first seen how badly she had been hurt, he didn't think she would live.

But Jill was in the best of hands. Dr. Rodziewicz, a Wayne State and Case Western Reserve University graduate, a member of the American Association of Neurological Surgery, the Congress of Neurological Surgeons and the New York State Medical Society and a fellow of the American College of Surgeons, headed up one of the top neurology units in the country. As the weary Russells gathered themselves together and departed to catch a few hours' sleep, he assured them that he and his staff would monitor Jill around the clock. They clung to the belief that if anyone could pull her through, he could.

Over at Community Hospital, where Jeff was having stitches put in his cut hand, Sergeant Dix had read him his Miranda rights just after 7:00 in the morning. "Do you understand?" he'd asked him. Jeff had said he did. Then he signed a Release of Medical Information form authorizing the police to see all the records of his treatment at the E.R. Half an hour later, Senior Investigator Maynard Cosnett and Investigator David Longo arrived at Community and suggested he accompany them to the Syracuse Police Department's Lafayette Station, where he could make a statement. "Fine," Jeff nodded agreeably.

While they were waiting for Jeff to finish with the nurse, Investigator Longo talked to Jim Cahill. He told them that Jeff had called him at 5:30 A.M. and said he'd gotten into a fight with his wife and they were both injured. Patty and Kevin had immediately driven to Spafford and stopped to pick up Dr. Kelly on the way. Jim said that Kevin had called for help. When they got to the station house, Detective Longo began the interview by checking that Jeff had been fully advised of his rights. Jeff said that Sergeant Dix had taken care of that and then poured out his chilling confession:

I reside with my wife, Jillian Catherine Cahill, and two children, Tim, age ten and Mary, age eight. Over the past several months my wife and I have been preparing for a separation. She was unhappy with the marriage, part of the problem seemed to be possible infidelity on her part. Over the last month or so Jill had awakened me maybe three times at night, grabbing my face and turning it towards her and then screaming or yelling at me. She also grabbed a twine necklace at one time and pulled it, causing a rope burn on my neck. She had also scratched my face at that time. I had discussed this with my parents and they advised that I should get up and get out, just get away from her. I also showed my parents the rope burns and the scratches.

Last night, April 20th, 1998, Jill went to bed around 7:00 P.M. She seemed down. I went to bed around 10 to 10:30 P.M., the same room and bed as

*her. She was asleep or appeared to be at that time.
Around 4 or 4:15 A.M. this morning, April 21st,
1998, I was awakened by Jill. She grabbed my face
and wrenched me over and then grabbed my arms
and held me down. She was saying words to the effect, 'I'm not going to live here. I can't go to the
P & C,' or something like that, indicating she no
longer had a life here. I then got up and went downstairs. She followed me down and was yelling at
me. Our daughter Mary came to the top of the
stairs and Jill went up and brought her down. Jill
then took Mary upstairs and put her to bed in our
bed and came back downstairs.*

*I went into the kitchen and was standing near
the refrigerator. Jill came into the kitchen. The argument continued. Jill went to the opposite side of
the room, where there is a counter and on the
counter was a Crockpot, which had several knives,
spoons and ladles in it. Jill picked up a knife from
this pot, sort of like a fillet knife with maybe a six
or seven-inch tapered blade. On March 30, 1998,
Jill had taken a knife and held it to her own chest.
She also took some kind of pills. I thought she was
going to do something like that again, threaten suicide. The knife wasn't very sharp but it was pointed.
I tried to take the knife from her. She struck me, cutting my left forearm. I got a hold of her, in a position with her facing away from me, with my arms
around her and forced her out the back door of the
house into a mudroom. As we were going out, she
was calling to the children, "Call the police. Your
father is trying to kill me."*

*I pushed her to the floor and we wrestled a bit.
She continued to call the children. I pushed up and
turned to get away. She was on the floor face down.*

I saw several baseball bats hanging on the wall and grabbed one. I turned to face her again and she was getting up facing me with her hands about chest high. She still had the knife in her right hand. I swung with the bat, hitting her on the left side of the head. As I swung, she raised her hands alongside her head. She started to move backwards and I swung again. This time she went backwards, falling out of the back door onto a concrete patio.

I went into the house. My daughter Mary was just inside the back door and I told her to go upstairs. Jill called to Mary, telling her to call the police, "Your father is trying to kill me." Mary started up the stairs and Jill came into the house. I could see she was hurt. There was blood on her left shoulder and side of her head. I still had the baseball bat in my hands and I swung again, hitting her on the shoulder. This blow deflected, also hitting her on the head. I swung two or three more times and she went down on the floor. I then tried to hold her down. She scratched at me, scratching my back and grabbed me by the balls.

Jill called for Tim to call the police. Tim went upstairs. I told Tim to get upstairs, to stay upstairs. Jill passed out or lost consciousness. She was moaning. I then called my dad and told him that Jill came at me with a knife, that I hit her and she was hurt real bad. He asked me if I had called SAVES. I told him, "No, please hurry." Dad said he would call SAVES.

My mother and brother Kevin then came to the house. It took longer for them to get there than I expected. After they got there, my dad came with a friend, Dr. Kelly. Dr Kelly checked Jill. After that SAVES came. Before anyone arrived, I went out to my car, a white Ford Taurus wagon, and got a rosary. Our black Lab was also outside, and I

*chased him down and got him back in the house. I
got some towels and packed them around Jill to try
and keep her warm. I also turned her head when
she started to vomit. I could see that she was not
doing good. I also went upstairs and talked to the
kids to try and allay some of their fears. I told them
that their grandparents were coming. I told Mary
that I got cut a few times, but that I was okay.*

When he was done, Cosnett read his Miranda rights again
and Jeff confirmed he had voluntarily agreed to give a written statement. After it was typed into the computer, it was
printed out and Jeff initialed each page "J.C.III" and noted
the time, 11:17 A.M.

While Jeff was in the process of outlining what happened, Cosnett had been in frequent touch with the investigators at the crime scene, and what he was hearing was
seriously out of whack with Jeff's version of events. Cosnett
was also very suspicious about the knife wounds that Jill was
supposed to have delivered in a frenzied attack. To the veteran cop's eye, they were self-inflicted. The detectives back
at the house had the likely culprit, a nail that was protruding
from a wall in the mudroom some 3'10" from the ground.

The investigators began picking holes in his story. "You
see," they told Jeff, "what you are telling us and what the detectives looking for evidence in your home are finding, just
doesn't match up. And these scratches, well, they are all on
your left side. You are right-handed, aren't you? And they
don't look like the slashes a knife makes. Such inconsistencies don't look good in a courtroom. Is there something you
would like to add to your statement?" He nodded and wrote,
"I would like to add the following statement I gave to Investigator Cosnett and Investigator Longo." Again he initialed it.

As Investigator Longo began to type the amended account into the computer, Jeff put a new slant on the horror

that had erupted just hours before. This time he said that he had helped Jill back into the kitchen before he went outside and got the knife and put it on the kitchen floor. He said he already had the baseball bat in the kitchen and he hit her with it at least twice more, with the knife on the floor. Then he said that this version wasn't right either and he'd like to make a third statement. Again he signed a note indicating he was making an amendment.

While I was arguing with my wife in the kitchen and after she pulled the knife from the pot on the countertop, I got Jill in a bear-hug-type position with her back to me. I got Jill out to the mudroom and down on the floor. I got up, got the baseball bat, and Jill was on her feet with the knife in her hand. I swung the bat twice at her, and on the second swing I hit Jill on the head. Jill fell back and out the door.

At that point I heard Mary inside. I yelled to her that everything was going to be okay and to go upstairs. I then thought Jill was hurt badly and I felt I should help her. I then helped Jill back into the house and into the kitchen. I then ran back to the mudroom and got the knife she had and put it on the floor by the stove. I got some towels from the kitchen area and helped Jill.

The argument started up again and Jill and I were wrestling again. That's when Jill scratched my back. I then got the bat, which I brought in from the mudroom and Jill tried to take it away from me. I got it from her and hit her in the head with it again. We continued to struggle and I again struck Jill in the head with the bat. I would say I hit her about two times while in the kitchen. Jill didn't have the knife during this struggle.

After hitting her, Jill was just laying on the floor

breathing very shallow. I then went into the base-
ment and got some towels and wrapped them
around Jill's head. While I was in the basement, I
realized what was going on and I could not believe
this was happening. After putting towels around
Jill, I went outside and cut a piece from a garden
hose, using a knife I took from the kitchen. Not the
same one Jill had earlier. I then set up the hose from
the tailpipe of my white Ford Taurus, from my white
Taurus station wagon to the rear window. I used
duct tape to secure the hose. When I was in the car,
I saw my rosary and decided that I couldn't kill my-
self.

I didn't know what to do. I could not believe
what had happened. I then went back into the mud-
room and found a nail. I then put the scratches on
my left shoulder and arm with it. I did this because
I wanted to make it look like there was more of a
struggle than there was. I was also afraid that Jill
was going to die. That's when I called my father
and talked to the children. I still don't know how I
got the cut on my left hand but I think it was some-
time during the fight with Jill.

Cahill read it over, signed it and noted the time:1:06 P.M.
He was led to the lockup, where he spent the rest of the afternoon and night.

While Cahill was copping to the brutal beating of his
wife, Detectives Douglas Gilmore and Dennis Burgos were
back at University Hospital hoping to talk to Jill, but she was
in no condition to give an interview. They were told she had
a brain hemorrhage and broken bones, and was going to be in
the induced coma for at least a week. Gilmore collected her
wedding ring, a large white towel, her pink pajama bottoms,

a sock, a piece of a white, green and yellow patterned sheet and a white tee-shirt and bagged the items for evidence.

The next morning Katy Price drove Debbie and the Russells to the bail hearing. The D.A. was asking for $200,000, the usual ballpark figure for bail in an attempted murder or a murder charge in Onondaga County. Jeff 's lawyer asked that it be set at a more modest $25,000. While they were waiting, they had looked for Jeff in the line of prisoners waiting their turn before the judge, but he wasn't among them. Dazed from the events of the previous day, and bone-weary after a sleepless night, they listened in disbelief as Jeff 's lawyer described him as "a pillar of the community." This glowing description was immediately refuted by Chief Assistant District Attorney Rick Trunfio, who trotted out the list of Jeff 's recent run-ins with the law. The judge postponed a decision and scheduled another hearing for April 29.

Rather than wait a week, Jeff 's father forked over $100,000 in cash and Jeff was sprung from jail that evening, much to the chagrin of the D.A. "In New York, a judge can only consider the person's likelihood of reappearing in the court, regardless of how heinous the crime is, but judges in most of the state look at the seriousness of the crime, although the law doesn't really allow it. Unfortunately, in our county we had a judge—no longer on the bench—who reduced the bail drastically. I think he cut it in half," said Bill Fitzpatrick. Anthony DiCaprio asked for and got an order of protection for Jill and the children. If Jeff went anywhere near them, he would be locked up again.

The day after the beating, Fred was by Jill's bedside with Katy, who was holding a one-sided conversation with her comatose friend. "I said something, and as soon as she heard my voice she tried to get up. The nurse had to hold her down. They gave her more stuff [medication] because they didn't want her moving, but it was the first actual inkling of something that was really positive in Jill's condition," he said.

Despite Fred's joy at that flicker of hope, they had a long road ahead of them. It was to be another two weeks before Jill came around. Her eyes remained closed, her legs were swollen, the only sign she was still with them was her tenacious grip when the doctor asked her to squeeze his hand. A couple of days after her initial surgery, her brain swelled up and she was put back on a ventilator. Even after she was able to breathe on her own, the big star-shaped cut was a major cause for concern. "Because we had opened up her head and couldn't put the bone back, the water [that supports the brain] was able to get out and leaked through this cut," said Dr. Rodziewicz.

Two days after Jill was hospitalized, Fred, Joan and Debbie saw the children for the first time since they'd arrived at Skaneateles. They picked them up from school and took them for ice cream. Tim got into the car and said, "Remember the night my mom and dad had the fight? My dad showed me where his wounds were," and pointed them out on his own body. Nobody said anything.

At 6:30 P.M. they dropped the children off at the Cahills' home, where they had been taken by Uncle Howdy (Kevin) on the night of the assault. Fred, Debbie and Joan were standing in the driveway when Patty walked over. Earlier, when Debbie had called to check on the children, Patty had told her, "It's God's will." "It was the first time we'd met since the attack," said Joan. "Patty never asked for Jill or said she was sorry, or said anything about what had taken place. She said, 'Now that this has happened we'll probably be seeing more of each other.' Then she turned to Debbie and queried: 'Why does Fred always drive?' Debbie just looked at her. So she asks me, 'Why is it that Fred does all the driving?' 'Because he *likes* to do all the driving,' I told her. Then she comes back with, 'Now if you had to, could you drive here from Tonawanda?'

"I said yes, I could drive here from Tonawanda if I had to."

"One of my sons is like that, he likes to drive," she said.

"And I am thinking, 'My daughter is fighting for her life in the hospital and you are going on about this stuff?' I asked her, 'So what the hell's the big deal?'"

In spite of the awkward exchange, the Russells left feeling that Patty and Jim were doing all they could for their traumatized grandchildren. They were grateful they had taken them and the dogs, Nick and Snoofy, under their wing, and in return, Patty thanked Joan and Fred for making the kids smile. Debbie talked to her about the order of protection and she promised that Jeff would not be allowed to see the children. She agreed to get them into counseling when the time was appropriate. Debbie felt it was important to keep the lines of communication open with his family, no matter what Jeff had done.

"We were just ordinary people living our day-to-day life in Tonawanda. Things like this just don't happen to us. And here you are caught in a situation that has you saying, 'Holy crap, how did this happen?' Not only are you dealing with what happened that day, you're having to deal with district attorneys, press, this and that—and the kids. At that point, we were like, 'They're with the Cahills, they're safe,'" said Debbie. What made them very uneasy was hearing that as soon as he was freed on bail, Jeff had called the hospital switchboard asking for Jill.

When they got back to her room that evening they were cheered a little by Dr. Rodziewicz, who said Jill had had a good day, although he was concerned that some spinal fluid was leaking and worried about her developing meningitis. He said they might put a drain into her to relieve pressure and convinced them it was a simple procedure that would bring big benefits. He also said that Jill would have an angiogram the next morning.

When they went in to see her the breathing tube was removed and some of the bandages had been unwrapped from her head. She was a pitiful sight—her head was covered in more stitches than a baseball, the left side of her head was gone, her face was purple with extensive bruising, her eyes were red and swollen. The full force of what Jeff had done to her hit them, and it was sickening.

8

The Hospital

Back at their hotel room that night, the Russells got a call from a friend of Jill's who said Mary had told a classmate at school that her mom had stabbed her dad. At half past eleven Katy Price phoned to say there was a rumor going around town that the Cahill brothers were looking for Tom Tulloch. Alarmed, Debbie rang Tom, who shrugged off the supposed threat, then talked to the Cahills, who assured her that they would not let Jeff anywhere near the children. She had already called the school on the advice of the police and informed the principal about the restraining order.

On Friday morning, three days after the assault, Fred and Joan gave the hospital permission to insert a feeding tube after Dr. Rodziewicz explained it would lessen the risk of infection. They also met with A.D.A. Trunfio and told him what they knew about Jill's marriage and separation. He emphasized that they had to make it clear to their daughter's in-laws that they must not discuss the case with Tim and Mary. When they got to the hospital, Tom was reading aloud from *Chicken Soup for the Soul* to Jill. He had also brought in a small compact disc player so she'd have her favorite music. He told them that his father had been out to dinner with Dr. Kelly, who had said that when Jim Cahill banged on his door, he said that the "kids" had been in an argument and needed his help. No mention was made of the severity of Jill's condition.

For two weeks Jill remained comatose, her lovely face swollen out of all recognition, the bones around her right eye splintered. For her distraught family, it was a scary sight. There were so many tubes attached to her: an IV line through which fluids, blood and food traveled was lodged in one of the big veins in the middle of her chest and another that measured her blood pressure was attached to an artery in her arm. An E.K.G. electrode registered her heartbeat and was linked to a screen at the nurses' station.

The sheer awfulness of it all had begun to sink in. Jeff, the son-in-law they had welcomed into their family with open arms, had used their beloved Jilly's head for batting practice, inflicting such devastating injuries that she would probably die, and if, by the grace of God, she did survive, the odds were that she would be brain damaged and confined to a wheelchair for the rest of her life.

Bill and his sister came down from Buffalo over the weekend. "You couldn't imagine how bad it was," said Rita. "We had no clue about what we were going to see, but when we walked in that room and saw her, we were so overwhelmed, we were speechless, and we couldn't break down because that would have made things worse for Fred and Joan. When we got out into the parking lot we looked at each other and said simultaneously, 'Oh my God, what was that?' We had never seen anything like that in our lives. She'd been given steroids, her neck was huge, she had stitches all over every corner of her head, all over her face. It was devastating and we were heartbroken." Bill, standing beside Joan, shook his head in anguish and told her, "At times like this it makes me ashamed to be a man."

While his wife clung to her life, Jeff resumed his, having been freed on $100,000 bail the day after he'd almost killed her. Mark put up half and his father ponied up the rest after raiding his retirement accounts. Jeff went to live with his youngest brother Tim and his wife, Kara, who had worked alongside Zaney Haux at Merrill Lynch.

It was a situation that angered the Russells. Why should this man who had readily admitted unleashing this brutal assault be walking around town while Jill suffered so? In the days after the beating, they were in no frame of mind to care for their grandchildren—their every waking moment was spent at Jill's bedside. But Rick Trunfio's caution about what their father's family might be telling the youngsters increased their growing unease over the kids being looked after by the parents of the man who had tried to kill their mother, and nearly succeeded.

On April 26 the Russells went shopping for socks and high-top sneakers to help support Jill's painfully thin ankles, and took Tim and Mary to lunch at the Sherwood Inn. Debbie had Tom's dictaphone with her and both kids recorded messages for their mom. When they got back to the hospital and played her the tape, her face lit up. Later that evening, Debbie went home to try to explain what had happened between their Uncle Jeff and Aunt Jilly to her own bewildered children. The day after, Anthony DiCaprio went to Onondaga County Family Court to seek an extension to the temporary order of protection for Jill and the children.

It should have been clear that Jeff Cahill's life had totally imploded. The wife who had been his first and only love was perilously near death, he had already lost her affection to Tom Tulloch and now she was in danger of slipping away forever. A judge had ordered him to keep away from his children and if Jill died, he'd probably never see them again. His business was a shambles, his bank balance was deep in the red, his truck had been repossessed and his customers were disappearing like lemmings now that his good-guy image was trashed by the gruesome news reports in the papers and on TV. He had brought shame, scandal and heartbreak to his own family, who, in the six days that had elapsed since the beating, had neither visited Jill in the hospital nor called to ask how she was doing.

And seven days after the attack, the cops finally got around to asking Kevin Cahill why he didn't hit 911 when he found Jill on the floor. He told them he had called FISH, a Skaneateles community organization where his mother worked as a volunteer, and asked for an ambulance. FISH, an acronym for Friends in Service Here, was not linked to the county's 911 emergency network and the response was not immediate.

According to detectives, Kevin said that Jill was lucid when he arrived at the house, saying: "Jeff, how'd we let this happen?" and "just clean me up and don't tell anyone."

Before Joan and Fred could even think of looking after the children, they had to find somewhere to live. Martha had been keeping a concerned eye on them, taking them out for dinner and trying to keep their spirits up when they were not at Jill's bedside. She called Cathy McDonald and told her, "You know that Joan and Fred are staying at the hotel up the road from the hospital. Do you have any room at your place?" At once Cathy got on the phone; she and her husband had a guesthouse on her property and although it was small, the Russells were welcome to it for as long as they needed to stay.

On Monday morning, they moved into the studio, about a mile or so along the road from Jeff and Jill's place. The quaint little house had been put up by the McDonalds to live in while their home was being built. With an odd angular shape, it had an open-plan ground floor from which an open staircase led to two second-floor bedrooms. It was the perfect solution, just big enough for Joan, Fred and the kids, and since Cathy and Tom had two kids of their own, Tim and Mary would have playmates on the premises.

The next day Jill's respirator was removed. She was able to answer a few questions, knew the names of her children, and called out for Joan when she briefly left her side. Anthony DiCaprio phoned Debbie and told her he had visited Jill and felt her spirit all over the room, and knew that she was going to get better. He advised that Joan and Fred should get a lawyer and gave her the phone number of Greg Monashefsky, who had been appointed the children's guardian in Family Court.

At the end of the week, it seemed her friends' and family's prayers had been answered: Jill woke up. Joan and Fred bumped into Dr. Rodziewicz in the corridor. "We're going to take the respirator away and see how she does without it," he told them. They stopped by the cafeteria to get something to eat and as they were on their way back to Jill's room, the doctor was coming down the hallway. "How is she?" they asked. "Why don't you go in there and ask her yourself?" he said, grinning. "She'll tell you."

"At the end of the first week she had just started moving and grabbing for your hand," said Debbie. "She went from a vegetative state to 'How are you doing?' the next time we saw her."

"During those early days, only the family and Tom were allowed to visit with her," said Martha Williams. "When I first walked into the room she just kind of looked over and said, 'Hi, Martha.' I was shocked she could talk. Her head was all bandaged up, but she had that big smile on her face and I just broke down and cried." Despite her horrendous condition, she had something on her mind, said Joan. "When Jill woke up she asked, 'Where are my kids?' We told her they were with Jeff's parents and she became visibly agitated. 'You get them away from there,' she said."

Incredibly, Jill kept improving. On May 1, when Debbie was visiting, she was "talking up a storm" and seemed to recognize everyone. When *Seinfeld* came on the TV she asked, "What are we going to do when he's not on anymore?" A thankful Debbie thought she was witnessing a miracle and put it down to all the prayers being said for her sister.

Jill was also riled that she could barely move. She was tied to the bed and fighting the restraints that kept her from doing any damage to her wounds, or her broken arm. "Every time I walked in there she'd ask for scissors," said Joan. "One day, she was ready for me and greeted me with: 'I need a pair of scissors.' I told her, 'They won't give them to us.' She glared at me and said, 'You have some in your purse, in your purse, Mother.' And I had. She knew I always kept a little pair there."

The next day Tim and Mary came over to inspect the studio and hang out in the pool and the Jacuzzi for a while before having dinner with the McDonalds. When Fred, Joan and Debbie got to the hospital, Jill was in fine form, her arm having been untied at last. Out of the blue she announced that she had chewed Tom's underwear and they all burst out laughing.

"I was at Hilton Head when I heard [about the attack on Jill]," said Michelle. "John had been down there too, but was back already. My sister called me and said, 'Something has happened to Jill.' I knew. It was the worst time of my life, I could not get home. I had my mother and the kids with me and an immediate airline flight out of there was like four thousand dollars. On the way home the next Saturday I overheard people talking about it at Atlanta Airport. I was in tears." By the time Michelle got back, Jill had been transferred to the seventh floor. "She was still unconscious, her head shaved, her face was blown up and purple, she was just lying there.

"Then one Sunday night, I was ironing when the phone rang. It was Jill. I said, 'Oh. Oh, Jill, hi, how are you?' She said, 'I'm in this room with this nice lady and she let me borrow her phone.' I was so astonished. She starts telling me she's in there to have some dental work done and still blames her parents for not giving her braces. 'I'm having a tooth fixed tomorrow and can you come by and pick me up at the front of the hospital?' she asked. I said, 'OK, Jill, no problem, I'll be there in the morning.' I called the staff and said, 'She's got a phone. She's out and about and doing things. Watch her.' "

"Her long-term memory was great," said Fred, "but she was having difficulty putting together why she was in this state. She kept saying, 'Did someone hit me on the head with a shovel?' I took her down to therapy to do some tests. I wheeled her in and this guy comes up to her and says, 'See that line in front of you, Jill? I'm going to get you out of the chair and I want to see what you can do walking down there.' And the next minute she got up. 'Wait a minute,' he said. 'No, I can do it,' she said and walked a straight line. The therapist muttered, 'I don't believe this.'

"She went through other tests. One doctor had her count backward. He told her he wanted her to count back from one hundred in sevens. She goes, 'One hundred, ninety-three,' and then stopped. 'That's as far as I'm going,' she told him. 'I hate math, I was an art student, I don't do math. That's why Michelle takes care of the books.' He asked her to write a sentence and she wrote a whole paragraph. Then he showed her some pictures and gave her a pen. 'Now draw what you saw,' he tells her. She begins to draw and he says, 'My God, these are better than the pictures.' "

Then she told her parents she wanted her purse because

she needed to go shopping with Katy. "The clothes I have here are all too casual," she told them. They were elated. Dr. Rodziewicz told Tom he was going to write a book about "our girl's" miraculous recovery. But Investigator David Longo had doubts that she would ever be able to help him build the case against Jeff. "When I went back to see if she could talk a little bit she was wearing a helmet and going through therapy and she was like a child. It was sad," he said.

It seemed the whole village of Skaneateles was pulling for her and rallying around the family. Every night when Joan and Fred came back from the hospital food would be waiting for them. The fridge was packed with meals, pastas, quiches, fruit and other goodies handed in daily, and Cathy had press-ganged her aerobics class to take turns in providing dinner. And on the nights when they couldn't face even loading up the microwave, Tom and Cathy invited them over to eat.

During dinner on May 5, Tom McDonald told them about a phone call he'd gotten earlier that day. It was from Jeff, who thanked him and Cathy for taking care of Jill's family before blundering into a rambling story about coaching the local kids. Then he had he reminded Tom how he'd warned him a couple of years before that Jill was unstable when she, Michelle and Cathy were going to buy the Skaneateles Nursery. Furious, Tom had cut him off. "Nothing could excuse what you did to Jill. You have destroyed so many people's lives," he told Jeff, and hung up.

This new development troubled them all, especially Bill. "He's trying to justify his actions somehow. He's behaving just the way he did before the assault," he told Debbie. In what turned out to be a haunting aside, she noted the conversation in her diary, adding that she hoped Jeff wasn't being left to his own devices. "Who knows what he's capable of?" she wrote.

Concerns were also growing that Jeff's family might be helping him circumvent the restraining order. Tim told the Russells that he had gone on long hikes with his uncles in the woods. Joan and Fred didn't know whether they were giving in to paranoia, or rightly suspicious; it just made them more anxious to get the kids into counseling as soon as possible. They still had not seen Jill. Their therapist was still advising against bringing the children to the hospital, cautioning that it was too soon and would be too traumatic for them to visit their battered mom.

Fred, Joan and Debbie tried to answer all their questions truthfully. They explained that Jill had had to have her head shaved before the surgeons could work on her wounds. Debbie told Tim about the plastic helmet-like protector his mom had to wear whenever she was out of bed, walking around or in the shower. It was with her all the time and Debbie had decorated it with pretty stickers. He had laughed at that and asked if his mom had a gash over her right eye, and pointed to his own head. Debbie told him she had and that it was healing well. He said he knew what the fight was about, but wouldn't tell. Then he blurted out that the reason for the fight was that his mother loved another man, and that man was "very, very bad."

They talked about Nick and Snoofy. Tim said that Nick, the black Labrador, spent a lot of time with his dad and Uncle Mark. Then he added something that made them freeze: he might get to see his dad in a couple of weeks. They passed on their fears to D.A. Fitzpatrick when they met him on May 5. Fitzpatrick told them he planned to make an example of Jeff, who should get no less than 20 years. Meanwhile Jill was beginning to mix up days and nights and faced surgery to repair her fractured eye socket.

Finally on Mother's Day, May 10, Jill was reunited with her children. An excited Mary climbed right into bed with

her. Tim became upset and after a little while Fred took
him home. On the way, Tim told his grandfather that his
dad had hit his mom with an aluminum bat and Dad was
now in trouble. Fred kept silent but his heart sunk. It seemed
what Tim was being told made him blame his mother for the
fight. Rick Trunfio had asked Joan to note down any conversations she'd had with the kids for the upcoming court hearing on May 11. She made sure he knew about her grandson's
remarks and also about Jeff's calls to Tom McDonald and to
the hospital.

The next morning, the Russells were back in Family
Court for a visitation hearing. Patty, Jim, Mark and Kevin
were there, and so was Jeff. They thought he looked rough.
The judge tabled another hearing for May 19 and ordered
psychiatric evaluations for him and the children. Anthony
DiCaprio remarked that he had never seen anyone appear so
unremorseful, and urged Fred and Joan again to seek legal
help because they would likely have to sue for temporary
custody.

Debbie talked to the children's guardian. He told her that
the Department of Social Services was trying to keep Jeff
away from the children on grounds of abuse and neglect, and
said there were inconsistencies between their account of the
incident and their father's. He said Mary had described in
sickeningly vivid detail the sound of her mother being hit
and promised her that should they be called as witnesses,
they would be questioned in judges' chambers with only the
lawyers and himself present. He too recommended that her
parents get representation.

Jill continued getting better. Her strength and coordination had improved tremendously and Tom Tulloch recalled
everyone tempting her to eat; he brought her a sumptuously
rich chocolate cake the same day that Katy came in with
chocolate chip cookies. Jill washed them down with chocolate

milk. Afterwards she felt good enough to suggest that Tom climb into her bed. But for all the hopeful moments, there were ominous signs that recovery was not just around the corner. She complained of the pain that engulfed her in waves. It was explained to her family that it was caused by pressure from meningitis and the bruising from her injuries.

Jill struggled with recent recollections. She still had no idea how she had landed in the hospital in the first place. Tom recalled one night staying with her until midnight and dancing around the subject. "She kept saying, 'Did someone hit me on the head with a shovel?'" The hospital psychologist told Joan and Fred that the time had come to level with her. On May 14, they read her the article from the newspaper. Tom, who arrived after she learned the unvarnished truth, said she took it extremely well. At first she was mad at Jeff, but her anger gave way to fear as the evening wore on. Along with her parents, Tom tried to soothe her, telling her she had nothing to be afraid of; she was in the hospital, and security had Jeff's picture along with notification about the restraining order. Tom stayed with her until half past one in the morning. The following day, Frank Sinatra, whose music they danced to the night they fell in love, died.

The doctors had warned that Jill would keep asking what had happened to her, but the next day when Joan and Fred walked into her room she greeted them with, 'Do you believe what that son of a bitch did to me?' Then she said something that chilled them to the bone: "He's going to finish me." Her father said, "Those were her exact words." She said the same to Debbie and Mallory when they arrived, and added, "All I ever did was try to help him." She reached for the white fluffy bear that they had bought for her to cuddle and instantly named him Tom Teddy.

That day she had a clear memory of the beating and wanted to tell Debbie about it. She said she remembered

Jeff swinging the bat from behind, and after the first blow, she covered her face with her hands and he hit her again. After she fell to the ground, he put his foot on her back to hold her down. She remembered being "dragged into the woods," and again said he had hit her with a shovel. She said she had noticed an adult-sized bat in the basement and had asked him about it. "It's in case any adults want to play," he'd told her. A couple of weeks before the attack he had tried to lure her down to the basement saying he wanted to show her some tools and she had refused to go. She also told Debbie that around Christmas, he had hit her and her ear bled.

But mostly she fretted over the children and what they had seen and heard that night. What she desperately wanted to do was just to see them and hold them. She was afraid Jeff would come to "get her and the kids" and she started at every noise out in the hall. "She kept saying, 'Where are my kids? Get those kids away from the Cahills, no more than four days with the Cahills,'" said Joan. Both she and Debbie assured her that the kids were fine, that they were being taken good care of. They left around 6:00 P.M. and returned at 8:00. When they got back she was still frightened and asked for Tom's number. He was away on a business trip to Palm Springs. Debbie remembered how hard it was to leave her.

A couple of days later Jill called in tears. "Why did this have to happen to me?" she asked. There was no reasonable answer. She was in agony and her head was swollen with fluid building up behind her right eye. She had had a CAT scan and endured a painful spinal tap to relieve it. She had another day after and broke out in hives reacting to a new drug. When Debbie phoned later, Jill was so out of it, she thought she was in a jungle surrounded by lions, tigers and gorillas.

Her parents and her divorce lawyer went back to court. Jeff wasn't there, but they learned he had been evaluated. The children still had received no counseling—their father's attorney claimed the kids had insurance and that Jill and Jeff had canceled their own coverage to save money. Joan was outraged; she and Fred knew that the health-conscious Jill, who they used to tease about being a hypochondriac, would never have agreed. "That's a lie," she blurted out. From then on Anthony DiCaprio dubbed her "Smokey" because watching her listen to the lawyer's excuses, he joked he could see smoke coming out of her ears.

The judge was incredulous. "You mean that woman has been in the hospital for a month without health insurance?" he asked, then ruled that Jeff was responsible for all her medical and psychiatric bills. The Russells just shook their heads, for they knew she'd never see a penny.

That night Patty called to say she wanted to take the kids to Cape Cod for the weekend. She maintained that Jeff would not be there, it would just be her and John with his family from Boston. Debbie willingly agreed; with Jill about to undergo surgery to repair her shattered eye the next day, she didn't think her parents could handle having the kids. "There will be absolutely no phone calls. After all, it's my dime," Patty continued. Debbie was speechless: their mother is fighting for her life, but don't expect any phone calls?

"The odd thing was, while I was talking to her, my cell phone, which I never used, was ringing and ringing. It was almost like Jill was reaching out from her hospital bed and telling me, 'Get the kids away from her.'" When she found out they were going, Jill became agitated, and her parents tried to placate her. "We couldn't do much else," said Joan. "Her condition had gotten so much worse and the doctors didn't know if she would live or die. We lied to her."

Next evening, after several delays, Jill was wheeled back

to the O.R., where the doctors opened up her stitches. She'd already had one surgery to replace the piece of her skull that had been "in storage." It was put back to protect her brain before she would be moved to rehab and begin learning to walk again. Again she developed an infection that meant it had to be removed a few days later and replaced permanently with a Plexiglas plate placed over the bone flap on her damaged right side. Debbie recalled thinking that Jill would be mad when she woke up and found her hair gone again. Her head was rebandaged and she was hooked up to an I.V. pumping fluids and antibiotics into her. Having spent twelve anxious hours at the hospital, Fred and Joan were exhausted. Tom arrived around midnight and persuaded them to get some rest even though he was just as tired. He too was by her side every day he wasn't traveling on business.

The next morning she felt better. But her head was half shaved and that made her look funny. That afternoon she kept pleading to be allowed to take a bath or a shower. Two days later, when Martha Williams was visiting and Debbie arrived with Rita, she was still going on about it. "I've been in here so long and all I want is a goddamn shower," she told them. Every time she was being wheeled to therapy or wherever, she'd ask, "Do you know where a shower is? I really need a shower." She lifted her arm and Rita told her, "Boy, you need a dip." "I do, I do," Jill said.

"I said, 'OK,' girl, we pulled the drape around her, showered her up, shaved her armpits and her legs and sprayed her with sunflower oil and put her in her Barbie pajamas. Debbie kidded she was Brain Trauma Barbie. That's when [Jill] told us, 'Jeff is lurking around the corners.' She said she saw him," said Rita. "But she also said she saw little pink elephants, so we just don't know. Now I think she was right."

In the shower Jill caught a glimpse of herself in the mirror.

They'd all been dreading her reaction when she would see her horrific injuries for the first time. She glanced in the glass and then peered at herself closely. Her long blonde hair was shorn, her face was crisscrossed with stitches and a huge chunk of her head was missing. "My God, there's a white hair in my eyebrow," she said. Everyone breathed a sigh of relief.

Over those first few weeks, she swayed between reality and semi-hallucinations. "She called me one night and said, 'Tom's coming over with the Jeep. Get me that dress we saw at Target, the brown one.' Then she said, 'Get me out of here, Mom and Dad can take care of me, they'd take better care of me than they do in this place,'" said Debbie. Yet there were days she was disarmingly lucid. "She had everyone in stitches at that damn hospital," said Joan. "They all loved her. A priest showed up one day and she told him, 'Look what your good Catholic boy did to me. I know I'm supposed to forgive, but excuse me if I don't right now.'"

By the end of May, it was clear that Jill's remarkable recovery was beginning to founder. The next few days were miserable. She underwent excruciating daily lumbar punches (spinal taps) to reduce the swelling on her brain, and passed out in the bathroom. She was moved back to the seventh floor I.C.U. Her pain was making her difficult and Joan spent most of the time in tears. Her temperature soared to 102, her neck and head hurt and she couldn't move an arm and a foot. She was put on morphine.

It didn't help anyone's mood when Amber Calloway reported that Jeff was back living at East Lake Road. She and her parents bumped into him out having dinner with his dad. He had given her a smile when he spotted her; she had wanted to rip his head off. Debbie was livid: "I am totally pissed off. It proves he doesn't give a rat's ass about what he's done. Would you show your face in public if you'd just bashed your wife's head in?" she vented to Tom. Zaney saw him pull up to a pizza place in town in Mark's flashy sports car. "I was absolutely appalled," she said. "I thought, 'You've got to be kidding me, she's in the hospital and here you are in the Jaguar with Mark, just hanging out?'"

By the beginning of June, Jill's fear of being attacked again was tangible. One morning she woke up Tom at 3:00, very upset. "Where are you? Why did you leave?" she asked him. "That was very difficult. She was afraid that Jeff was lurking around the hallways and could I come and get her? It tore at my heartstrings," he said. "She called a couple of times to say she was scared. I kind of chalked that up to short-term dementia, or whatever, after what she'd been through. I thought it was craziness, especially given the level of security supposedly in place there and having his mugshot hung up by the nurses' station close to her room."

Three days later, her amazing progress had totally stalled. Tom told Debbie he had taken Jill on a dinner date to the hospital cafeteria. She had been exhausted, headachy and bothered by her badly damaged eye, and was having difficulty with her balance. The next morning Debbie got a call at work wanting to know when she was coming for her. Debbie played along, telling her that she couldn't leave until Friday evening after work. "Can't wait," she was told. Then Jill wanted to know if Debbie had a pen because she needed to make a list of things for Joan and Fred to get for her: a pea coat, a fur headband, earmuffs and the dress from Target. They talked for fifteen minutes, covering everything from the kids and how they were coping, to Jill's terror of Jeff. Debbie later recalled telling her not to be afraid, that they were all there to make sure she didn't get hurt again.

But unknown to anyone, by the end of the first week in June when she was on another downward spiral, lethargic, uncooperative and in pain, Jill had every reason to be very afraid. Back on May 11, the day the first Family Court hearing was held to decide what was best for Tim and Mary, Jeff had logged on to his home computer, clicked on to the Internet and started checking out Web pages that contained information about lethal poisons. Eight days later, after the second hearing, he honed in on cyanide sites and browsed recipes detailing how to prepare a fatal dose.

9

Custody

A short distance from the hospital, a grand jury had been impaneled and was now hearing evidence. Debbie called Rick Trunfio, who assured her the case was coming along nicely. She told him about Jeff grinning at Amber. "Well, he won't be smiling much longer," Rick said.

When they met at the end of the month Trunfio had told her that the grand jury had accepted all the evidence and wouldn't need Jill's testimony. Debbie told him that if she was well enough, she was sure Jill would want to tell her side of the story. Trunfio added that Jeff was claiming self-defense, but he wasn't buying that scenario for a minute. The police investigation showed she was hit the first time as she was running out the backdoor into the yard and that she had been dragged back inside. That jelled with what Jill had told her family. Trunfio said they had found a counselor to see the children, but nothing had happened yet because Jeff had not put the money in escrow to cover the cost.

Just before the grand jury brought in a decision, Martha Williams called Jeff. "I got this strange idea in my head that

I had to get Jill's Christmas tree ornaments—she was like me, a nut about Christmas. I called him to tell him I wanted to come over to the house to pick them up and he started telling me how she was seeing someone, how bad that felt. I told him, 'I don't care if she was fucking the whole football team in the yard, that didn't excuse what you did.'" Nobody knows his side of the story, Jill had said terrible things to him and called him names, he had bleated. Martha told him she didn't want to hear any more. He told her to give Jill's hand a squeeze from him. "No," she said and hung up. "I was furious. He was trying to lay the blame on Jill."

On June 12, Jeff Cahill was indicted on multiple counts of assault, aggravated assault, use of a deadly weapon, disfigurement and depraved indifference to human life. The Russells got the satisfaction of seeing him on the TV news, being carted off in handcuffs. The day before, they had discovered that the insurance he had been required to take out on the kids didn't cover counseling. That was going to have to come from the Victims of Violent Crime fund. Jill had spent the day in the O.R. having a shunt put in. When she was wheeled out of recovery she gave her tearful parents a thumbs-up.

Four days later Jeff was arraigned. Cathy McDonald, Martha Williams and Michelle Morris joined Jill's parents and sister at the courthouse in Syracuse. Jeff arrived flanked by his lawyer, Richard Priest. He was wearing a suit and an arrogant sneer. He said "hi" to Martha as he passed by her. Judge William J. Burke listened to the charge and looked at him. "So he's out walking the streets? On a bond or cash bail?" he asked Priest incredulously. "Cash," the attorney replied. The judge shook his head and asked for a plea. "Not guilty," Jeff answered. A hearing was set for the judge's chambers for June 25.

Standing on the courthouse steps afterward, Rick Trunfio asked Jill's family to have faith in the system. It wasn't a good day for him to ask that. Jill was regressing, she was lethargic, she could no longer talk and was communicating only with her eyes. Her doctors decided that the shunt in her head was causing the problem because it was draining too much fluid and had caused her brain to shift. A new valve was ordered, but didn't solve the problem. On June 24 Fred and Joan got an early morning call from the hospital asking permission to replace it with another one.

A couple of days later, Jill was back in the I.C.U. having difficulty breathing. She underwent an M.R.I. that revealed that the new shunt was also causing problems, probably putting too much pressure on her brain stem. "After six weeks she developed meningitis," said Joan. "Every time they opened her head to fix it she would get meningitis. Then they couldn't get that shunt going to drain the fluid from around her brain and she got hydrocephalus." Her parents were nearly at the end of their rope and Debbie cried herself to sleep.

The one bright spot in those dark days was that David was able to juggle his job at the Garrison Bight Marina in Key West to let him fly up from Florida once a month and stay for four or five days at a time. Sometimes his buddy Kevin Killian, who had lived in Fort Lauderdale with David, Greg Owens and Jill, drove up from his home in Maryland. "She was like a sister to him, when they all lived together," said Joan.

A few days later, the shunt was removed from Jill's spine and another was put in her head on the opposite side from the bone flap. Again the family, her friends and Tom endured a long wait outside the I.C.U. Even when she was well enough to be transferred to the rehab unit, the problems recurred. "Some people just have a lot of trouble finding a system that works for them and unfortunately Ms. Cahill did. It took many, many operations, many, many times back to the operating room before we were able to get her through the infections," explained Dr. Rodziewicz.

In all, Jill underwent fifteen surgeries. As she was moved between intensive care and rehab, Dr. Rodziewicz and his staff kept the family informed of every single development; he talked often to Tim and Mary to explain what was happening with their mom. The visits from them seemed to give her the will to survive and to withstand the grueling months of recovery. The children talked about Jill to Joan and Fred, but they never mentioned the horrific incident that had put her in the hospital. One time Mark Cahill brought them to see their mom after visiting Jeff's parents and Debbie showed him a picture of Jill she had taken after the beating. He betrayed no emotion as he glanced at it briefly and told her that he had seen worse at Memorial Sloan-Kettering [the New York cancer hospital] where he volunteered.

The next day Mark called and asked if the kids could go to Cape Cod with Patty until July 6. He asked how Jill was doing and Debbie recalled being brutally honest with him. "I wanted him to know what that S.O.B. did," she said. "I told him taking the kids away depended on their counseling schedule. He was not aware that there was a schedule and seemed to think it was a one-time meeting. I explained this was going to be ongoing therapy for them." To herself, she thought, "These people are absolutely clueless."

Greg Monashefsky, the children's guardian, had arranged for them to meet with counselor Mary Kuhn and after that, he okayed the trip to the Cape. He told Debbie that Mary was a real professional and that Rick Trunfio was thrilled to have her. He said he had been in Family Court on June 18 and Jeff's petition to visit with his kids had been postponed until August.

The ordeal was taking a toll on all of them, Joan especially. She worried about Jill's fluctuating condition, about the children and what was shaping up to be a nasty custody battle. From the moment they got the call, the Russells had disassociated his family with what Jeff had done to their daughter. In the days that followed the beating, as the Russells kept a round-the-clock vigil by her bedside, they were grateful to the Cahills for taking care of Tim and Mary. But as the days progressed, it was natural that his family would draw the wagons around Jeff, no matter what he had done.

It seemed to the Russells that Jill's in-laws were playing fast and loose with the court order that stipulated that Jeff must not contact his children. There were the hikes in the woods—how hard would it be for Jeff to meet them away from prying eyes in Skaneateles? There were reports from neighbors and friends that they had seen the Jeep he was now driving parked outside stores when Patty was inside with the youngsters. And although they had complied with Rick Trunfio's demand that they warn the Cahills not to talk to the kids about the case, it was clear that the youngsters still believed that Jill had attacked Jeff with a knife. They had told the counselor that God wanted their father to do what he did and their mom deserved everything she got.

That was a prevailing sentiment held by more than Jeff's family. D.A. Bill Fitzpatrick, an avid golfer, encountered the "she asked for it" opinion when he dropped by the popular local golf store where Kevin Cahill worked. "I am in there, a friend of mine who I've known for years came up to me and said, 'I'd like you to meet somebody, his brother is in a bit of a jam.' I told him I'd really prefer not to do that and said, 'Why don't you have the guy's lawyer contact me? What kind of a jam is he in?' He said, 'Well, he was involved in an assault with his wife and your office is making a big deal out of it. We think the guy needs probation and counseling.'

" 'What's his name?' I asked. He tells me the name and I looked at him and said, 'My God, are you talking about the guy who beat his wife half to death with a baseball bat? Get a grip on reality here, he's not getting probation or counseling and he's going to state prison for a long period of time.' "

It also seemed that Jill's in-laws had little sympathy for

From left to right: Jill, Debbie, mom Joan and baby David in 1959.
Photo courtesy Russell family

Jill in her senior class picture at Tonawanda High School, New York.
Photo courtesy Russell family

ABOVE: Grace the Wonder Dog in Skaneateles. *Credit: Katy Price*

LEFT: Twenty-one-year-old Jill water-skiing in Fort Lauderdale. *Photo courtesy Russell family*

Jill with Barrington, her pet rabbit.
Photo courtesy Russell family

Michelle Morris, Jill and Amber Calloway
in Amber's store.
Credit: Suzanne Haux

Amber and Jill together,
the best of friends.
Photo courtesy Russell family

Amber, Jill, Susie Birchenough, Jill's sister Debbie
and Flower Fairies partner Michelle Morris.
Credit: Suzannne Haux

Jill and Jeff at Katy Price's apartment in Skaneateles.
Credit: Katy Price

Jeff and Jill at a party in August 1987.
Credit: Katy Price

Jill with Tim in the paddling pool, summer 1988.
Photo courtesy Russell family

Jill, Tim, Mary, and Nick the black lab on the porch of the old farmhouse at 2444 East Lake Road, Spafford, where the Cahills lived with their two children.
Photo courtesy Russell family

Jeff Cahill looking contemplative about his future.
Credit: The Post-Standard

Jeff Cahill in handcuffs at the courthouse.
Credit: The Post-Standard

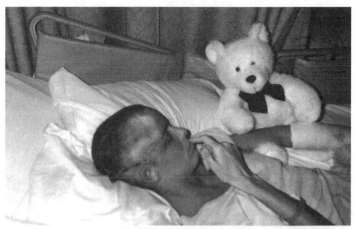

After the April 21 beating: Jill with her teddy bear at University Hospital.
Syracuse 1998.
Photo courtesy Russell Family

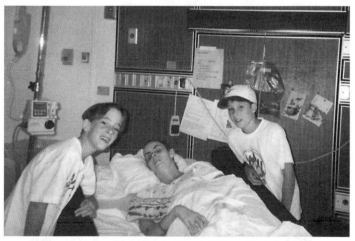

Nearly six months after the beating: Tim and Mary visit their mother at
University Hospital. She had just relearned how to say their names.
Photo courtesy Russell family

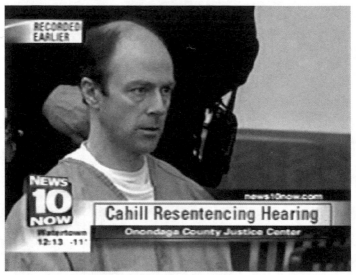

Jeff Cahill at his sentencing.
Courtesy Channel 10 News. Frame grab by Jason Homler.

Joan and Fred Russell, Debbie and Bill Jaeger in Tonawanda.
Credit: Marion Collins

the ordeal the Russells were going through. But to some of their friends, the Cahills' behavior was callous. "After Jill is in the hospital, the rich brother, Mark, the rich stockbroker, sends her parents a bunch of parking tickets, saying that Jill racked them up while she was in New York borrowing his Jeep eight months before. It turned out that not only was she not there at that time anyway, but just the gall of a millionaire sending these grief-stricken parents parking tickets to pay; how heartless can you get?" said Katy Price.

On the last day of June, the hospital called to say Jill was back in surgery and had meningitis again. All day the family waited at the hospital for news. By midnight she was in the I.C.U. on a ventilator, where she'd be kept until she was stabilized. It was the third surgery that week and the next forty-eight hours were crucial. The new drain in her head seemed to be working, but she was now being fed with a tube into her stomach since she was so malnourished. Her family was worried sick. Joan and Debbie called Rick Trunfio and told him Jill was back on the critical list.

Fred, Joan and Dave, who was visiting from Key West, called the kids at the Cape and kept them on the line as long as possible on Patty's "dime." Mary chattered excitedly about her upcoming birthday. On July 12, the whole family, along with Tim and Mary, met with Dr. Rodziewicz and their counselor. The doctor told the children how important it was that they help their mom's recovery as he explained her latest upcoming surgery.

That weekend was beautiful, and back at Camp Jill (their name for the McDonalds' guesthouse) they were hanging out at the pool when Debbie spotted Jim Cahill. "I walked back to the house to do something and I saw him in the driveway," she said. "I went to tell my folks and when I went back he was gone. Tom McDonald phoned him to ask if he was looking for anything. 'No,' he said, 'I was just checking up on the kids.' Jim then said he had come to take Tim to the Pizza

Hut—not 'the girl,' just Tim. He always called her 'the girl.'
'We should talk sometime,' he told Tom, who said, 'Fine, but
call first.' " Later that night Kevin called to arrange to take the
kids to 9:30 A.M. Mass.

That set the counselor into overdrive. Under no circum-
stances should the children be alone with Uncle Howdy
(Kevin), she stressed; she had concluded he was feeding
them negative information.

July 15 was Mary's eighth birthday. The family did their
best to make it a happy one by having friends come over to
the McDonalds' house and the next day they had a party in
Jill's room. The nurse had told Joan that Jill was humming
along with the radio that morning. Debbie had bought a
Beanie Baby for Jill to give to Mary and when they sang
"Happy Birthday," her heart monitor peaked. When they said
goodbye, her eyes filled with tears. None of her father's family called or sent Mary a card, but Cathy McDonald got a call
from a Cahill family friend who told her that Jeff "is very re-
morseful and loves Jill very much."

The next weekend Kevin called again wanting to take the
kids to church. When he was told the Russells would
take them, he asked if he could pick them up afterwards to
take them to Patty's to give Mary her (four days late) gifts.
Joan told him he would have to bring them to the McDonalds'. Why? he asked. She reminded him that the legal
guardian had said that he could only see them when Joan
and Fred were present. The phone rang again. Joan picked
up and Kevin began yelling at her. She hung up.

A few minutes later Jim Cahill came whipping up the
drive. "What's going on?" he demanded. Joan led him into
the back yard where everyone was sitting and said, "We've
got company." Tom McDonald stood up and asked, "Who the
hell are you?" and laced into him about his announced visit
earlier that week. Then the Russells let Jim Cahill know exactly what was going on, how desperately ill Jill was, what

they were dealing with. They told him Tim and Mary would not be going back to the Cape because it was crucial for them to be near Jill. Fred boiled over and lashed out: "You never even sent her a damn card. I don't care if you hated her, she's your daughter-in-law."

Jill's condition worsened. When her parents arrived at the hospital on the 19th she wasn't responding. Another CAT scan revealed fluid building up under the bone flap and pushing on her brain and Dr. Rodziewicz scheduled immediate surgery. They called Tom, who came rushing over. Although the doctor said he was optimistic she'd pull through, they waited, immobilized with grief and worry, while Jill went back to the O.R.

"At the time we were going through two or three surgeries in a week and we hadn't gotten to see the children, and I was in tears," said Joan. "Then Patty showed up [at the studio] and I remember her sitting there telling me that Jeff really loves his children and there's proof. 'Remember the time when Mary fell and cut her head? Jill stayed home with Tim and I went with Jeff to the hospital and Jeff passed right out cold and that's a sign of his love for her,' she said.

"I said, 'Was it a true sign of love when he took the baseball bat to Jill?' I was so upset that day and I am thinking, 'I've got Jilly in there, not knowing if she is going to live for another minute and you are talking about Jeff loving his kids.' I couldn't wait to get her outside. It was Jeff's fault Mary hurt her head in the first place, he was roughhousing with her."

Three months to the day after she had arrived at University, Joan and Fred learned that when one of the nurses told Jill her mom and dad loved her, she had replied clear as a bell, "I love them too." It was the first time she had spoken in over four weeks and they were overjoyed. Joan shed tears of happiness. Two days later she had a temperature of 104 degrees and was battling another potentially fatal bout of meningitis. For Fred and Joan the tension was nearly unbearable, but they stayed with her the whole time, going home only twice, once in July so that Joan could have a mammogram—she'd had cancer eight years before and the doctor had found a lump in her other breast which, mercifully, turned out to be benign, and in September, to attend a wedding.

Mary Kuhn called Debbie. Since starting counseling, Tim was more open and forthcoming. He understood that his mother was gravely ill and that his dad might not be around for a long time. Mary was still in denial, and one social worker described her as "Pollyanna on Eggshells." She had turned to Debbie for hugs and kisses during their week at camp. The counselor had also met with Jeff. He thought that April 21 was just another day and didn't see why the kids would have any problem dealing with it.

At the beginning of August Fred and Joan hired lawyer Marilyn Miller to petition for custody. Jeff was supposed to be paying $400 a month for child support and they hadn't seen a cent. Patty, who had taken herself off to Cape Cod, raced back home. The Russells met with her and Mark to decide how the kids would spend the rest of the month. They said they understood that the children needed to be in town to keep their weekly visits with their counselor and to see Jill and that they would be living at the McDonalds' home. Debbie felt sorry for Patty, who looked thin, weary and heartsick, and thought both Mark and his mother were doing their best for Tim and Mary.

In the middle of the month, when Jill was scheduled to have the first of many surgeries needed to repair her broken eye socket and caved-in skull, the Cahills cross-petitioned, claiming that they were closer to the kids, and that they had more money and could take better care of them; the fragile truce between the two families foundered. The discussion was postponed for a week with Fred and Joan getting custody until then. They had been horrified to discover that the children had been taken back to the home where they'd seen their mother battered senseless, to use the pool.

The families brushed against each other at one of Tim's basketball games. Mark came up to Fred and said his dad wanted to speak to him. Then they walked right by without saying a word. "I was there with my son David," said Fred. "I said to him, 'This is bullshit, I'm going over to see what they want.' I said, 'Hello, Jim, you wanted to talk to me?'

"He said, 'I want to take the kids to church this weekend.'

" 'No,' I said. 'They're with us this weekend. You want to take them to church, take them next weekend.'

" 'Well, Patty and I wanted to take them.'

" 'No,' I said. 'The answer is no,' and walked away."

"They gave us such grief," said Joan. "I turned up at school one day to pick up the kids and the principal said, 'You can't take them. Mrs. Cahill is in charge of the children.'" He said he had a letter from her son Jeff, who had granted temporary guardianship to his parents in an affidavit he signed two days after being arrested. That was the last straw for Fred, who went straight to the court. He came back with the papers showing we had been awarded custody. 'That's all I wanted to see,' said the principal."

"They took the kids to the crime scene," said Debbie "took them to swim in the pool, took them on trips out in the woods with the uncles in violation of the court order. A friend said she had met the kids at the hairdresser's. Patty had taken them for a haircut and their father was in the Jeep outside. That was a violation of the court order of protection that barred Jeff from contacting his children." To Debbie, they acted as if they were above the law.

Marilyn Miller took the Russells' reservations about Jill's in-laws to Judge Anthony Paris. The children had divulged what they were being told by the father's family without prompting, she said. "There is no reason to believe that the children would be making up these stories. We never had a trial on the custody issues, so a lot of the things that the Cahills allegedly did that would make your skin crawl were never tested in court. We had a wonderful judge who listened to me and/or the law guardian when we told him that we had information to believe that 'thus and so' had occurred and he acted on it."

At one point in the proceedings when both sides were in chambers the judge had a question for Mary Kuhn. Miller dialed her number on her cell phone and handed the phone to the judge. "That call blew Jeff's attorney and his parents' attorney out of the water—they had no arguments that would stand up to the children's therapist's recommendations," she recalled.

On August 18, when Jim and Patty Cahill decided to countersue for custody, Jeff's lawyer was up in arms. If the case went ahead Jeff would be required to testify for the first time under oath about the night of the assault, as would his parents, and with the criminal trial looming, he was not about to allow any of them to take the stand in Family Court. Two days later, as Joan and Fred were with Marilyn prepping for cross-examination and Jill was undergoing her fifteenth surgery, the Cahills dropped their suit. To give them a welcome break from what had been a trying day, Tom took Joan, Fred and Debbie out on a boat ride. When they returned Jill was back in her room, trying to talk and squeezing their hands.

She was fighting back from her latest operation as a visitation agreement was still being hammered out. Throughout the hearing, Joan was unnerved by Jim Cahill, who, she said, winked and pointed at her whenever she spoke. Then he took umbrage at his lawyer and asked him to leave. Patty insisted he stay. When it came her turn to speak, Patty denied she'd ever said the kids didn't need counseling until Joan challenged her and repeated their conversation. According to Joan, she then backtracked, blaming the paperwork for the delay.

"Mary Kuhn wasn't there for some reason," said Debbie. "It ended up just about half and half and the Cahills were happy about that. Then when Mary heard about it, she was livid. 'That's way too much time for those children to be with the Cahills,' she said. "We were back in court next day. I could see the sparks coming out of her eyes and ears as she talked to the judge. 'I can only give you so much information, but if you subpoena me, I'll give you all of it.' she said."

She cited the Cahills' failure to get the children therapy until ordered to do so by the court two months after seeing their mother beaten, and their insistence that it was a family matter that did not warrant the help of professionals. The children were told not to show emotion, despite the horror of what they had witnessed; the Cahills had made inappropriate comments to the children despite the court order which forbade them to discuss the case and had allowed Mark to have unsupervised visits with them.

When the judge read her report, he ruled that the Cahills could have the children every other weekend from 9:00 A.M. Saturday until 4:00 P.M. on Sunday and after school until 7:00 P.M. on Wednesdays. Uncle Howdy (Kevin) was to have no contact with them at all. Uncle Mark (Nipper) could only see them if Patty or Jim were present.

"The next time Tim and Mary were to go to Jeff's parents', Kevin's twin, Brian Cahill, arrived to collect them," said Debbie. "He has been away from the family for twenty years. He was very nice and concerned about Jill and told us, 'I can't tell you how sorry I am about this.' Fred and Joan showed him pictures of Jill they had taken in the hospital and he seemed very moved."

At last Jill was slowly improving. "For most of the summer she was in—they didn't call it a coma—sometimes you might see her open her eyes a little," said Martha Williams.

"The nurses would say, 'We're sure we saw her tapping her feet to that Tom Petty song,' so we made sure she had that Tom Petty tape she loved. They'd say, 'She said something today,' but for the most part when I was going up there, I was talking to her and she was laying there as though she was napping and if her eyes fluttered, that was a big deal. There were many times when I'd get a call at two in the morning saying she was going into brain surgery and I'd say to myself, 'This is it, she's not going to make it.'

"I remember a time when she was coming out of it, in early September, she couldn't speak very well and she was a lot different from how she'd been when she went in—then she was joking about having to shave her legs and she was just like Jill. I took my little niece to see her and she was a little apprehensive, but as soon as she walked into the room Jill said, 'Oh, Julie, how nice of you to come up and visit me.' Even though she had a shaved head and terrible bashes in her skull, she was just herself. But when she woke at the end of the summer she wasn't herself and then we were really nervous that she would ever make a recovery, that she would ever live outside a nursing home."

Tom called Debbie and told her he'd visited Jill and when he put his head on her shoulder she had reached up to touch his face. On August 20 she got out of I.C.U. Physical therapists were working with her daily and she was infection-free at last. The following weekend, Patty called to check whether the kids had attended church. Joan told her Tim had been sick all night and Mary didn't want to go, so she hadn't taken them. Patty said, "I'll take them, after all, it is their upbringing." Once again Joan told her that no, she couldn't. The court order was clear when she could see the kids and this wasn't one of the days. Mary Kuhn told Debbie after the children's weekly session that Fred and Joan had all the authority now and they should use it.

She also told Debbie she was recommending that the

children see their father, not for his sake, but for theirs. She had made clear what he had to tell the children: what happened back in April was between the adults, Jeff did something very wrong, he's sorry for it and it had nothing to do with them. If he varied from the approved script, the visits would stop.

While Fred and Joan were relieved to have the custody situation settled, they were running on empty. Despite the McDonalds' generosity in providing a place for them to stay throughout this nightmare, their Social Security income was stretched to the limits. They had shelved their retirement to become parents to two children who had witnessed unimaginable horror, were desperately missing their mom and dad and had been exposed to all sorts of confusing information, and they were bearing the brunt of the youngsters' hurt, anger and frustration. Mary Kuhn advised them, "You have to treat them as if they were your own."

10

Cyanide

It was four months since Jeff's father and brother had bailed him out of jail. He was seen driving around town and going in and out of the house on East Lake Road. And at last he had regular employment doing add jobs at a car dealership in Fayetteville owned by his brother Tim's father-in-law. At any rate, he did not keep a low profile and the incident with Jill continued to polarize the affluent village, with the jocks who had grown up with Jeff deciding she'd had it coming, and the folks who knew her saying Jeff Cahill should be locked up and the key thrown away.

But while his neighbors were arguing about him, Jeff was busy on the computer. After his first couple of forays on the Internet that coincided with Family Court hearings about the children, he began his research in earnest. By the beginning of July, he had narrowed his choice of toxin down to cyanide potassium. He surfed through on-line cyanide sites to find out how to concoct a deadly mix and where to obtain the ingredients.

Over the next few weeks, after 68 hits, he became

extremely knowledgeable about cyanide and devised a plan. Although he could order it on line, he knew that buying poison was not exactly like ordering a sweater from L.L. Bean; it was not going be delivered to his door with a friendly smile and a wave. What he had to do was to get between the mailman and a seemingly legitimate purchaser. He came up with a solution when he lighted upon an outfit that used cyanide in manufacturing, and was just a few miles away in DeWitt, an eastern suburb of Syracuse.

The company in question, General Super Plating, was a third-generation family-owned business that had been in operation since 1932. Now it occupies a 75,000-square-foot plant, has 200 employees and specializes in very high-quality work using chrome, copper, nickel, palladium and even gold to finish plastics and metals for all kinds of industries. Among its customers are giants of aerospace, electric, cosmetics and military hardware manufacture whose brand names read like a Fortune 500 list: Chrysler, Grumman, Harley-Davidson, Chanel, Calvin Klein, Motorola, Kodak, General Electric, Avon and Victoria's Secret. How perfect was that?

He did a dummy run to see how easy it would be to persuade a United Parcel Service guy to part with a package. He was watching on July 7, as 34-year-old Robert Leo pulled his UPS truck behind the Home Depot store at 5814 Bridge Street across from the lot from General Super Plating around 9:30 A.M. From the seat beside him, Jeff lifted a well-worn maroon-colored baseball cap with a logo in front and stuck it on his head, covered his eyes with a pair of blue-tinted dark sunglasses and walked over to the brown van. Leo was in the back of the truck checking his list of deliveries when he heard Jeff approach and looked up inquiringly.

"Do you have a Next Day Air package for General Super Plating?" Since he was smartly dressed in a dark-colored pin-striped, button-down shirt, Leo assumed that he was an employee of the company and handed him a pile of packages. Jeff quickly rifled through them, picked out one with a California return address and made off quickly. Leo yelled after him: "Hey, I need your name and you have to sign for it." Jeff shouted back, "It's Smith," and kept going. Leo typed "Smith" into his handheld computer.

Jeff couldn't believe how simple that had been, and chuckled all the way home, where he got back on line to find a source for the chemicals, choosing an outfit in California. Next he hit the phones, contacting Bryant Labs of Berkeley, CA, to find out the procedure for buying them. Another call provided him with the name of the employee at GSP who placed orders. Then he made a copy of the GSP logo and printed out his own crude reproduction of it to use as a letterhead. On it he put an order number, 5076, and addressed it to Bryant Labs, misspelling the city twice as "Berkley" before typing in his request for 1 lb. KCN (Potassium Cyanide) at $29.85 and 125 grams of sodium formate costing $14.50. He added $50 for shipping and handling and another $26.50 to cover the surcharge for dispatching hazardous and poisonous materials.

He wrote that it was to be paid for C.O.D., and delivered via UPS to General Super Plating on July 10. At the bottom, he signed "Tracey Jones." The next day the order was forwarded from Bryant Labs to its main supplier, Spectrum Labs, who shipped it by ground on July 9, and then, realizing they'd made a mistake, sent out another batch by air.

That same day, Jeff attended a pre-trial hearing on the assault charges. On July 10, 13 and 16, Spectrum Labs received three more orders supposedly from General Super Plating and dispatched them all by UPS.

Every other day for the next couple of weeks, Jeff would be lurking near the General Super Plating building as Bob Leo made his regular stops at Bally Matrix, Chimney's Video, Kayser Beauty Supply, Home Depot and General Super Plating, and each time, he'd ask if Leo had any packages for the company. The first couple of times there were none; Leo had changed his routine and had made his delivery to the plating firm before Jeff showed up.

One time Leo was driving on an access road between Niagara Mohawk and Falso Heating Co. when he noticed a black Jeep Wrangler parked on the hard shoulder. "It was dirty and I saw the rear window had either some sort of smudge on it or it was broken," he told the cops. As he passed, he recognized the driver as the guy who'd been pestering him. Jeff began signaling him to stop, but Leo had ignored him and kept going.

Oblivious to the fact that the driver was growing mightily suspicious and might turn him in, Jeff made another attempt to intercept him. On July 17 Leo was making a delivery to McDonald's at 3207 Erie Boulevard in DeWitt around 9:00 in the morning. It was a warm day and he had opened both doors of the cab. He had just come out of the restaurant and was about to step into the driver's side when he noticed Jeff standing outside the passenger door. By this time Leo, who at nearly seven feet tall is an imposing figure, was fed up being accosted.

"I was mad to see this man outside my truck because he had been bothering me for the past week or so about packages for General Super Plating and I said, 'I was already there. I made the delivery. Go over and talk to Cindy Brenno,'" he later said in court. He told them that every time he appeared, Jeff was smartly, but casually dressed, and always wore the same maroon cap with the logo in front and sunglasses.

That same day, Leo shared his suspicions with Kevin Keenan, a General Super Plating truck driver working the early shift in shipping and receiving. When the UPS van arrived, it was Keenan's job to check the delivery list, sign it and distribute the packages to the various departments. Keenan told the police that Leo had said some guy was trying to pass himself off as one of their employees and steal packages. Leo had given him a detailed description of Jeff and his vehicle.

Around lunchtime he was driving from the warehouse back to the shipping dock when he pulled up abruptly. "I saw the vehicle that Bobby had described to me. The black Jeep was parked right there. It kind of caught me off-guard. The man inside it, who was wearing exactly the same outfit Bobby had described, waved at me." Keenan looked at the license plate that had caught his eye because it was askew. As soon as he got inside the shipping office he wrote down the tag number, S18-7MT, on the notice board.

It wasn't the first time that Jeff had shown up at the plant. Aware that Leo had altered his schedule, he placed his third order for the deadly toxins on July 13 and asked for it to be sent by two-day service. Two days later, he had watched from his vantage point in the parking lot as the brown van pulled in, then drove away. As soon as the shipping clerk took off to make his rounds, Jeff slipped in and stole a package. It contained more than enough to do the job. His return trip to the plant to try to steal the last delivery was just for insurance.

Keenan took his suspicions to accountant Tracy Jones and discovered that he wasn't the only one at General Super Plating who smelled a rat. She had been trying to make sense of two packages of chemicals she had received; she hadn't ordered them and as far as she could make out, no one else in the company had either. As soon as they had arrived she had sent them over to the lab, but when she dropped by later, she was told that they contained stuff they never used.

She checked to see where they had come from. The invoices were from Spectrum Labs, and were for three 500-milligram bottles of potassium cyanide and a container of potassium formate. The company never ordered chemicals in such small quantities—when General Super Plating ordered cyanide, they got two or three 1,600-pound containers of it at a time. She called Bryant Labs, who provided proof of delivery from UPS. There was another mystery: a third package had been entered into the General Super Plating shipping log and it was missing.

"I called trying to find why they had been sent to me with my name on them and to find out where they had gotten my name. We had never ordered anything from this company. They said I had faxed them a letter requesting this order. I asked them to fax it back to me," Tracy said at the trial. When it arrived, the order was obviously a fake. All orders from General Super Plating are written on a standardized requisition form, the company's letterhead bore no resemblance to the real thing and her name was wrong, spelled "Tracey" with an "e." The order also listed her as Purchasing Director, a position that didn't even exist at GSP.

She thought back to July 17 when Cindy Brenno from the shipping department had called and said a man wearing a red baseball cap and sunglasses was looking for a package delivered by UPS from California. Cindy had sent him to the front desk and Tracy remembered that he'd never shown up. She reported what had been going on to her boss and the company's attorney, who told her to call the DeWitt police. Around 2:20 P.M., Officer Mark Roberts drove out to the plant and took statements from Tracy, Kevin Keenan and Cindy Brenno. He left the cyanide and the fake fax with her and went home at 3:00 P.M. when his shift ended.

The next day Officer Roberts traced the license plate of the black Jeep that had stalked the UPS driver to a Mark W. Cahill, of 666 Greenwich Avenue in Manhattan. He ran the name through the police computer and came up with nothing; Mark Cahill was clean. With the city police and the state cops not having access to each other's data banks, a situation that has been addressed since 9/11, his search did not spit out that he was the brother of Jeff Cahill. And incredibly, the name Cahill did not ring any bells in the DeWitt Police Department despite the beating of Jill Cahill having been widely reported in the local news.

Even more incredible is the fact that someone had illegally obtained enough deadly poison to cause several agonizing deaths, and this didn't motivate the DeWitt police to track down the culprit. In a mind-boggling oversight, no one called Mark Cahill to ask him why he (or someone driving his Jeep) was trying to relieve a UPS man of packages of deadly chemicals in upstate New York. Officer Roberts, a fifteen-year veteran cop, submitted a four-page report stating that the packages had been missing for three weeks, and the amount in question was too small to be used in the manufacture of drugs. Why he mentioned that is a bit of a puzzle. Experts say cyanide is never used in the manufacture of recreational drugs, since killing the user would diminish the market. "There is, however, enough to use as a poison," he added ominously, and sent out a description of the Jeep along with its owner's name to all local police districts including Onondaga County. No one bit.

Roberts handed the report to his supervisor, who stuck it in a non-active file. "The officer made the assumption that the person reading the number plate had juxtaposed some numbers and gotten it wrong," said Bill Fitzpatrick.

On August 18, Jeff's lawyers finally rolled out their case. They would plead self-defense and insanity and moved to suppress not only his confession, but also all the blood and forensic evidence. "The judge just rolled her eyes," said Debbie. Trunfio warned her they'd be in for a fight. "Good," she said. "I bet the jury will be harder on him than if he took a plea bargain." If anyone was insane, she told him, it was Jill, for putting up with all his crap for the last six years.

Two days later, the custody battle for Tim and Mary was back in Family Court where Judge Paris awarded temporary custody to Jill's parents, visiting rights to the Cahills, and limited the access Jeff's brothers had to their nephew and niece while his case was unresolved.

The Cahills would be allowed to see their grandchildren every other weekend, one afternoon and one evening a week. He also ordered that Kevin Cahill would have no contact with the children at all and his brother Mark could only see the children in the company of his parents. He stipulated that the children would remain in the Skaneateles school district. Judge Paris put a gag order on the proceedings and warned both sides they'd be in trouble if they breached it.

While the custody question was settled for the time being, the Russells were still struggling to keep their financial heads above water. The children were getting no support from their father, and Fred and Joan were already stretched to the limit and faced with growing legal fees. With Jill's medical bills mounting up, they were forced to apply for Medicaid.

They were also conscious that Jeff was uncomfortably close. Cathy McDonald tried to get the children onto a different school bus after she found that the one that picked them up was stopping in front of their old house, where he was living with the two dogs. "He was right down the road from us," said Joan. "We only saw him once when he drove past one day while we were waiting for the bus to drop off the kids." They never spoke to him again. It was bad enough that they had been forced to face him in court during the protracted custody battle. "At one of the hearings Jeff was there and for a few seconds, his eyes locked with mine," said Joan. The exchange had not gone unnoticed by the lawyer representing the Russells. "She told me, 'That bastard has no remorse.' It was true. I felt, the way he stared at me, he could have killed me too."

While her husband was plotting to obtain poison and her family was fighting for her kids, Jill lay in a twilight world, drifting in and out of consciousness as her body battled the effects of her multiple surgeries, and the parts of her brain that were not damaged struggled to take over the functions of the brain cells that had been killed. From time to time she seemed to understand what was being said, but mostly, she lay in what seemed like a terminal sleep. Joan rarely left her side.

Her friends Zaney, Katy, Michelle and Cathy visited her whenever they could. Tom was by her side every moment that he was not at work or on a business trip. He learned more about brain trauma than he'd ever wanted to. "There were so many complications and probably the most frustrating thing was the meningitis, which would come and go. And it was real difficult to see her slip out of this miraculous recovery post surgery," he said.

"I don't think anyone gave up hope even though we knew it would be a long hard path, given what she had lost. Basically she was paralyzed on one entire side of her body. She went from jumping out of her bed a week after the assault and from having full use of all her faculties to being bedridden and half-paralyzed and withering away. The number of operations she endured through this whole process were more than any human could ever stand."

As the months wore on, some of her early visitors fell by the wayside, unable to take the sadness. "She was pretty normal for a while, but after they put a shunt into her head she started looking pretty scary, because the whole side of her face was sunk in so bad, and I think a lot of people stopped visiting her at that point because they couldn't bear looking at her and they were thinking, 'This isn't Jill,'" said Katy.

"I went every day. I worked ten minutes away and so I could go on my lunch hour. For some reason they couldn't get her to eat and she would eat if I fed her, but she wouldn't if anyone else did. A lot of times I went when no one else was there, when Fred and Joan had already gone back to Skaneateles and she'd be sitting in this room freezing, her skinny little arms, which were like sticks at this point, sitting on the arm of the wheelchair with no padding or pillow under her, and she was uncomfortable. It was just like [the hospital] forgot about her. She used to say to me, 'You know, Katy, Jeff's been in here,' and I would say, 'No, Jill,' and I really didn't believe her. When I look back, I kick myself for that, because he probably went in right after I left."

Another loyal visitor was Chris Tormey, her friend from the airline. He had also spent time at University Hospital after suffering serious brain injury in a 1993 auto crash while driving one night to Cazenovia, New York, from Washington, D.C., where he had been X-raying mummies at the Smithsonian.

"I was drinking and driving and I went off the road. The vehicle rolled twice, then hit the shoulder and then I am in the opposite lane facing backwards. A guy came around the corner speeding and hit me head-on. He got out of his Dodge Caravan and it blew up. The last thing I remember was this semi-trailer coming at me. I got my seat belt undone and moved to the back. They got me out of the vehicle and airlifted me in a coma to University."

Chris wanted to boost Fred and Joan, to show them that with brain injuries, recovery is possible. "Every area of my brain had trauma, and my point was that I had sustained that severe damage and I recovered to the point that I did." Chris went on to major in political science at SUNY–Albany.

At the beginning of September Jeff was back in court objecting to the prosecution's request for a blood sample. His attorneys, Dick Priest and his sidekick Gary Miles, argued in all the pre-trial conferences and motions before the court that Jeff had acted in self-defense. Rick Trunfio said they had already matched some of the blood to Jill, but finding out exactly whose blood was found where was crucial to either confirming or debunking Jeff's claim that he'd hit his wife to save his own skin. While they were at it, Trunfio added, they'd like saliva, pubic and head hair samples. The court ruled that Jeff had to comply.

Jill was now under the care of Dr. Stephen Lebduska in the coma recovery unit where she'd been moved at the end of August. At the trial, he described how the athletic, vibrant Jill had wasted away in the months after the assault. "She looked like she was starving. Although she was receiving adequate nutrition, it was all going intravenously because she had complications and multiple surgeries.

"She wasn't moving much, there was some very slight movement in her upper right arm. She couldn't speak when she came to us in August and was just partially opening her eyes. We continued with aggressive nutrition and this coma stimulation program and over the two months she was my patient, she slowly but steadily improved."

But although to her family the progress was agonizing, by the time fall rolled around Jill was fitfully awake and conscious. "By October, she could tell me the names of her children, she could answer simple yes or no questions fairly consistently. She occasionally asked questions and that's a sign of even higher cognitive function," said Dr. Lebduska.

Nurse Julie Labayewski remembered that Jill's room was festooned with pictures of her kids and of her gardens. "She couldn't talk when I first met her. In the last four or five weeks before she died she began to say some simple words, one or two at a time. She would follow you with her eyes when you were in the room. If you had a picture she could look towards that picture, look at people who were near her, but initially, she couldn't communicate back to us."

Julie described how she cared for Jill and the other couple of patients in the unit. She gave them their meds, helped them with meals and bathing, and guided them through the exercises prescribed by the therapist. "We would get her out of bed, give family members ideas of what to do so they could work with her, like making sure they stood at a certain side to make her turn her head, make her try to reach for something. Initially she was on the sixth-floor Coma Recovery Unit, then because there was some construction at the hospital, she was moved to the second-floor rehab.

Jill had also made her first trips outside, with her father pushing her in a wheelchair around the hospital grounds. And Jill was determined to help herself. She tried to wash her face and comb her hair. "It was like she was coming out of a stroke," said Joan.

In clinical terms, Jill's progress was being measured weekly by the coma recovery scale, which goes from 0 to 25. At the beginning of May she had registered a 5 and by October, she had moved up to 23. Her devoted nurses shared her joy with each new accomplishment. Some of them burst into tears when she stuck out her tongue four times on command.

The first week in October, Patricia Cahill showed up to see her daughter-in-law for the first time since she'd watched her loaded half-dead into an ambulance months before. She had called Joan saying she would like to visit Jill, and Joan had consulted the counselor who told her it might be good for Patty to see the damage Jeff had done. Joan told Patty she would speak to the doctors and let her know. The next morning Fred and Joan headed over to the hospital around 11:00 A.M. "When we got off the elevator, she's sitting there with her Bible and rosary and a little cooler with some yogurt. I had told her on the phone that Jill was starting to eat Jell-O and pudding," said Joan.

"I went to talk to the nurse to see if it was OK. 'Son of a bitch,' I said when I walked in the room. 'What's the matter?' she asked. 'Her mother-in-law is here and wants to see her,' I began, then I turned around and she's walking in with Fred! I was mad at Fred. She walked over to Jill and said something. Jill didn't answer, she just looked at her. Then she stuck to the wall and watched the nurses talking to Jill and taking her out of bed to put her in the wheelchair, and all the way down to therapy, Patty's pushing her and going on about her cataracts!"

While Jill was inching her way back to her old life, Cathy and Michelle and her friends in Skaneateles were organizing a fund-raiser to be held on Sunday, October 25. "Put Out the Pumpkins, Bring In the Bunnies" was billed as a harvest festival with a silent auction to help the Cahill children. It had been weeks in the pipeline and everyone had worked around the clock to make it a success.

"We started out with a handful of people and a mission to raise money for the children. They weren't getting any support from Jeff's family and Jill's parents needed help," said Michelle. "Some people were reluctant to give, as they weren't sure that the money was going to the kids. We had to do a lot of convincing in the beginning that the money raised was only for them. We had about five or six weeks to pull this off. Cathy and I hit the streets of Skaneateles and Auburn soliciting donations from local merchants."

Cathy and Michelle ordered up a bunch of specially printed tee-shirts for the event and were so thrilled with the results, they wanted to show them to Jill. Michelle is haunted by the conviction that there was something more pressing on Jill's mind that night than looking at shirts. "We stopped by the hospital and Tom was there," she said. "She was sitting up, at this point she was still not talking, but I think that she pretty much knew what was going on. I felt she knew. I was showing her the newspaper article about the fund-raiser and she kept smacking the paper down and trying to tell me something and I couldn't understand what it was. I am sure now that it was that Jeff had been in there."

Nurse Julie also noticed that Jill was disturbed. "A couple of days before she died she was more tearful than normal, very tearful at times, saying her kids' names, she was saying 'Mary' a lot. You could always tell that whatever she was doing, it was for her kids. Brain injury patients can be very emotional. Sometimes you don't know whether it's frustration, fear, or what's going on."

On October 24, Tom McDonald saw Mark Cahill at the soccer field. The hood of his convertible Jaguar was down, and in the back seat, looking for all the world like Princess Diana, was Mary. Despite the court ruling that Patty or Jim had to be present when Mark was with the children, they were nowhere to be seen and Mary wasn't wearing a seat belt. Mary Kuhn suggested that Cathy call the Cahills and tell them about the upcoming fund-raiser.

The event was a huge success. Held at Hobbit Hollow Barn on West Lake Road, about a mile out of town, it drew nearly 1,000 people and all the local press. It was a beautiful, warm day and the foliage was picture-perfect. There was a country & western band and the local high school kids sang. There was face painting and pillowcase painting for Trick or Treat bags, a huge bake sale, a chili cooking contest and a silent auction. The final tally was close to $66,000.

Zaney had also seen Jill just prior to the event and couldn't get the visit out of her mind. "I was flustered because I knew Jill was trying to tell me something. I was trying to figure out what it was and I was trying to be friendly."

While the fund-raiser was in full swing, a TV crew went out to 2444 East Lake Road. "They knocked on Jeff's door and when he opened it [they] provoked him: 'What do you think about having this fund-raiser for your family?' He slammed the door without saying a word. They showed it on the evening news. Now his embarrassment was out there publicly," said Michelle.

On Monday, Cathy and Jill set up shop at Cathy's house to distribute all the items from the auction. They had organized a bank account and used a PO box for collecting donations. That afternoon, Patty met her granddaughter at the school bus and handed her a paper bag. Mary had been making a model of a bug for a science project at school and Fred was helping her. During her weekend visit to her Cahill grandparents she had started making another one while she was there and Nano said her dad would finish it for her. The Russells believed this was another deliberate flouting of the court order that banned all contact of any kind between Jeff and his children. Debbie called Rick Trunfio and told him. "I don't fucking believe it," he said. That evening Patty arrived at the door with blueberry muffins for Mary.

On Tuesday, Michelle went back to Cathy's, where they worked all day winding up the fund-raiser. Around 4:00 she saw Jeff driving the Jeep in the village and later remembered thinking, I wonder where's he going now.' That night she decided to go to an aerobics class that all the friends had gone to before the assault, thinking that it was time things began to get back to normal.

After school, Joan, Fred and Debbie took Tim and Mary to visit their mom. As they went past, Debbie noticed that the police mugshot of Jeff had been posted at the nurses' station outside her room. The kids walked right by without reacting.

11

The Arrest

Jill's last day was one of her best. Her face had lit up when her brother walked in, having flown from Key West for the fund-raiser. The whole family's spirits had been buoyed by the generosity of the people of Skaneateles. They had been with her every step of the way, often in tears and despair as she was taken to the operating room for yet another critical surgery, suffered as they watched her frustration to communicate and do the simplest things for herself, and been overjoyed at every sign that she was reclaiming some of her faculties. Her children were her life line and she clung to it desperately. She was determined to be around to see them grow up.

Jeff Cahill had other plans for her. His freedom depended on a jury believing his version of what had gone on that night back in April when he had nearly killed her. If only he had finished her off then, he could have stuck to his mantra that he had been afraid for his own safety. He could have painted her to be an adulterous wife and a bad mother without any fear of rebuttal or her spilling out all that stuff about him that only she knew. Who wouldn't sympathize with all he had suffered? At best he would get a slap on the wrist, at worst he'd have to serve a short stretch of time for what was, as any jury would quickly recognize once he'd made his case, justifiable manslaughter. It had been a domestic dispute that had gotten out of hand, that's all.

But that wasn't the situation. Against all the odds, the damn woman had survived. Now she was beginning to speak; his mother had told him that she'd seen her whisper to the nurses. And she had described how awful Jill looked—she bore scant resemblance to the healthy, energetic and beautiful person she had been before he had picked up that bat. Later that week he was due to appear at a hearing on the assault charges. Jeff must have realized that if Jill was wheeled into a courtroom with her face disfigured, her head misshapen, her limbs wasted and atrophied, paralyzed on one side, and croaked out her damaging testimony, he was cooked.

He had no intention of letting that happen. He had been caught off-guard on Sunday when the TV crew came pounding at his door. Now the whole town had seen him for what he was, a remorseless deadbeat who refused to pay for the children he had professed to love so dearly. He brooded about it that evening and all day Monday.

By Tuesday he had made up his mind; it was time; she had to be silenced. He went into the yard and retrieved the cyanide from where he had hidden it weeks before, came back inside the house and went over to the drawer where Mary had put the stuff she had bought for Halloween and where Jill kept art materials. He found just what he was looking for, small plastic containers full of glitter. He emptied the green sparkles from one of them down the sink, banging it against the edge to make sure none stuck to the sides. Unsealing the cyanide and the potassium formate, he mixed them together as instructed in the recipe he had taken from the Internet and carefully filled the little tube with the deadly formula before replacing the cap. Then he returned the rest of the poison to its secret location.

He checked the time. It was just after half past eight and dark outside. He stripped off the sweatpants he was wearing and changed into the blue polo shirt and off-white chinos he wore whenever he wanted to slip unnoticed into the hospital, laced up his work boots and clipped a plastic ID card to the shirt. From a bureau drawer he took a reddish-brown wig and checked it out in the bedroom mirror. That would do—it sure didn't look anything like his thinning hair. He put the wig in a bag along with the little bottle that would solve his problems, if everything went as planned.

Around 9:00 he got into the Jeep, checked the selection of dark glasses he kept in the glove compartment and started the engine. He drove slowly. He wanted to stay cool and collected; the last thing he wanted to do was to attract attention. He drew into the parking area at University Hospital half an hour later. The lot was fairly empty with only a few visitors' cars and the usual staffers' autos in the employees' section. He parked away from the main entrance in a quiet spot where there was no one else around. He took the wig from the bag and using the rearview mirror, pulled it on, making sure none of his own hair was visible. From the back seat he removed a disposable mop cover from a packet he'd bought weeks before and patted his pocket to make sure the little bottle was still there. He got out and strode purposefully to the entrance.

This was the tricky part. All visitors to the hospital had to check in with the security officer at the main desk. Jeff had always gotten in without any trouble before, but there was always the chance that there would be some anally officious guard on duty who would insist on checking his I.D. closely and raise the alarm. If that happened and they matched him to the police mugshot the hospital had on its Do Not Admit list, he'd be in trouble.

The beauty of the place was that there were plenty of distractions: the lobby was usually packed with people and right beside reception was the hospital store that was always full of visitors looking for supplies and gifts for the patients. Taking a deep breath, Jeff strode up to the desk where security officer Justin Hamlin was beginning his second month on the job. Hamlin glanced up and asked for I.D. Jeff flashed a tag with the hospital logo, but without a photograph, and was waved through, but he left a lingering impression on the rookie guard, who recalled later, "I couldn't forget his eyes. They were very hollow and very distant."

So far, so good. Jeff made for the basement where he knew all the janitorial supplies were kept. He'd been there before too. He knew that there would be no one around; on a previous foray he had checked that the night porters had already started their rounds. He grabbed a mop, covered it with the dustcover he had brought with him in case the supply room would be locked, and headed up the fire stairs until he reached the door on the second floor. He was banking on not running into any of the regular housekeeping staff, who might have asked awkward questions; if his surveillance paid off, they would already be scattered throughout the building.

He made for the rehabilitation unit, keeping close to the wall and pushing the mop in front of him. Halfway down, he saw someone coming down the corridor towards him. As they met, Tyrone Hunter slowed and gave him a leery stare. Jeff sunk his head on his chest and kept mopping the floor. Cleaner John George saw him, and wondered about the blank I.D. Cynthia Jones approached him to clean up a mess, but he ignored her and she went in search of someone more willing. Nurse Marie Morley saw him heading towards the nurses' station. It was 10:00 P.M. when he reached the middle of the unit, where another nurse was busy filling a medicine cart. She looked up and said, "Hi." He glanced up at her, but didn't reply, taking off towards the coma unit at the end of the floor. As a safety precaution, Jill's name was not on the door, but he knew where to go—he'd already been in the hospital that day. Quickly looking around to check that no one was following him, he ducked into room 2206.

Jill was lying on her back asleep. He took the bottle out of his pocket and sat down on the bed while he unscrewed the top, then reached for her mouth. Suddenly, her eyes flew open, and panic spread across her face when she recognized him. She clamped her lips shut. He tried to pry them open with his left hand, holding the bottle of poison in his right. Summoning up all her strength she tried to turn her head to the side. Roughly, he grabbed her by the jaw and sunk his nails into her lips, cruelly scratching her chin until he'd forced a slight gap between her teeth and threw the contents of the bottle at her mouth. Some of the deadly potion hit the target; the rest spilled on her neck and chest. As quietly as he had come in, he slipped out, running down the stairs and out into the cool clear night.

Before he was out of the building, Jill was gasping for air and Julie Labayewski was performing CPR. A code blue had been called and a crash team was racing towards her. Security had been alerted and the police called.

Syracuse Police Department Detective Dennis Murphy was on the 4:00 P.M.–to–midnight shift. An hour before he was due to go home, he was called in by his sergeant and told to partner up with Detective Mike Dillion. He knew about the incident at the hospital—as soon as it was called in, a buzz had gone around the station house. Everyone there knew all about Jeff Cahill. "Go to his home, 2444 East Lake

Road in Spafford. If this guy is there, pick him up," he was told. On the way, Murphy called the sheriff's department and asked for support. He and Dillion teamed up with a deputy and a cop from the Skaneateles police and Lieutenant Ted Botsford. It was just before half past midnight when they arrived.

When they pulled up in front of the house, it was completely dark—there were no streetlights and none of the neighboring homes had inside or outside lights on. Murphy saw the black Jeep parked in the driveway and walked around the right side to the back of the house, stopping about ten to fifteen yards away to duck behind a tree. They had no idea if Cahill had a gun or how dangerous he was. With Murphy providing cover, Dillion and Botsford approached the front door.

Dillion knocked. A few seconds later, a light popped on in a rear upstairs bedroom. Through the glass they could see a man coming down the stairs pulling on a flannel shirt. Murphy joined the other two at the door. When the suspect opened it, Dillion identified himself and his partner as Syracuse detectives investigating a crime that had taken place in the city and said they'd like him to go with them to the Criminal Investigation Division to talk about it.

"OK, let me put on some clothes," Jeff said. He went back upstairs and dressed in jeans and sneakers, put Nick and Snoofy in separate rooms, then found his spare key and locked the front door. He was handcuffed and put into the back seat of the unmarked Chevy Lumina. Botsford, who walked over to check out the Jeep, called over to Murphy, "His car is still warm." Murphy went over and put his hand on the hood and the radiator grille. On such a crisp fall night they should have been cool to the touch. There was heat coming from both.

Murphy made a call to Time and Temperature and was told it was 12:44 A.M. and 55 degrees. During the thirty-minute trip to Syracuse, Jeff was silent. As he drove, Murphy glanced in his rearview mirror and saw that, far from being nervous or worried, the suspect had fallen asleep, his head nuzzled comfortably on the headrest. At 3:45 A.M., Jeff was read his Miranda rights and charged with the attempted murder of his wife. This time, Jeff, who had been so eager to paint himself as the wronged husband trying to fend off a crazed knife-wielding woman when he was charged with assault back in April, was saying nothing. It struck the cops that for such a horrible crime, he was unnaturally calm.

Investigator Longo, who had interviewed Jeff after the beating, was asleep when the phone rang. "I was called by one of my bosses. He wanted me to go down and see if I could assist the investigation in any way. I got dressed and went to the Syracuse Police Department. I saw Jeff there, in an interview room. I didn't speak to him, I saw him through a glass. He was sitting in a chair with his legs stretched out in front of him, relaxed and defiant. He refused to talk. He requested an attorney right away."

At 5:12 A.M. Detective Christopher DeGerno was standing in front of a judge asking for his stamp on a search warrant for the house, any structure attached to the property or on the grounds of the property and the Jeep. On DeGerno's wish list were a brown hairpiece or wig, eyeglasses, work boots, a work shirt, blue jeans, hospital uniforms, toxic/caustic materials and an identification card.

In his affidavit he cited statements police had taken around midnight from hospital employees John George, Marie Morley and Justin Hamlin, all of whom had picked Jeff Cahill from the mugshot as the man they had seen in the north wing. When he finished, DeGerno filled out a second search warrant application, this time specifically for the Jeep, explaining that detectives had reported finding the car outside the house and said it had been driven shortly before police picked up the suspect.

After dropping off the bags with the hospital bedding and

the other evidence he had collected at the hospital, around 4:00 in the morning, evidence specialist Officer Fred Baunee joined the team already at the house. On a table behind the couch in the living room, he found some small tubes of green glitter, the kind of thing kids use in arts and crafts or for putting on their faces at Halloween. The little plastic container looked exactly like the one hospital security chief Jeffrey Hood had given him and the tops were the same as the cap Hood handed to him inside a latex glove. When Baunee opened a dresser drawer in the mudroom, he pulled out four wigs in various colors and styles—two were black, one was brown, the other silver with a red tint.

A few hours after Jeff's arrest, another search warrant was issued, this time to Syracuse Police Detective Steven Stonecypher. He was looking for any light-colored slacks in the house, citing Cynthia Jones' description of the bogus staffer wearing white or beige pants. He asked for permission to recover all capsules, vials, containers and caps that could be used to transport the toxic substance that had caused Jill Cahill's death. He was also interested in Cahill's computer. He wanted to seize the machine along with its external and internal drives, storage equipment, terminals, monitors, keyboards, point modems, hard and floppy disks, cassettes, videocassettes and diskettes. He explained to the judge that the Internet was fertile ground for anyone looking for information on how to obtain harmful substances.

By the end of the day, police had removed an IBM Aptiva 330 computer, a Hewlett-Packard Officejet model 500 printer/fax/copier along with the manuals and software for it, an IBM computer monitor, a Microsoft Windows user guide, a Microsoft Windows 95 upgrade package, a Brother computer mouse, a telephone cord, a Lin-Shiung computer printing cable, a SI Waber power strip, monitor power cables, an IBM computer keyboard, 3 WinFax Lite, 3 Sony and IPM diskettes, Canon BJ series Bubble Jet Printer diskettes and CD-ROMs of Tie Fighter Wars, Galaxy of Games Arcade Action, R.B.I. Baseball '94 and Animal Planet along with 2 Canon Creative CD-ROMs and a Microsoft Encarta CD-rom box.

Also taken into evidence were a pair of silver FosterGrant sunglasses, a Disney kids' pair in lilac and brown Perry Ellis wire-rim glasses, a spiral notebook with pictures of two children on the front and back covers, a Mead Five-Star perforated page notebook, a National Laboratories pocket folder containing typed and handwritten papers, a Welch Allyn information folder containing printed and handwritten papers and two pairs of light-colored pants.

Using the police onis computerized ID system Detectives Edward Taglialatela and Joel Cardone put together a photo lineup of six guys who resembled Cahill and showed it to the staff members on duty the night before who had reported seeing the stranger. Nurses Marie Morley and Vicki Dunning picked Jeff Cahill out without hesitation, as did Tyrone Hunter, Cynthia Jones, Justin Hamlin, John George and Donna Holloway. All signed their names beneath his mugshot, which was on the bottom right side of the sheet. Only one employee couldn't be sure.

Around 10:30 the phone rang in the McDonalds' house. Tom transferred the call to Fred and Joan in the studio. "I felt I had a cold coming on and went to bed early," said Joan. "The bed was right in the kitchen, Dave was on the couch and the kids were upstairs. Tom came on the intercom and he says, 'The hospital is on, pick up.' Fred grabs the phone, I fly out of bed, Dave bolts off the couch and I hear sirens and look out the window and here are all these police cars outside and Tom's yelling at the police. Dr. Kramer said somebody had broken into the hospital and done something to Jill. The police were going to give us an escort to the hospital, but it was late enough at night that we wouldn't run into traffic, so they let us go in by ourselves. Tom took Tim and Mary to the main house."

For what was an agonizing time, Joan, Fred and David waited. "The doctor kept coming out and telling us, 'It's very grave, we can't get any response from her, from her brain stem,' and I said, 'Well, that doesn't sound good,'" said Joan. "When we finally got to see Jill, I just looked at her and said, 'She's dead.' We had to stay quite a ways back because they were still cleaning her up, but you could tell she was gone. She looked beautiful, but it was the respirator that was keeping her breathing. The cyanide shut down every organ in her body. And we had her go through all that crap. These scratches on her chin and mouth, she went out fighting."

Cathy McDonald called Debbie at 5:30 A.M. the next morning and told her that Jeff had gotten into the hospital and poisoned Jill. "She's in stable condition, but hurry," she said. When she and Bill arrived with their children that afternoon, several of Jill's friends were already there. "They were still working on her. I had no idea about the severity of it," said Debbie. "I had no idea that she was being kept alive on a ventilator. I was like, 'Hey, c'mon, snap out of it, you've got through worse than this.' Then Michelle told me that she was on life support and that there was no brain activity."

They sat at her bedside all day, hoping and praying for a miracle. Michelle had been asleep when Cathy called her saying, "Something has happened at the hospital, they think it's Jeff, but they don't know where he is." Michelle immediately jumped out of bed. "We leave our house totally unlocked all the time, the car's in the driveway with my purse and keys in it—this is Skaneateles. But I was just totally panicked, I ran out of the house, went around and locked everything, then we took the kids to my mother's. We drove by the

Cahills' place and noticed his parents' car in the driveway, picked up Cathy and got to the hospital at two in the morning. When we arrived all these people in hooded garments were dealing with her, a contaminated person. It was just awful. I knew at that point she was just not going to make it."

"Cathy called me around six A.M." said Katy Price. "I knew when I got there, there was no hope. As soon as they took her off life support, she died. We were all there with her that afternoon. The priest arrived and gave her the last rites. And the kids were there. It took a while because [Joan and Fred] didn't know what to do about them. They finally decided during the afternoon that the children would need to be there."

At 3:45 A.M. Jeff had been charged with attempted murder and aggravated criminal contempt and arraigned before City Court Judge Timothy Higgins, who ordered him held at the Onondaga County Justice Center on $1 million bail or $2 million bond. This time, there was no rush by his family to raise money to free him. District Attorney Fitzpatrick announced that if Jill died, he would seek the death penalty.

The McDonalds brought Jill's children to the hospital. Their counselor arrived shortly after and stayed throughout the rest of the day with them. Joan recalled Tim and Mary struggling to keep their composure. "When they brought the children in and sat them next to me, I told them, 'Do it. Cry. It's OK to cry.' How do you know at that age how to deal with any of that? Especially when you've had all that brainwashing, been told, 'Don't cry, be a soldier.' Mike came over to me and said, 'Mame, I hate him, I hate Uncle Jeff.' I told him, 'It's OK, he's not your uncle anymore,' " said Joan.

"It was awful," said Katy. "I kept looking at Mary out of the side of my eye. She was so little, she was just looking at Jill. It wasn't a terrible, dramatic scene at all. The kids were

just saying prayers and looking at their mother, who was lying there so still. And I remember the whole day, I kept praying to any God that would hear me, 'Just open your eyes,
Jill.' "

Dr. Rodziewicz found out what had happened when he
arrived at the hospital that morning. He had checked on Jill
daily since April. "He was at the I.C.U. and asked, 'What is
she doing here?' He immediately canceled his schedule and
spent the whole day with us," said Joan. "We kept talking to
her, although we didn't really know if she could hear. They
did a bedside Mass for all of us so we could say goodbye to
her."

Jill's doctor shook his head. She was being kept alive
only by a respirator. He could offer them not even a glim-
mer of hope; she was brain-dead, and no amount of prayers,
medical science or willpower was going to make her well
again. They would need to decide when to let her go. Heart-
sick, Fred told Joan and Debbie that he would take care of
Jill one more time. She had suffered enough. At 6.45 P.M.,
three hours after her husband's arrest, with her family gathered around her bedside, Jill Cahill died. She was 41 years
old.

"Fred stayed with her and they came out and said she was
gone," said Joan. "Dr. Rodziewicz grabbed me. He was crying, I was crying, and I said, 'I can't go in there, I can't see
her like that, am I a bad mother? Am I a bad mother?' And he
said, 'No, Joan, you're a wonderful mother.' When she died,
Fred went in there. He said it was the most horrible thing. It
was OK when they pulled the plug, and then he stayed for another forty-five minutes and when she started looking weird,
he just lost it. I didn't know that until a month after, he said
he wished he hadn't gone back, but he couldn't leave her,
couldn't let her die alone."

Zaney summed up what everyone was feeling: "Here's
this wonderful person just trying to raise her children,

abused with this horrible, horrible injury. After the first month when she seemed to be recovering, she would have a relapse because there was too much fluid being taken from her spinal cord or she would have a mini-stroke and she'd recover. She was always able somehow to recover. I remember June 24, my birthday, she almost died that night and I was afraid she would die on my birthday. It was meningitis, but she came out of it. It always seemed that something bad would happen and then she'd be in recovery and you'd see progress, then something else would happen and then you'd see progress.

"I always thought she'd be able to enjoy her children. She might be in a wheelchair, but she could enjoy a glass of champagne, and with rehabilitation, eventually, she would be able to watch the kids. I was always hopeful that would happen. I never thought that she would be a vegetable. I don't think any of us thought that she'd be a vegetable. I think with the doctors and the staff and the kids there that she would have grown old with the kids."

Michelle had not been so optimistic. "I felt she was making strides. Was she ever going to get back to where she was? No, I didn't believe that. She had five bouts of meningitis. That takes its toll. About two weeks after she went into the hospital, one of the nurses told me, 'Oh, she's got meningitis, but she'll be OK,' and I thought, 'No she won't.' I knew as a former nurse, and being married to a doctor, that too much damage had been done."

The day after, the Russells received a call from Tim Cahill. "Jeff's truck had been parked at his lot and although it was Jeff's, it was apparently registered to Jill. The day after she died he called up and said, 'Get this goddamn truck out of here or I'll throw it out on the street,'" said Joan.

At his brother's trial Mark Cahill claimed to have found out that his sister-in-law had been poisoned and his brother had been charged with her murder when he opened his morning newspaper at his New York apartment on Thursday, October 29. He claimed he called his parents at once and headed home. On the way to Skaneateles he took a left onto Route 41 and drove past Jeff's house around 2:00 P.M. He pulled into the driveway, got out and walked around to the back yard, where he found his mother standing alone, crying. He went over and put his arms around her, trying to comfort her. She told him she had been to the jail, to see Jeff. "C'mon, Mom, let's go home," he told her.

At the same time that Mark was consoling his mother, Medical Examiner Mary Jumbelic was conducting an autopsy. She said that Jill had died of suffocation caused by cyanide poisoning, and ruled it a homicide.

On October 30, the Russells held a wake for Jill. That morning, Patty and Mark went back to the house. "It was Friday, the day of Jill's wake and Patty Cahill was at Jill's house digging up plants. They weren't supposed to be taking anything for five years, that was in the separation order, because the plants belonged to Jill and Michelle's business," said Joan. "Jeff and Jill's neighbor saw the car arrive and came by and they spoke to them for a few minutes before they left."

While the Russells and their friends grieved for Jill, the police were making sure they had a watertight case against her husband. Detective Steven Stonecypher was talking to UPS driver Bob Leo, who told him about the intercepted packages addressed to General Super Plating. He had thought it odd that Jeff turned down several before taking away a 10"×12" envelope. Stonecypher then spoke to Kevin Keenan, who had seen Jeff in the black Jeep and written down the license number, and to Cynthia Brenno, who had directed him to the front office to locate an overnight package. He talked to Tracy Jones who had reported the missing packages to the DeWitt police.

Armed with their affidavits, Stonecypher brought a fourth amendment to the original search warrant to Judge Norman Mordue at 10:09 A.M. on Saturday, October 31. He wanted to search Jeff's home for a maroon baseball cap, a pair of bluish-green oval sunglasses, all packages from Bryant Labs and Spectrum Quality Labs, all documents that contained his handwriting, any UPS delivery receipts, any and all cyanide containers or packages, all OfficeMax letters and receipts, any dark-colored, long-sleeved, pinstriped, button-down-collared shirts and all paperwork with the name General Super Plating Company on it.

At 7:30 A.M. that morning Detective Tom Derby was assigned to the East Lake Road house while the search warrant was being executed. When he got there, he turned the car to face the road, parking two thirds of the way up the driveway where he sat for the next three hours, getting out several times and walking around the property.

At 10:30 A.M. a silver minivan pulled up. Inside were a man and an older woman who Derby recognized as Patty Cahill. She rolled down the window and introduced her son Mark. "What are you doing here?" the cop asked. Mark said he wanted to look around to make sure the place hadn't been vandalized. "There's a search warrant being executed in there and no one is allowed in," he was told firmly. "I want to pick up a shirt for my son. He's cold in jail," said Patty. Derby told her to go home and get one of her husband's shirts for her "poor cold son."

But instead of leaving, they drove around to the back yard. The cop followed them. "What are you doing? I told you to get out of here," he said. Mark said he wanted to check a piece of equipment, a brake that Jeff used for putting new siding on houses; it was stowed behind the shed. Derby shook his head in disbelief: "What part of 'get out of here' don't you understand?" he asked them. They took off empty-handed.

Derby made a quick note of the conversation and called his boss back at the station house. A couple of hours later, Sergeant Don Hilton arrived to execute a search warrant of the grounds and outbuildings. Derby repeated his exchange with the Cahills, especially the part about Mark Cahill's interest in the shed. Detectives Mark Abraham and Gordon Quonce were directed specifically to the small shed at the back of the house and the area immediately surrounding it.

They moved a mowing tractor out of the way so they could make a thorough search. "Behind the shed there was a couple of sawhorses with a metal construction brake covered by a blue tarp," Abraham said at the trial. The shed was propped up on upright cinder blocks with gaps between them. They moved some bricks that were partially hidden with leaves and in the right-hand corner, way in the back, he found a blue-and-white bottle of potassium cyanide. The bottle was labeled "Spectrum Quality Company."

Early evening, just before 6:00 P.M., Detective Quonce went to the judge with a fifth amendment. This time he wanted to remove a TDK microcassette from the kitchen, having found it during that afternoon's search. By the time they had finished combing the house and grounds, the cops had unearthed a damning array of evidence. Steven Stonecypher bagged and labeled each one for testing, filled out a "blue" card for each item, put them inside evidence bags that he sealed at the top and dropped them into the trunk of his car.

In the incriminating haul was a half-burned wig, a box of Tec wall grout, a box of Laticrete wall grout, a bottle of potassium cyanide with the brand name Spectrum Quality Co., a pair of blue rubber gloves, three pairs of tinted sunglasses with black wire frames, two with brown wire frames and five more assorted pairs and several checks belonging to James and Jill Cahill with his signature on them. There was a maroon baseball cap with a "Cornell" logo on the front—Detective Derby had found that in an alcove at the top of the stairs—a maroon cap with "Titleist" on it, a computer book containing several Internet addresses, a blue Sony computer disk and a TDK M-60 microcassette with "End of Cheating" written on the spine.

12

A Jury of His Peers

"We are here to celebrate the life of a young woman who loved life and her friends, her family, her children and had a great love for the rest of God's creatures as well," the Reverend Thomas McGrath told the four hundred mourners packed into St. Mary's of the Lake on October 31. Beside her picture on the altar was a massive bouquet of five hundred pink roses from Tom Tulloch. Everyone who had known Jill knew that Halloween was one of her favorite holidays, and none of them missed the bitter irony of the timing of her funeral. For her family and Rita and Tom Winkowski, it brought back the party exactly one year before, when the man responsible for all this pain had dressed up as O. J. Simpson, hung a doll around his neck and told Bill Jaeger, "It's Jill."

But heartbreaking though it was, the service was not without moments that would have made Jill smile. John Eppolito recalled her "classic dog bark imitations" which their dog had difficulty differentiating from the real thing. He told the story of his and Michelle's 3-year-old son Benjamin, who wanted to know where she was. "She's with the angels," his mother had told him. He went to the phone and began dialing: "Hello, angels?" he'd said. "Can you put Jill on?"

Debbie read a favorite passage from Corinthians 1:13, one often recited at weddings, but which seemed to describe her sister perfectly:

> *Love is patient, love is kind. It does not envy, it does not boast, it is not proud. It is not rude, it is not self-seeking, it is not easily angered, it keeps no record of wrongs. Love does not delight in evil but rejoices with the truth. It always protects, always trusts, always hopes, always perseveres.*

Tom sat directly behind the Russells and Debbie. With him were his parents, his sister and brother and members of his extended family. "I cried through the entire service," he says. "There wasn't an empty seat or a dry eye in the place. It was horribly sad; words cannot describe how sad it was. Even to this day it's something I think about all the time. She was very straight and full of life. The cup was always half full for Jill. She was beautiful inside and out. You don't meet someone like that every day and I loved her to tears."

The same day, Family Court Judge Anthony Paris barred Jeff, his parents, his brothers and his extended family from "any and all contact, direct or indirect with Tim and Mary Cahill and Joan and Fred Russell for any purpose, in any manner," including attending Jill's funeral. He also scheduled another hearing to decide whether the children needed an order of protection from their father's family, citing affidavits from a social worker and the Russells' lawyer contending that Patty and Jim Cahill had allowed Jeff to help Mary with a school project and let Mark drive the children unsupervised in direct violation of his August ruling.

Through their lawyer, the Cahills railed against the restriction, calling it "a knee-jerk reaction to what happened."

The family had intended to take Jill home and bury her in a plot reserved for her parents at a cemetery in Tonawanda. "I had even picked out the gravestone and everything," said Debbie. "Fred and Joan had her urn in a box at their house, then one day Joan and I were talking and we both were thinking the same thing, we couldn't put her in the ground. She loved life and all the beautiful things that went along with it. I wanted her at our house with her children. We talked to the kids about it, and they were not bothered by having her around so we brought her home for Christmas 1999. It probably sounds weird to the average person but we feel good having her there. We even have a Halloween mask for her (her second favorite holiday) and a halo for her at Christmas."

Immediately after Jill's death, the outcry over Jeff's waltz through the front door of the hospital decked out in an outfit that screamed for attention and displaying a laughably bogus I.D. tag, became a deafening roar. To make things worse, at least one employee told the police she had seen him there before. The director of public safety claimed there was nothing that would have made anyone raise the alarm in the visitors' book; after 6:30 P.M., everyone had to show identification and after 8:30 P.M., they also had to be okayed by the nursing supervisor before being allowed onto the floors.

Neither was there a reasonable explanation for how he got by unchallenged when there was his mugshot taped to a marble ledge in the main lobby and a copy of it hanging just a few yards from Jill's bed at the nurses' station. The security chief confirmed they were there that night. "How did he get past security?" asked Fred. "Even though everyone knew who we were, we stopped every time we came in. It was, 'Hi, Joan, hi, Fred, how is Jill today? Let me see your I.D.' But Jeff got in there. It's still unbelievable to us."

In early November, more questions were raised when the local paper, the Syracuse *Post-Standard*, got wind of the De-Witt Police Department's failure to connect the dots in their halfhearted investigation. General Super Plating had done everything right, holding an internal audit, then calling the police when they realized a pound of cyanide ordered in its name was missing. The paper quoted the then DeWitt Police Chief James DeLapp's baffling assertion that "Ultimately there will be more praise than criticism for the way the case was handled." The expected praise was not forthcoming. Rick Trunfio said he was not aware of General Super Plating's report until a week after Jill was killed, and kept silent about DeWitt's bungling. "That was pretty bad, It's not a great leap of logic to say the officer should have investigated further," says Bill Fitzpatrick.

On November 17, Fred and Joan went back to Family Court to ask for sole custody of the children. They needed to take Tim and Mary home. The only thing that was keeping them in Skaneateles was Judge Paris' ruling that the youngsters remain in the local school district. If they were to have any chance at a normal life, they had to make a fresh start away from a place where they'd always be known as the kids whose mom was murdered by their dad. The judge agreed. "When we got custody, the judge, everybody told us. 'Take the children and get away from here,' said Joan. The Cahills put up no fight and agreed that it was in the best interests of their grandchildren to have no contact with them until Jeff's fate was decided at trial.

Fresh in the Russells' minds as they petitioned the judge was the disturbing find they'd made when they and some of her friends were clearing out Jill's belongings. "It was the coldest, grayest feeling you could ever feel. The house was a total shambles," said Michelle. "It was a very old house and that's such an eerie feeling. It was just so cold. Jill did everything she could to make it beautiful, she had no money, she had left-over furniture from whomever and she made it look great. You never really saw how bad the house was." Shivering, Tom McDonald had said, "Why don't we light a fire?"

"Everything was taken off the walls and most things were put in boxes," said Debbie. "The Cahills had access to the home prior to us. We had to get their permission to go that day. My cousin, Cathy Hance, found this piece of cardboard in what looked like Jeff's writing attached to the back of one of the pictures stacked up against a wall. It contained all this weird sexual innuendo, homosexual stuff about gerbils, just sick. We still are shocked by its content," she said.

There was a pink Post-it note attached to it which said, "I'm the king of fucking with someone else's handwriting. This is how I did it," and a small piece of pink paper with what appeared to be the original note before it was enlarged. Michelle told them she had seen the vile card before. Jill had found it the winter before when everything was falling apart and shown it to her, saying, "Can you believe this?" To their great disappointment, what they didn't find was any photo albums or videos of Jill and the kids.

Two days later, a grand jury indicted Jeff on two counts of first-degree murder, two counts of second-degree murder, second-degree burglary, aggravated criminal contempt and fourth-degree criminal possession of a weapon. He was arraigned the following morning and pleaded not guilty to all seven charges.

There was still some pending business in Skaneateles for the Russells before they could move back to Tonawanda. On December 2, they were in Onondaga County Surrogate Court facing another battle with the Cahills, this time over who would handle the children's financial interests. Joan and Fred asked Judge Peter Wells to appoint them "guardians of the property." Jeff, who didn't attend the hearing, and his parents objected, asking the Court to consider co-guardianship between both sets of grandparents. "They wanted joint control over any money as a result of any [future] wrongful death suit," said Debbie. Three days before Christmas, the Court of Appeals in Albany threw out the New York 1995 death penalty law that encouraged defendants to plead guilty and submit to life without parole to avoid a lethal injection, on the grounds it violated their constitutional rights.

As Jeff prepared to celebrate his first Christmas behind bars, the Russells said goodbye to the people of Skaneateles, especially the McDonalds, who had opened their hearts and their home to them. They went back to Tonowanda. The children were going to live with Debbie and her family near Buffalo and she and Bill refinanced their home to pay for an extension that would accommodate a family about to double overnight. On New Year's Eve, D.A. Fitzpatrick announced he would be seeking the death penalty.

In January, Jeff's lawyers launched a pre-trial campaign, burying the court with motions aimed at sabotaging the state's case. First they tried to stop the assault and the murder being tried together. Judge Burke ruled against them. He heard from the cop who had taken statements from Jeff. At issue was his claim that the fight between him and Jill had erupted at 4:00 A.M. Jeff claimed to have no recollection of being Mirandized at Lafayette state police barracks, but Burke held that there was plenty of credible evidence that the cops had followed the book, and their testimony would be admissible.

With the trial looming, Priest and Miles filed another round of motions that smacked of desperation. In one they claimed that Fitzpatrick was seeking the death penalty only to appease the Russells; in the next they said that there were worse offenders out there; then they carped that Jeff was only facing execution because Jill was white and middle-class. They attacked the motive, saying there was no need for him to have murdered her to stop her testifying since he had already conveniently beaten her into a coma and rendered her incapable of giving evidence. Then they contended that the death penalty was unconstitutional, questioned whether the hospital employees who had identified Jeff from a photo or actual lineup were biased because they had seen his mugshot, and claimed that the orders of protection were not properly served.

Rick Trunfio batted aside all of the motions and told the judge that Jeff had been present when the Family Court judge issued the restraining order, and that Judge Burke's August 7 order extending it had been delivered to Priest, as his lawyer. He added that when he was arrested, Jeff had admitted that he wasn't supposed to be at the hospital. Priest and Miles then wanted the cyanide evidence dismissed, complaining the search warrant had been limited to the house despite the fact that the cops' affidavits had specifically mentioned outbuildings. Lastly, they wanted a transcript of the medical examiner's report.

On April 27, the Russells filed a $40 million wrongful death suit against Jeff and Doyle Security Systems, the Rochester-based company hired by University Hospital. It sought $10 million for Jill's pain and suffering, her mental anguish and fear, her loss of enjoyment of life and employment, and medical expenses incurred by the assault; $20 million for her pain and suffering from being stalked and poisoned in the hospital and $10 million in punitive damages. The suit said that Jeff Cahill had made several visits to the hospital and sued Doyle for a further $10 million for failing to act on reports he'd been seen there.

In a May 4 ruling, Burke upheld the death penalty law and the validity of the search warrants, but threw out one charge of aggravated criminal contempt, agreeing that the orders of protection were not served correctly. It made no difference to the capital case; Jeff Cahill could still end up on death row.

At the beginning of May 1999, some 1,000 Onondaga County residents woke up to find jury summonses in their mailboxes with instructions to show up at the Civic Center on May 26. Some of the 565 citizens who answered the summons arrived as early at 7:30 A.M. on a pouring wet morning, and were ushered into the Crouse-Hinds Theatre to be addressed by Judge Burke.

They were given a 30-page questionnaire aimed at measuring their "death qualification." Not only were they required to divulge personal details, they had to say whether they had been on a jury before and tell what they had read or heard about the case. They were also asked if their religious beliefs pitted them irrevocably against the death penalty—the idea being to quickly dismiss both the people who would "fry the bastard" themselves and those who maintained that taking any life was wrong for any reason.

At 9:00 A.M. Jeff had been brought to the judge's chambers to explain why he had opted to miss the proceedings.

"Mr. Cahill advises me that he waives his presence for the morning," Richard Priest began.

"Is that true, Mr. Cahill?" asked Burke.

"Yes it is," Jeff replied.

"You've talked this over with your lawyer? You know you have an absolute right to be present at every stage of your trial?"

"Yes, I understand that and I have talked it over with Mr. Priest," he answered.

"Mr. Cahill, let me ask you how old you are?" asked the judge.

"Thirty-eight."

"And what's your highest education?"

"Through college."

"Are you on any medication of any sort?" asked Judge Burke.

"None."

"And you are comfortable here with the decision you're making?"

"Yes."

Turning to Priest, Burke then wanted to know: "Is this the decision now, that he's going to waive his presence throughout the course of this trial?"

"No, Judge, just for this stage, we'll discuss the future after that," said Priest.

"Just today," Burke repeated, looking dismayed. "If your purpose is to pop in each morning for me to have a calendar call to have your client decide whether he wants to come today or not, I'd rather not, OK?" Jeff was led back to his cell.

The judge then addressed the jury pool. "This is a strange setting. I am a little bit not at ease," he admitted, looking around the 2,117-seat auditorium. "I have never done anything like this in my life. But for our purposes today, this is my courtroom, as big as it is."

He swore them in and introduced the prosecutors, District Attorney William Fitzpatrick, Chief Assistant District Attorneys Domenic (Rick) Trunfio and Stephen Dougherty and the team of Richard Priest and Gary Miles for the defense. Then he warned, "I don't want you to talk about the case for any reason. You're not to watch it on television or read about it in the newspaper. Put it aside. Don't look at it. If you are selected here, you're going to hear it firsthand yourself and you don't need those fine ladies and gentlemen of the press telling you what's going on.

"The purpose of this questionnaire is to assist the attorneys and the Court in selecting a jury that can decide this question fairly, impartially and according to the law. "Therefore, please fill out the questionnaire honestly and candidly." He then said they would be recalled in small groups for further questioning and announced that the trial would start, barring any last-minute hitches, on August 2.

Two weeks later, 290 people were divided into groups of ten to appear at group interviews. This time Jeff and his father showed up. Then Priest and Miles, who had imported a jury-selection expert from Kansas at a cost of $30,000, tried to scuttle the entire jury pool, claiming it did not include enough African-Americans, Latinos, women, poor people or young people. They also complained that the uniformed guards on duty at the Civic Theatre prejudiced potential jurors against his client. Telling them he was fed up with their continual petty griping, Judge Burke angrily tossed out the motion.

On June 17, Richard Priest phoned Fitzpatrick with an offer. "My client is willing to plead guilty and spare everyone the ordeal of a trial in exchange for life without parole," he said. Fitzpatrick sat down and fired off a letter back: "I have to be candid with you and tell you unequivocally that I believe your client should be put to death for his crimes. However, I have decided to respect the [Russell] family's wishes and possibly put an end to this matter," he replied. "But if Mr. Cahill thinks he is going to dance around a full and complete confession, he should forget this strategy now."

He then went on to lay down five conditions: Jeff would admit in court that he'd battered Jill and forced cyanide down her throat; he would give up his right to appeal; he would surrender all parental rights to the children, contacting them only through Jill's family; he would put $100,000 in trust for them; and he had to cooperate in any civil lawsuit brought by his father-in-law. "These are not negotiable," Fitzpatrick concluded, adding, "I hope the deal does not go through." He gave Jeff until June 26 to reply.

Four days later Priest said they liked the offer, but there was a sticking point—Jeff was broke. Fitzpatrick withdrew the offer. Immediately, Priest filed a motion claiming bad faith and demanding that the D.A. be thrown off the case. His client had agreed to all the original stipulations and might manage $50,000 for his kids. Fitzpatrick retorted, "Dick, if I said twenty thousand dollars, you would have come back with twelve thousand." Priest claimed the only reason his client was no longer being offered a deal was that he had no money. After being advised that the Court of Appeals might agree, Fitzpatrick dropped the financial demand.

Then Priest said Jeff might not agree to admit he killed Jill to stop her testifying. Exasperated, Fitzpatrick declared he would not let the defendant "pull a stunt" like he did at the pre-trial hearing where he claimed amnesia about the assault. Gary Miles said Jeff wouldn't cede his parental rights. That had the judge steamed. "You know, Mr. Priest, something that always troubles me about this case is the lack of your client being present at any of these proceedings," he said. "I think it's about time he was here and hearing what's being said about this case, in front of me." We are keeping him fully informed, Miles assured him. "I understand that, and he's not listening to you, is he?" said Burke.

While the legal wrangling went on, Jeff's parents sold the little green farmhouse to a young couple from Auburn, Ohio. The Reverend Deron Milleville, 33, and his 26-year-old wife Julie, had moved to Skaneateles when he was appointed to Holy Trinity Lutheran Church. They told the Syracuse *Post-Standard* that they had been driving along East Lake Road when they spotted the For Sale sign out front. They loved the view and had discovered a birdhouse that looked like a miniature model of their church hanging from the branch of a tree. When they learned about the house's bloody history, they had been concerned the purchase might seem ghoulish, but they took the birdhouse as a sign from the Almighty they were meant to live there. And at $92,000, it was a bargain.

By the beginning of July the jury pool was whittled down to 66. With only a few days remaining, the defense tried another tack. This time, Priest went to the New York State

Supreme Court to ask that the trial be moved out of Onondaga County. With all the publicity surrounding the case, everyone has already decided Jeff is guilty, he declared.

Priest had already been turned down by the Appellate Court in Rochester for a change of venue, but the Supreme Court offered a ray of hope: if the jury selection process ran into trouble, they would reconsider. Well, the pool was stacked with pro–death penalty jurors, Priest objected. "If we are going to start killing people, at least let us walk in front of people who don't know the facts of the case."

Rick Trunfio responded by outlining the scrupulously orchestrated selection process. He pointed out that even if the Supreme Court judge decided in the defendant's favor while the trial was taking place, or even after, there was nothing to stop them relocating it to another county. Since the end result would be the same, why delay? It took the court less than half an hour to decide to go ahead with the exisiting date, Monday, August 2. For Jeff Cahill, the day of reckoning was coming.

Three days before the trial, Priest sent another letter to the district attorney:

> *Mr. Cahill does not wish to evade or deny his responsibility for this murder. He understands that a trial will have consequences beyond his own fate and will subject his family and Jill's family to immeasurable pain and suffering. A trial of this sort will exact costs to all concerned . . . these costs include the emotional toll which will be borne largely by the Cahill children and Jill's family.*

Priest enclosed a 5-page affidavit signed by Jeff copping to first-degree assault and first-degree murder, but he would not admit he had poisoned Jill because she would have been a compelling witness at his assault trial. Fitzpatrick unequivocally turned down the offer: the deal had to be on his terms or it was off the table.

Early on August 2, the jury selection survivors filed into the court to be questioned again by both sides. By 9:30 A.M., seven men and five women and six alternates (one woman and five men) had been chosen. Throughout the proceedings, Jeff Cahill listened impassively. From their places in the packed spectator seats, so did several members of his family, Joan and several of Jill's friends, along with observers from Vera House, a not-for-profit family crisis center operated by Syracuse/Onondaga County. Fred and Debbie were not allowed to be in the courtroom since they were to be called as witnesses.

Facing his brother-in-law for the first time since his sister was beaten senseless was almost too much for Jill's brother Dave to bear. "He's a spineless piece of crap. He's gutless. The first day of the trial Bill and I were in the first row, he was just eight feet away from us. It was very tempting to jump up and strangle him," he said.

All eyes were fixed on Bill Fitzpatrick as he rose to begin his opening remarks to the jury. "April twenty-first, 1998, for the majority of you people, was just another day. It was a day when we were planning things in our lives. It was the beginning of spring. We might have been thinking about weddings or graduations, or just about choices that we have to make in our lives every day. But April twenty-first, 1998, was the day that the life of Jill Cahill turned into a devastating and tragic, and almost incomprehensible nightmare," he began.

"She was, prior to that date, a beautiful, talented, forty-one-year-old woman, mother of two wonderful children and at that time, the wife of this defendant, James Cahill.

"The defendant and Jill met sometime in 1987, Jill then being about thirty years old. She's coming off what would fairly be characterized as a bad relationship. The defendant was almost twenty-seven years old at the time. He was single.

He was a member of a well-known and large family in the Skaneateles area. And two people, like it happens every day in America, fell in love, began a relationship, and on July ninth, 1987, with Jill pregnant with their son, they were married in a small religious ceremony right here in Onondaga County, in Skaneateles, New York. The defendant made many promises to his new bride that July wedding. And the evidence is going to show that he would live to keep very few of them.

"Their son Timothy was born on February second, 1988. He is now a tall, handsome, athletic boy who is living happily and safely with Jill's sister, who you will hear from, outside the city of Buffalo, New York. Their second child, Mary, was born on July fifth, 1990. She was then, and is now, a golden-haired beauty, like her mother. And she is also now living with her brother and her aunt and uncle.

"You will hear evidence that the marriage became strained, and that whatever deep love there was between these two people had subsided significantly. Intimacy for Jill Cahill was a thing of the past with this defendant. Bills were not being paid, one family car was actually seized because of lack of insurance, forcing the family to borrow another car from the defendant's brother Mark. And debts mounted. One might ask the question: who is to blame? And the People's response to that is: who knows and, frankly, who cares? Because the evidence will be this: what could have been an idyllic marriage was no longer a storybook marriage.

"You'll learn that against this backdrop, in the fall of 1997, Jill became romantically involved with another man. I hope you choose not to pass judgment on that, as we obviously have been denied the opportunity to hear Jill's version as to why this infidelity occurred, but it is, nevertheless, a fact that will be brought out at this trial."

Fitzpatrick described the couple's fair and amicable separation agreement, how Jill, after an Easter visit to her sister with the children, had returned home despite the sister's misgivings, to start her new life. Then just before 5:30 A.M. on the morning of April 21, her husband had made a frantic call to his parents telling them something terrible had happened: they had fought, and Jill had been hurt very badly.

"This defendant's parents rushed to the home, along with a family friend, who you will hear from, Dr. Kelly. His brother Kevin also rushed to the home. And eventually, eventually the authorities are called."

Fitzpatrick told how, even as heroic efforts were being made by doctors at University Hospital to save Jill's life, her husband gave a three-page statement to New York state police in which he claimed he battered his wife in self-defense. But the search of the physical evidence did not gel with his story and when faced with the facts, he had admitted his wounds were self-inflicted.

"You will hear testimony to the effect that several of the blows to Jill Cahill were inflicted when she was lying helplessly on the floor. And you will see that baseball bat and you will see the horrible condition it is in and how that resulted with the defendant being indicted for the crime of Assault in the First Degree and Criminal Possession of a Weapon in the Fourth Degree.

"I must prove to you that Jill Cahill suffered serious physical injury—of anything in this trial, you will have no doubt about that whatsoever. From that point on, the trial will begin to focus on the brief remaining, but horrific life of Jill and the scheming of this defendant to murder her. For the next six months of her life, she lived at the Health Science Center. Why do I say that she lived there? Because the People must prove to you, as one of the elements of the crimes, that the hospital was Jill Cahill's dwelling—and of that you will have no doubt. She ate there, she bathed there, she slept there and she was attended to there as she crawled her way back to humanity.

"You'll hear proof in this trial that in May of 1998, the defendant's assault case was being presented to a grand jury. What was the defendant, who was out on bail, doing? You will hear proof that in May of 1998 he began an exploratory search on his computer for information about poison. Cahill was left in no doubt that he faced a severe term in a state penitentiary. That's when he chose cyanide potassium as the poison he would use to eliminate his wife.

"But he doesn't act immediately," Fitzpatrick continued. "Because in August, fluid begins to build up in what's left of Jill's skull and she suffers a relapse. The odds are stacked against her surviving this relapse. But again she fights valiantly and by the beginning of October is well enough to be moved into the rehab unit where she gets her first visit from any member of the Cahill family, her mother-in-law, Patricia. I ascribe no evil motive to Mrs. Cahill for not visiting her daughter-in-law before.

"She sees Jill Cahill in the hospital, she sees Jill is able to talk; that she's making progress. About two weeks later, she has a conversation with this defendant and he asks her a very, very telling question, to the effect, 'I wonder if Jill will tell the truth at the upcoming trial.' Because don't forget, the defendant's initial reaction is that this was an act of self-defense. Cahill, wearing a crude disguise, gains access to his wife's hospital room, where he is confronted by a nurse and leaves. A week later he's back, and this time, he kills her with the deadly poison."

It was clear from his lawyer's opening remarks that Jeff's not guilty plea didn't mean he had not assaulted then killed his wife: Gary Miles' strategy would be to chip away at the prosecution's contention that this was a capital case. "Jeff Cahill is not a cold-blooded murdering monster," he said.

"Whatever else he did, he is not unlike you and I, he is a man who tried his best to love his wife and be faithful to her. He loved his children and cared for them. He loved his family and he loved his God.

"April twenty-first was by any account, a violent and dangerous altercation between Jeff and Jill Cahill. [The prosecutors] are going to ask you to consider the second event, when they allege that Jeff entered the hospital for the purpose of committing some other crime, other than killing his wife—I don't know what that is, and I submit you'll never know what that is—and he killed her. And from these events, they are going to ask you to assume that his motivation was one, to eliminate her as a witness, and two, to further the commission of a burglary.

"Think very carefully about that. As Mr. Fitzpatrick said, people will tell you Jeff was in the hospital a week prior to the time he's supposed to have administered the cyanide, in poor disguise, an orange wig, which literally every person in the hospital who saw him noticed, but he didn't kill her then. He had the cyanide, according to Mr. Fitzpatrick.

"But on October nineteenth or twentieth, this man, with a burning desire to eliminate his wife before she could testify against him, didn't administer the cyanide to her. That, I submit, is a telling point.

"What the prosecution don't want you to consider, in fact, on the morning of April twenty-first, over the course of several hours of interrogation, Jeff Cahill gave a full and complete and voluntary statement to state police investigators. He gave not only a three-page statement, but a subsequent one-page statement. And he told the investigators exactly what they wanted to hear. What Mr. Fitzpatrick did not tell you was that Jeff's main concern, and the concern he communicated to everyone that morning, was, How is Jill? How are my kids? He did also not tell you that following this altercation with his wife, Jeff went to his car, cut a length of garden hose, took duct tape, and attempted to kill himself. He didn't do that, but he tried.

"I think what you're going to find, if you go beyond and behind that incident of this six-month period in the life of a then thirty-eight-year old man, you will find that when his wife came at him with a knife on April twenty-first, Jeff Cahill snapped. And he struck his wife with that bat; no one is going to argue that. He struck her repeatedly. And he, in fact, may have struck her with it after it was no longer necessary to do so. When a person snaps, they break. And when some people snap, they break so badly that they can never be put together again.

"You will hear that, when faced with the prospect of losing not only the only woman he had ever loved, the only woman with who he had ever had an intimate relationship, but with the prospect of losing the two children who defined his life, and by who as a man he was defined, he broke. He broke so badly he couldn't get back together again. And no one saw it. No one saw it." As if on cue, Jeff briefly burst into tears.

13

The Trial

The first witness called by Fitzpatrick was Anthony DiCaprio, the divorce lawyer Jill had retained with the help of Tom Tulloch and Michelle Morris Eppolito. He caused a few nervous titters when he put his right hand on the Bible and had it replaced with the left one by the court officer. He testified that while drawing up the agreement that was to effectively end their marriage, the couple had seemed friendly, there were no problems over custody—Jeff would have the children every other week—and arranged to divide their financial responsibilities fairly.

He was followed by NY State Trooper Tom Haumann, who had responded to the 911 call on April 21. He described the stomach-churning sight that greeted him in the pretty country kitchen. His professional cop delivery couldn't disguise the horror he still plainly felt. Jill was lying on the floor in a pool of oozing blood, writhing and moaning in agony, her head and face a bloody mess of crushed bone and tissue. He had noticed that someone had tried to clean up; he'd found a bucket and blood-soaked washrag in the sink.

Her mewling husband said she attacked him with a knife and he had retaliated with a bat. Both weapons were introduced into evidence.

On cross-examination Dick Priest asked him, "As part of your investigation, did you determine that Jill had threatened Jeff with a knife about three weeks before?"

"I was told that by Patricia Cahill," Haumann replied.

Evidence specialist and Senior Investigator William Ambler told the court that blood was liberally showered throughout the lower half of the house and he had called in state police blood-spatter expert Eli Shaheen to decipher what had gone on. Shaheen had snapped off six rolls of film with thirty-six exposures each to document the scene. As Shaheen testified, Bill Fitzpatrick clicked blown-up and graphic photographs of the carnage onto a large screen. Some of the jurors gasped and others looked away—the walls were literally dripping with blood. It was hardly believable that so much could have exploded from just one person. Jeff had opened his wife's head like a sugared-up kid splits a birthday piñata.

As image after sickening image flashed before them, Investigator Shaheen took the jury on a virtual walk through the farmhouse, pointing to the blood on the outside wall, on the barbecue grill and on the patio, the spatters and hair swipes and the pool of blood in the mudroom. In the kitchen he indicated spattering on the walls, on the lower kitchen cabinets and the puddle of blood on the kitchen floor.

The patterns, positions and trajectories of the spatters told the story of where and how the brutal attack had taken place, he said. Jill had been hit at least once in the mudroom, and tried in vain to flee out into the yard, but her attacker caught up with her on the patio and hit her again. He dragged her into the mudroom and delivered another blow while she was slumped against the doorjamb. She either crawled or, more likely, was pulled back into the kitchen. There, as she lay collapsed and defenseless on the floor, he hit her again and again and again and again. And he hit her with such force that her blood shot up to the ceiling.

When he finished, the courtroom was deadly quiet. Some of the jurors dabbed their eyes, but the man accused of such savagery stared straight ahead. Not once did he glance at his handiwork. For the Russells, it was devastating. They knew what had happened, they'd dealt with the repercussions of the violent beating for months. "But it was so horrible to sit there and see all that blood and then to see her in the pictures of the autopsy," said Joan.

Dr. John Kelly took the stand. He told the court that he was wakened by pounding on his front door at 4:30 A.M. When he switched on the light and opened it, his old college friend James Cahill was on the step, pleading for help. There had been a fight between Jeff and his wife and both were hurt; his son was cut. When Dr. Kelly arrived, Jeff was sitting in the living room. "He had a cut on his arm and was bleeding a little, but he seemed to be sound, he seemed to be healthy and he was in possession of his facilities, so then I walked into the kitchen," he said.

"Did you administer any treatment to Jeff Cahill?" asked Assistant District Attorney Trunfio.

"No, I did not."

"Why not?"

"He didn't need any at the time," replied Kelly.

"When you walked into the kitchen, would you describe to the ladies and gentlemen of the jury what you saw?"

"I saw Jill Cahill on the floor. I think it was Jill. At the time I wasn't sure who it was, but judging from what [the Cahills] told me, it was Jill. She was in a pool of blood, unresponsive. I couldn't get her to respond to anything I did to stimulate her."

"Can you tell the jury what you did to get her to respond?" asked Trunfio.

Kelly said he examined her and tried to talk to her. He called her name loudly and when she had not reacted he had resorted to what he termed "painful stimuli" to try to rouse her. That didn't work either. He had wiped the blood from her face and from her head to see better how badly hurt she was. That's when he noticed that her skull was bashed in. He knew right away that she had to get to the operating room at Upstate as soon as possible.

"Was there anything you could have done at that point, as a surgeon, to help Ms. Cahill?"

"Nothing," said the doctor.

"She had a pulse?"

"She had a pulse."

"Could she speak or move her head at all?" asked Trunfio.

"She couldn't move anything," replied Kelly.

"Was she unconscious?"

"Yes."

"What did you do after you made the decision that she needed to get to University Hospital?"

"Called an ambulance. I asked someone to call the ambulance."

"What did you do after that?" asked Trunfio.

"I helped her get into the ambulance when it came."

Before Kelly stepped down, Jeff's attorney rose to his feet. "Did you notice the fact that Jeff was crying and upset like that?"

He wasn't crying, but he was upset, replied the doctor.

It was clear to the D.A. that Dr. Kelly was still disturbed by his friends' disregard for their daughter-in-law. "He was a very decent guy and a very, very powerful witness for us. He got there expecting to find a cut lip or a bruise and instead found a woman in the condition Jill was in, and his reaction, which he expressed very clearly to the jury, was, 'What the hell is wrong with you people? We have to get an ambulance here, and the state police,' " said Bill Fitzpatrick.

Rick Trunfio turned to the next witness, Trooper Richard Dix. When he got to Spafford, Sergeant June Worden from the Elbridge Barracks of the New York state police was on the porch. She'd told him to head over to Community General Hospital, find Jeff Cahill, read him his rights and wait for the investigators to arrive.

Investigator Maynard Cosnett told of sitting at the computer at Lafayette Barracks typing in the statement Jeff had dictated as he sat beside him. When he'd finished and printed it out, Jeff signed the last page. Cosnett testified that he wasn't buying the confession; he had been on the phone several times with the detectives who were sifting through the evidence back at the house while Cahill was pouring out his story, and the information they gave him made it clear that there were some glaring inconsistencies.

"When you say 'information,' you mean physical evidence?" asked Trunfio.

"Correct," replied Cosnett. "Also the injuries that Mr. Cahill suffered appeared to be very minor. And in my estimation, based on years of experience in investigating crimes, I thought that there was a possibility that they were self-inflicted rather than the way he has described that they had occurred."

"And you decided to reinterview him?" asked Trunfio.

"Correct."

Cosnett said he had first met Jeff in the treatment room of Community Hospital where he was having a wound on his hand dressed, around 8:00 in the morning. His father was with him. Cosnett checked with Trooper Dix that Cahill had been Mirandized before taking him to Lafayette Barracks to continue the interview.

James Cahill followed them to the barracks in his car. Cosnett testified that he had glanced out of his office window while he was interviewing Jeff and saw him standing outside. "Didn't you make a decision that you were not going to let the father see the son at that time?" Priest asked.

"It was not a conscious decision. But if he had asked me

if he could come in and speak to him, I would have told him he would have to wait until we were done," replied Cosnett.

Priest stressed for the jury's benefit that, throughout all this time, Jeff had been cooperative.

Cosnett said he had already decided to reinterview him: "I explained to him that I wanted to go back and clarify certain points and we would be taking an additional statement if Mr. Cahill was willing to continue talking to us." Priest's questioning could not shake the veteran cop. His partner, David Longo, testified that he had been suspicious about Cahill's injuries from the start.

"What is it about them that made you question him about the self-inflicted injuries?" asked Trunfio.

"First of all, they are very superficial. Second of all, they're all on the left side of his body and they were curved, which indicated that they were pulled across or down," he said.

"You asked him if he was right-handed?"

"Yes."

"And he indicated to you that he did this with a nail?"

"Correct."

"And when did you complete that second statement?"

"At one-o-six P.M."

"And that's when he signed it?"

"Yes."

"What did you do after the defendant signed this second statement?" asked Trunfio.

"He was eventually arrested."

"What time was he physically arrested and taken in custody?"

"Officially about one-fifteen P.M., one-thirty P.M."

Day two of the trial began with the court hearing how Cahill had gotten his hands on the cyanide. Two weeks after the assault, he had sat down at his computer in the home he'd shared with Jill and tapped into dozens of Internet sites in his search for deadly poisons. When he hit on fast-acting potassium cyanide to do the job efficiently, he found it was readily available and could be ordered by mail. Some more research revealed that cyanide is used in electroplating; that was extremely useful information, since he was familiar with General Super Plating in DeWitt.

This information swirled around his head until July, when it looked like Jill might not die from her wounds after all. That's when Jeff concocted a requisition form and ordered a pound of poison. On July 9, 1998, 500 grams of potassium cyanide and sodium formate were shipped by UPS Ground to General Super Plating. On July 10, realizing the order was supposed to have shipped overnight, the California supplier, Spectrum Labs, dispatched a duplicate order. Three days later they fulfilled another order and three days after that, on July 16, they provided 125 grams of potassium formate from their branch in New Jersey.

UPS driver Robert Leo testified that he had been near Home Depot when he was approached by a man who said he was picking up overnight packages for General Super Plating. Convinced he was an employee, Leo handed over an envelope. He described how a couple of days later, the same guy, driving a Jeep Wrangler, had tried to flag him down. He had driven on to his next stop, McDonald's, where the man caught up with him and asked for a Next Day Air package. Leo had told him he'd already made his deliveries. Suspicious, he had driven over to General Super Plating and conveyed his misgivings to Kevin Keenan.

Several employees of the company took the stand to describe how they became aware of these orders. Keenan told the court that Bob Leo had described a stranger who drove a black Jeep passing himself off as an employee to intercept packages. When he noticed the Jeep outside the plant, he'd noted the license tag number and reported it to Tracy Jones, who had since married and was now Tracy Fuller. She told the court that she had been tipped off that something was amiss when she received deliveries she hadn't ordered.

Looking at a copy of the letter sent in her name, she said: "The company logo was wrong, the address of the letterhead was wrong and that's not my signature at the bottom. My name is spelled wrong. [Whoever sent this] included an 'e' in my first name."

"You are not in the habit of misspelling your first name, I guess?" Trunfio asked her.

"No."

"What about your title, Purchasing Director, under your misspelled name?"

"There's never been a person with that title at General Super Plating," she told him.

Tracy said that she was still trying to find out where the missing packages had gone when she was told that a guy had turned up looking for a UPS package from California and she called the DeWitt Police Department. An officer arrived, he took statements and that was the last she heard. "Did you give them any of this material, the fake fax, the cyanide?" asked Trunfio. "No. I had shown them it all at the time, but they did not take anything with them. I kept it all in my possession."

She thought no more of it until October 29 when she was watching an early morning news show which led off with a woman being poisoned with potassium cyanide. "When I got to work I contacted the DeWitt police, thinking there might have been a connection," she said. "They told me that the Syracuse Police Department were on their way over to speak with me." When a detective arrived she handed over all her records and the chemicals.

Investigator Joseph Donahue of the Computer Crimes Unit in Albany produced a document downloaded from Cahill's printer and he read it out.

Two words were misspelled, said Donahue, "Tracey" and "received." He read another order for the poison. This time, the order was for "one hundred twenty-five grams of sodium formate, fourteen dollars fifty cents; shipping/handling, fifty dollars; hazardous/poisonous, twenty-six dollars sixty cents; total one hundred twenty dollars eighty-five cents." It was dated July 10, 1998, and again was to be sent to Ms. Jones. Each document downloaded from the defendant's computer contained the same spelling mistakes.

First Chief Assistant District Attorney Glenn Suddaby for Onondaga County was sworn in. He had received the initial call on the April 21 assault on Jill and testified that he thought he'd be looking at a homicide, given her condition. He told the jury that when Cahill was arraigned on June 16, he was looking at a jail sentence of 25 years. Could Cahill have copped a plea? Dougherty asked. Even if he had pleaded guilty he was still facing 10 to 20 years, Suddaby said. Dougherty then asked him if he knew from talking to Rick Trunfio back in October whether Jill Cahill was expected to be a witness if there was a trial. "That was totally dependent on her medical condition and the advice of her doctors," he replied. "It was our intention to call her if she was capable, if her doctors said it was OK."

That made Gary Miles attack. He claimed that Dick Priest was negotiating for a lesser sentence and maintained that there was no indication the case would have gone to trial. Suddaby replied that the shutoff date of July 9 had come and gone with no deal and a pre-trial hearing date had been set. Miles tried a different tack.

"Do you know why no law enforcement officers bothered to see if Jill Cahill knew anything about the assault?"

"Chief Trunfio was monitoring that situation daily, and

we were waiting for the doctors' permission to speak to her."

"Wasn't it a fact that, based on what you folks know, Jill Cahill had no recollection of the assault whatsoever?"

"That's not true, sir," said Suddaby.

"And in fact, are you aware that as of that point in time, October twenty-seventh, she was just starting to remember the names of her two children? You wouldn't have even needed Jill Cahill to be wheeled into the courtroom in order to prosecute the Assault One case, because there are well-documented photos and medical records of her injuries, aren't there?" asked Miles.

"It's always better to bring the victim into the courtroom before a jury," Suddaby replied.

Next the jury heard from the heroic surgeon who saved her life. Dr. Gerard Rodziewicz testified that she had arrived in the emergency room in a horrendous state. It had taken him and his team an entire hour to sew up cuts and staunch the heavy bleeding before he could begin to operate on her. As pictures of her in the E.R. flashed onto the screen, he told the jury that she'd needed ten pints of blood. He described the hours of surgery to remove the large blood clot on her brain.

He told the jury about her many setbacks over the ensuing months. Yet despite it all, she had survived and each time she recovered, then regressed, and she'd fought back. "Every time you gave this woman a chance to get better, she did," he said.

She had recovered so well that six months after she'd first been admitted, she was in a rehab program. She would have eventually been able to have some sort of meaningful life again. He told how all his efforts and Jill's brave fight had come to an end October 28 when he walked in to find her back in intensive care, brain-dead, being kept alive by a respirator.

Also to the grisly photographic backdrop of Jill's wounds,

medical examiner Dr. Mary Jumbelic told the jury that not only was Jill dealt life-threatening repeated blows to her head on the night she was beaten, she'd suffered other injuries: bruising on the right side of her neck and on her left breast; the skin was scraped on her right shoulder, her right elbow, her right forearm and on her wrist; her right hand was badly bruised and swollen and the nail on her middle right finger had been ripped off. She had a smaller wound on her left thumb, and her right arm was broken. Dr. Jumbelic left the jury grappling with a toe-curling image of what happened the night Jill was attacked. She had not gone down easily; as grievously damaged as she was, she had fought for her life as well as she could, given that she was overpowered by a man striking her with a metal bat. It was Dr. Jumbelic's estimation that at least four of the blows had hit Jill squarely on her head.

Dr. Stephen Lebduska told the court about the progress Jill had been making in his recovery unit. He was followed by Fred Russell, who movingly described the six-month-long vigil he and Joan had kept for their daughter; they had put their lives on hold to be by her side every day. By October, she was inching forward to recovery. Debbie broke down on the stand when she was asked to identify a picture of Jill, just days after she had been beaten, and another one of her sister and her father in the rehab unit, taken just before she was murdered. As they watched and listened to her, Joan and Jill's friends sobbed.

Throughout their testimony, which had the jurors reaching for the Kleenex, Jeff showed no reaction; he looked almost bored. "I've tried dozens and dozens of people for murder and I have never seen a guy so detached, so very unemotional," said Bill Fitzpatrick. "He didn't appear to have a great relationship with his lawyers. A lot of defendants scribble notes or whisper in their lawyers' ears or try to make a point about something. This guy did none of that."

On Thursday, August 5, Patricia Cahill testified. As she walked to the witness box, she gave Jeff two thumbs up, which infuriated the incredulous Russells. She was questioned about her conversation with him in mid-October after she had visited her daughter-in-law in the hospital. It had taken place as they were walking in Jill's flower-filled garden at Spafford, she said.

"Did he say anything about his wife during this conversation?" asked Fitzpatrick.

"Yes."

"What did he say?"

"We were looking at the flowers and the plants and determining what goes where and he remarked, 'Jill designed this garden a certain way and I hope that when this is all concluded that she can tell the truth about what led to the breakup of our marriage.'"

Fitzpatrick began to question Patty about the testimony she had given to the grand jury, but was stopped by the judge. He tried again: "Getting back to this conversation, you told your son Jeff about your physical observations of your daughter-in-law, Jill. Is that right?"

"Yes, sir."

"And he expressed concern as to whether or not she was going to tell the truth. Is that right?"

"When I was telling Jeff about Jill, he said nothing," she replied. She was asked to read from her prior testimony to refresh her memory and seemed to be befuddled by the request, but the jury took the D.A.'s implication on board: Patty Cahill had told her son that Jill could speak; not well—it was a huge effort and it tired her—but she could talk. And Jeff was afraid of what she would say.

"I'm done with this witness," said Fitzpatrick testily, tired of playing cat and mouse with her.

"You are dismissed, Mrs. Cahill," said the judge. Before she retook her seat, she walked from the witness box straight over to Jeff and flashed a two-thumbs-up sign in front of him again.

WHTV Channel 5 reporter Donna Adamo, who covered the case and attended the trial daily for her station, recalls that the tension in the court was tangible. "There was a very strange atmosphere in the courtroom. It seethed with it. There was a very strange relationship between mother and son. She was intimidating. I sensed that in the courtroom. I think Dick Priest was intimidated by her. It was obvious she controlled everything and everyone in the family—the husband seemed terrified of her. And I think Jeff hated her for that.

"Mrs. Cahill and his father came to the trial separately and they never sat together. They would be at opposite sides of the bench and never spoke to each other. They were a strange family. Kevin, I hated. John was the nicest one. He said he couldn't say anything, but told me, 'We are not all the same,'" Adamo said. "The Cahills hated me. I reported as fairly as I could the events in the trial each day and I was told they watched the broadcasts at night. I tried to talk to them often, I wanted to get as balanced a report as I could. One day outside the courthouse I met Mrs. Cahill and she stuck her tongue out at me. I thought, 'How stupid is that?'"

Mark followed his mother into the witness box. He was asked what he and his mother were doing at Jeff's house after his brother had been arrested.

"Do you recall going to your brother's home on the morning of October the thirty-first, 1998?"

"Yes."

"Had you visited your brother in jail prior to that date?" Fitzpatrick wanted to know.

"I believe so, yes."

"Was anyone with you?"

"My mother."

"Did you meet anyone at the house, sir?"

"It was a . . . he was a detective, I believe."

"What did you ask the officer when you arrived at the scene on that date, sir?"

"We wanted to get some tee-shirts for my brother."

"Anything else?"

"I wanted to check the house, make sure it hadn't been vandalized, and I wanted to see a piece of equipment up in his back yard."

"And the piece of equipment that you wanted to go see was what, sir?" asked Fitzpatrick.

"It was called a brake," answered Mark Cahill.

Fitzpatrick showed him a picture of the brake to verify it was the tool in question. "And the structure behind the brake is what?" he asked.

"A shed."

"And the brake and the shed and the grass and the leaves and the boards and everything in the photo are located where?"

"My brother's property."

"And can you tell the jury why it is you wanted to see the brake that morning, sir?"

"Wanted to inspect it, see whether, if it was in good condition."

"For purposes of . . . ?" queried Fitzpatrick.

"Probably going to sell the brake."

On Friday, the last of the prosecution's forty-two witnesses were called. In the morning, five University Hospital employees pointed across the courtroom and testified that Jeff Cahill was the bewigged, broom-pushing stranger who had masqueraded as a hospital cleaner and fled when challenged by Donna Holloway two weeks before when she discovered him in Jill's room. Many of them had seen him on her floor, near Jill's room the night she died.

Nurse Julie Labayewski said she ran to Jill's room after being told about the suspicious-looking cleaner, and found her gasping for breath with the cyanide granules scattered on her neck, chest and bedclothes. She said she had found a small white plastic cap in the bed and after she had stopped working on Jill, when Jill was taken off to the I.C.U., Julie had felt her hands burning.

Syracuse Police Department forensic scientist Tamara Danner testified that when she received the sheets from Jill's bed, there was such a strong odor that she had put brown paper in the laboratory's chemical hood to remove any toxic fumes. She said that the vial found in the hospital was a cut-down version of the little green glitter tube she had been sent—it was made out of the same plastic and appeared to be identical to the one she had received from the house. The caps of both tubes were also the same, with the number 4 on the inside. She also told the jury that she had been asked to look at a partially burned wig that had been taken from the Cahill home.

Dr. Timothy Rohrig, Onondaga County's director of the forensic toxicology, DNA and criminal labs, testified that the vial and the substance found on Jill's neck and chest had both tested positive for potassium cyanide. "Cyanide is a very potent, rapidly acting poison, that in very, very small quantities can cause death," he said. "It's the cyanide portion of the potassium cyanide that stops the body using its oxygen and the cells essentially suffocate to death."

Dr. Rohrig explained that the mixture would be quickly dissolved by the acidic stomach contents. Jill's stomach contained just 13 milligrams of cyanide. "That amount in itself is probably not fatal, but just the finding of that amount of cyanide indicates that she received a large dose of it, because it's rapidly absorbed. The cyanide remaining [in her stomach] is a very significant and very strong reading."

He added that the blood sample taken in the E.R. on October 27 had 15 micrograms of cyanide per milliliter. One microgram is a fatal dose. Jeff had researched his poisons well. Just five or six hours later, only 2 micrograms were detectable in her blood. If Jill had lain undisturbed all night, any trace of cyanide would have been lost. "I think he was looking for something that would be incredibly lethal, quick, because he realized he is going to be poisoning her in a hospital, so if he used something slower she might have been brought around," said Rick Trunfio.

Dr. Jumbelic was recalled to the stand to give evidence about the night Jill died. She confirmed Dr. Rohrig's finding that Jill had suffocated to death, her body starved of its own oxygen. Dr. Jumbelic had conducted an autopsy at 5:10 P.M. the following afternoon at the medical examiner's office. She noted at least ten scrapes on Jill's chin, and more on her lips. Fitzpatrick flashed a blown-up picture of Jill's lips and jaw on the screen. "Is there anything about the injuries on her chin that are consistent with medical intervention to save her?" he asked.

"No," she told him.

Gary Miles leaped to his feet to suggest the marks on her mouth might have been caused by a feeding tube. The medical examiner was having none of it. The only tube in her mouth had been inserted at the side. "Do you have an opinion, within a reasonable degree of medical certainty, as to whether these wounds are consistent with the forcible opening and/or closing of her mouth?" asked Fitzpatrick.

"They are," she replied.

"What was your opinion as to the cause of death?"

"She died of cyanide intoxication, and another significant injury was her blunt head trauma, due to a prior beating."

Detective Bob Teater testified about finding the partially burned wig stuffed into a 55-gallon drum during the Halloween execution of a search warrant issued after Detective Tom Derby refused to let Mark and Patty Cahill into the house or to check the brake in the back yard, and the maroon baseball cap Cahill had worn when he waylaid the UPS truck. Evidence technician Police Officer Fred Baunee described

discovering the little glitter tubes on a table in the living room
and four wigs in the mudroom. Detective Mark Abraham told
of removing the blue-and-white bottle of cyanide from under
the corner brick of the cinder blocks on the base of the shed.

"Can you tell us the distance, as best you can, between the
brake and where you found the bottle?" asked Dougherty.

"It's less than two feet, sir."

14

Verdict

The prosecution wrapped its case at the end of the first week after parading 42 witnesses and 120 exhibits before the jury. On Monday morning, August 9, after their motion to dismiss the charges was rejected by Judge Burke, the defense team produced just one person to testify for Jeff; Dr. William Scott Allyn was called on to establish Jeff's state of mind before he "snapped."

Allyn told the court he was a family doctor in Skaneateles and had known Jeff Cahill since they were children. He said Jeff had called him early one Saturday morning back in April 1998, worried about his health. Allyn had told him to consult his colleague who was on call that morning, but Jeff wanted to speak with him. Dr. Allyn had told him to come to his home. When he arrived, Jeff said he couldn't sleep.

"Why did he think he was having difficulty sleeping?" asked Gary Miles.

"He said his marriage was breaking up."

"Did he express any concern about family members?" asked Miles.

"He did, about his children. I believe that Jill and the children were in Buffalo and he raised concern about their being away."

"Did Jeff make mention of, in any further detail that you recall now, how the status of his marriage was affecting him?"

"Yes. He said he was under some stress."

"Did he mention any specific difficulties?" prompted Miles.

"Yes, he related in general terms to me that there had been some incidents that had occurred where there had been quite a bit of fighting between them. I recall him relating many incidents of marital discord, fighting and yelling."

Miles tried to coax details from the doctor, but Fitzpatrick jumped in repeatedly and successfully had him silenced. Then he began his cross-examination.

Jeff wasn't a regular patient, he discovered. In fact, Allyn hadn't treated him since giving him a tetanus shot two years before.

"Had he ever called you on a Saturday before April the eighteenth?"

"No, sir."

"Now, when you met with him, did the defendant tell you that he had been aware for at least two and a half months that his wife had been unfaithful to him?"

"I do not recall him specifying a time, no," said Allyn.

"Well, he certainly wasn't trying to tell you that he had just recently found out about it, say, within the last several days?" reasoned Fitzpatrick. "Did the defendant tell you on April the eighteenth that he had not been intimate with his wife for the previous six years?"

"No, sir, not that I recall."

"So his primary concern, as far as you were concerned as a doctor, was that he was having difficulty sleeping?"

"That was the reason he gave for wanting to see me, yes."

"And then he talked in general terms about some discord, some violence in the marriage, is that right?"

"That's correct," replied Allyn.

"And three days later, Doctor, he beats his wife's head in with a baseball bat. Did you learn that?" Fitzpatrick asked.

"Yes I did, sir."

"Did you feel like you'd been set up by your friend?"

"I really can't answer that," protested Allyn.

"Crossed your mind though, didn't it?" said Fitzpatrick.

Allyn then said he had prescribed the sleeping pill Ambien for Jeff.

Miles leaped up to redirect. He asked Allyn to recall what Cahill had told him about his wife's infidelity. Miles handed him a note Allyn had written at the time and asked him to read it over to refresh his memory. The doctor said that Jeff had told him that Jill was having an affair and that he'd claimed to have discovered this from the phone bill.

"Did he state who was the originator of any violent acts between them?" asked Miles.

"He spoke in general terms about times when Jill would become irrational, drink too much. He spoke in general terms of her anger and rage." After one confrontation Jeff said he had taken the children to his parents' house and when he went home, his wife threatened to kill herself with a knife and threatened him with a knife. "According to Jeff, she said, 'If I stab myself, they'll think you did it,' which I put in quotations," Allyn testified.

This all happened three days before Jeff almost killed her with a bat, Fitzpatrick reminded the doctor. Was it possible that Cahill used Allyn to create a defense and that he was planning to kill his wife all along?

"I have no way of knowing what Jeff was thinking," replied Allyn.

After he left the witness box, the defense called for a

fifteen-minute recess. Then Priest stunned the court by announcing the defense would fold—at one time he had noti-
fied the court he would call seven witnesses. Jeff would not
take the stand.

After the doctor's testimony, the decision not to bring Tom
Tulloch into the mix was puzzling to many. While nothing
would have exonerated Jeff Cahill's murderous actions,
there might have been at least a shred of understanding for a
guy whose wife was about to leave him for a younger, handsome and more successful man. But Priest chose not to go
that route.

It was a decision Bill Fitzpatrick understood. "I think it
would have been a tactical error to bring him in. Prying into
Jill's sex life would have opened the door for the prosecution
to open the door to Jeff's, and that would have told the jury
about the condoms, the makeup. If Jeff wasn't having
sex with his wife, who was he intimate with? If he tried
some sort of psychiatric defense or 'by reason of diminished
capacity'— but the killing was so cold-blooded that I think
that raising Tulloch may have backfired." He added that the
defense may have been worried that he would have brought
up conversations about her husband between Jill and Tulloch
during cross-examination.

With no motive offered by his attorneys for the beating
and subsequent murder, Fitzpatrick had his own theory to
explain the unfolding of events: "Jill was a very beautiful
woman and the marriage was really precipitated by her pregnancy with Tim, then followed by Mary relatively soon. We
were never able to get this out in trial but there were two
things that relate to my theory of what precipitated the murder. One was that Jill had told all of her friends that after the
birth of Mary, that their sexual intimacy stopped, so that was
a period of eight years. Yet Jill had found the condoms."

Although during the course of the investigation he didn't

come across even one man who claimed to be Jeff's lover, Fitzpatrick is convinced that he was having homosexual trysts and couldn't face his mother finding out. "I don't think there would have been anything more devastating to the defendant's mother than a nasty divorce proceeding and for Jill to reveal that Jeff was gay. [His mother] would just have reacted very, very forcefully to that."

On Tuesday, August 10, the jury heard closing arguments. "You carry with you the responsibility to determine not only how Jill died, who caused her death, but why," began Gary Miles. "If you find reasonable doubt to the motive of those acts, do not permit the prosecution to slip out from under their burden. The terrible and brutal nature of the assault of Jill with a baseball bat, no matter how it started, who started it, whether someone had a knife, the terrible brutal nature of Jeff's reaction, the horrible wounds and terrible suffering of Jill for six months, her helplessness in the hospital, the horrific means and mechanism of her death, the premeditated nature and steps involved in bringing about that death, do not constitute first-degree murder.

"As Jill's attorney said, she wanted out of her marriage. After ten years and two children, it wasn't working anymore. And there is no blame to be laid for that. Absolutely none. It's no one's fault that the relationship broke. But I think you know that relationship, those two children of that relationship, were Jeff Cahill's world. The impending breakup of that relationship caused him to seek counsel from his childhood friend. 'Scott, I can't sleep. I feel so much stress. Jill is leaving me. My life is breaking up and I don't know what to do about it. Give me advice, Help me sleep.'

"And Scott gave him advice. Avoid any confrontations with your wife, sleep somewhere else, get out of the house. Jeff tries to follow that advice when an argument in the early hours of April twenty-first escalated and became physical. He went downstairs and the argument went downstairs. And the final piece broke. Jeff snapped. A kind, loving, gentle husband and father took a baseball bat to the head of the woman he loved, conduct so completely out of character that no one saw the potential for what happened later on.

"When Jill decided to leave Jeff, she had the lawyer draw up a separation agreement. And on April ninth, he signed away his world. He permanently signed away a part of his life as he had known it. You can read that agreement. It's in the evidence. It's in a very real way a testament to the disintegration of a marriage, a family, and ultimately a man who was defined by those two concepts of marriage and family. Look at it. It shows the financial stresses that were on Jill and Jeff. What is allocated in that agreement are not things of monetary value, but pictures, shrubbery, everything that defined the Cahill life. It states in black and white, when, where and how Jeff Cahill was to be permitted to continue to be a father to his children."

Miles told the jury that the D.A. had used gory photos to whip them into such outrage over the brutality of the attack and the murder that they would no longer be capable of considering reasonable doubt. "They call Patricia Cahill, the mother of a man who may be on trial for his life," he said incredulously. "They ask her to testify against her son in a case which could lead to his execution. In some sort of an attempt to supply the motive of witness elimination, they want her to talk about a conversation she and Jeff had in the gardens of his home on East Lake Road as Jill lay in the hospital.

"And what does Patricia Cahill tell you? He doesn't say: 'Mom, I hope she does tell the truth.' He says: 'Mom, I hope when it's all over, she can tell the truth.' Is that a man who fears that his wife is going to testify against him in a criminal proceeding and that she might lie—or a man who fears for his wife because he has put her in a position where she may never be able to tell anything to anyone ever again?

"More tellingly, the prosecution gives us evidence of the

course of two Family Court proceedings, order of protection against Jeff involving Tim and Mary, his children, and visitation and custody matters involving not only Jeff but his parents. The connection between cyanide and the computer is not the criminal case. The connection is what's going on in the Family Court and the fact it's becoming obvious to Jeff that not only are his children being taken from him, but from his parents as well. That's Jeff's motive. Not the assault case. Jeff convicted himself of assault. Tim and Mary are lost, Jill lies in the hospital. This man completely breaks apart. His children and his wife are gone, it's his fault, he knows it and he doesn't know how to deal with it.

"And look what he did. He leaves a ton of information on cyanide in his computer. And he leaves a jar of potassium cyanide right where it will be found. He goes to SUNY Health Science Center in a disguise that fools no one on at least two occasions. Everyone who sees him tells you this man was seriously out of place. He goes home on the twenty-seventh of October and he waits for the police. And when they come, he goes with them. That same blind disturbance that appeared on April twenty-first never left this man. It stayed with him until the night he killed his wife. And no one noticed."

Telling the jury that they were the most closely scrutinized group of jurors in recent history, he cautioned them against the prosecution's bid to inflame their emotions. After offering a roundabout apology to the Russells, he concluded: "Hold Jeff responsible for what he did, but my God, don't attribute motives that aren't there."

After Miles sat down, Bill Fitzpatrick took the floor. "You have been asked to stare into the face of unspeakable evil. That's what this case is about, ladies and gentlemen. It is numbing in its inhumanity and chilling in its planning and execution—the elimination of a woman that he claims he once loved, to simply save his own skin.

"I would like to make some comments on the points Mr. Miles made. I want to talk about Jeff waiting for the knock on his door on October twenty-seventh or twenty-eighth. There isn't a single shred of evidence that Mr. Cahill went home waiting for the knock on his door. If he did not perform this murder competently, I make no apology for that. If he got caught, that's his problem, because he wasn't waiting for any knock on the door when Officers Dillion and Murphy got there. He was coming down the stairs out of bed, putting his shirt on, and the cyanide was hidden by the shed and his wig was burning on the trash. And this case has been about his efforts to cover up his crimes from April twenty-first.

"Let me talk about his lawyer's representation that his two children are his whole world. Oh, really? Oh, really? Were Tim and Mary part of his world when they were upstairs looking at what he was doing to their mother? Is that his whole world? Well, then, it's a God-awful world, ladies and gentlemen.

"They told you at the beginning of this case, 'He's just like you and me.' Well, he certainly ain't like me, and I'll be damn sure he's not like any of you. 'Go upstairs, Mary,' reads his statement. 'Go upstairs, Timmy,' and all the time Jill is calling out for her two children to save her life and call the police.

"He snapped. These statements are voluntary? Why did we need a second statement? Why? Because he never once accepted his responsibility for what he did in April and what he did in October. Not one single time. The police got a second statement because the first one was a pack of lies.

"They want to know on October nineteenth or twentieth why he didn't kill her. I'll tell you why he didn't kill her. Because Donna Holloway gave this woman another week of life, that's why he didn't kill her. Donna Holloway smelled something fishy about this guy and she never took her eyes off him.

"And you remember Mrs. Cahill? Now they want you to

know that, 'Well, what he really said was: "I hope when it's all over she tells the truth about the breakup of our marriage.'" Hello. Hello? He's got one hundred twenty-five grams of cyanide in his house while he's talking to Mommy in the back yard. He's not hoping she's going to tell the truth, because he's going to kill her.

"They brought Dr. Allyn to testify about a conversation he had with the defendant three days before the baseball bat assault. Do I believe Dr. Allyn? Frankly, I have no reason not to believe him. But I'll suggest to you, and when I heard his testimony for the first time, I opined during my cross-examination of the doctor that this was a setup. Think about the words he used: 'I'm going to stab myself and make it look like you did it.' Think about that. If Jill said that to him, and I don't suggest there is any reason to believe that she did, isn't it likely on April twenty-first the first person that ever touched the knife wasn't Jill Cahill, but Jeff Cahill?

"The savagery of this assault: I have a very, very deep disagreement with Mr. Miles as to what happened on April the twenty-first of 1998. She had to have been struck outside while she was trying to get away. You can see the physical evidence of the hair swipes right in front of you, the helpless woman being dragged into that room, and she was struck again in the mudroom. And we know she was struck while her head—the source of the bleeding—was very low to the ground, because the blood spatter is also very, very low to the ground. She crawls back into the kitchen and the brutality there speaks for itself."

As he was talking, his voice rising, Fitzpatrick picked up the dented metal bat and walloped it into his outstretched hand. "Did he snap during the first blow?" He slammed the bat as hard as he could down on his hand again. "Did he snap during the second blow to her head?" He smacked it down seven times in all and asked, "Or did he snap during the multiple, *the multiple* blows to her head?"

Donna Adamo recalled the electricity in the room as the district attorney swung the bat. "The jury flinched with each blow. It was incredibly dramatic. Half of them were in tears. They really looked shell-shocked," she said. "Jeff sat cold. No emotion flickered across his face."

"And I want to talk about these self-inflicted wounds, because that's what they are, self-inflicted," Fitzpatrick continued. "The defendant says so under oath in his statement. Look at the linear patterns to them. Tell me in the name of God how someone who, coming at you with a knife, is able to get perfectly covered lines on only one side of your body. Reenact it with a ruler or something. It's impossible. What's he doing standing there while Jill is taking the tip of the knife and scratching him? Where are the slash marks on his arm as he's trying to defend himself from the horrible assault from this knife?" He held up the bloodstained sweatshirt Jeff had worn when he beat her and asked the jury where the holes were; were they really supposed to believe she was slashing him when there wasn't a single nick in the fabric?

"And let's talk about time for a moment. The fight starts between 4:00 A.M. and 4:15 A.M., but the first call to the police isn't until 5:34 A.M. and it's not from the defendant. He called Mommy and Daddy, OK? That's an awful long period of time between when he says this fight started and when the police get there. And when Dr. Kelly gets there, the first thing Dr. Kelly does say is, 'My God, has someone called an ambulance?' This is a guy that's so concerned, he's sitting there, trying to get his ducks in order. He concocts this suicide attempt and he couldn't do it because he saw the rosary beads. It starts with Dr. Allyn, continues at the scene, the smearing there of the blood. It continued with the self-inflicted wounds.

"Dr. Gerard Rodziewicz said, 'Every time we gave her a chance to get better, she did.' I don't know if there was a more telling comment in this trial." He talked about the restraining order. Maybe he had his ears closed. Maybe he had earmuffs on. Maybe he looked away. I don't know, I can only prove it to you beyond a reasonable doubt. For crying out loud, the guy was in court ten, a dozen times, talking about an order of protection. He knows he's not supposed to be in that hospital, never mind in her room."

It was vital to understand that her hospital room was Jill's home, Fitzpatrick went on. Jeff had broken into it as surely as if he had broken into her house, and that was why he was guilty of murder in the first degree. They should also convict him on the count of murder in the second degree, Fitzpatrick told them. He's over 18, he intended to kill his wife, he did kill her and one of his motives was to prevent her testifying at his trial.

He took them through the chronology: "On May eleventh, Jeff is in Family Court talking about his children and what's going to happen with them. And during the proceeding on the eleventh, Rick Trunfio says the criminal case is proceeding before the grand jury. And what does the defendant do when it's concluded and he's in there talking about the future of 'his whole world,' Tim and Mary? He logs on to the Internet and begins to plot the murder of the mother they loved.

"On May nineteenth there is a Family Court record indicating that a psychologist is about to interview his two children, 'his whole world.' Again the defendant was present," said Fitzpatrick. "And what does he do? On May nineteenth he logs on to the Internet again and he begins now to search how to order cyanide. Now he's already learned, that of the million ways there are to die, there aren't many more horrible than dying by potassium cyanide.

"On July seventeenth, 1998, after ordering it on the eighth, the defendant finally has his cyanide in his possession. The day after he ordered it, there was a pre-trial hearing in Criminal Court. He realizes that the case isn't going away and he is going to be looking at serious hard time in Attica. 'Me, Mr. Jeff Cahill, Cornell graduate. I have to go to Attica for this?' " mimicked the D.A.

"On October 5th his mother visits Jill for the first time in the hospital and two weeks later she tells him what she saw." Fitzpatrick again faced the jury and asked them if they thought it was coincidence that on that date, or the following day, Jeff Cahill was positively identified at that hospital. "The case is going to trial, there's a hearing scheduled for November second. And he kills Jill less than a week before.

"He burned this wig, put the cyanide by the shed by the brake, and—guess what happened?—Mark and Mom come up on the day of her daughter-in-law's funeral and they decide, 'Hey, we got to go check out the brake at Jeff's house.' 'You have to what?' asks Officer Derby. 'We want to check out the brake, we're going to sell it.' Officer Derby said, 'Check out the brake, boys.' And guess what? There is the cyanide. And there you have it.

Fitzpatrick compared the reactions of the two families. He noted that Mark Cahill, who couldn't seem to recall exactly when he heard about his sister-in-law's death, cried as he talked about his mother. The defendant cried when his lawyer said he snapped and when his mother testified. "Debbie Jaeger cried. I want you to compare that testimony of that woman to the testimony of the defendant's brother and his mother," he told the jury. "Knowing what he had done to her sister, I asked her, 'Was he a good father before April of 1998?' With no fear of contradiction—and she could have said practically anything she wanted—she said, 'Yeah, he was a good father.' "

Jill's parents and sister wept as he wound up: "To Fred and Joan and Tim and Mary and Debbie and David, most importantly, I'll leave you with these final words. They're words, not of hate, they're words of love from *Romeo and Juliet*: 'When she shall die, I will cut her out into little stars and she'll make the face of Heaven so fine that all the world will be in love with night and pay no worship to the garish sun.' " To the jury he said, "God speed to you people. It's never too late to do the right thing."

After Fitzpatrick wrapped up on this poetic note, Judge Burke began to instruct the jury on the law. To convict Cahill on First-Degree Murder they had to find him guilty of killing his wife during a burglary at University Hospital. Burke explained that the prosecution's position was that Jill lived at University Hospital for the last six months of her life— Cahill was well aware of the restraining order, yet entered her room with the intent to commit a crime there. If the jury bought that, they must convict. If they didn't accept that premise, they must acquit.

He explained the charge of Criminal Possession of a Weapon in the Fourth Degree. A person is guilty if he unlawfully obtains a dangerous instrument capable of causing serious injury or death, in this case potassium cyanide, with the intent to use it against another person. They must not take into account what could happen to Cahill. "You, the jury, should not permit the question of punishment to influence your judgment," he warned.

Burke apologized for being repetitive and appointed the first person seated and sworn, Michelle Terry, as the jury foreperson. "Before you can say guilty or not guilty, all twelve of you must agree. Your verdict has to be unanimous," he added.

"If there's a question among yourselves, Mrs. Terry, you write that question out and you sign it and I'll bring everyone back in here, I'll get all these folks gathered together again and I'll make sure that each and every one of you understands absolutely what the law is as it applies to this particular case."

With the jury gone, Priest went back to the courtroom to object to the verdict sheet Judge Burke had prepared for each member of the jury. Far from simplifying their decision, "the language is confusing," he complained. The judge agreed to rethink the wording over lunch, but refused to hold up the deliberations until it was reworked. Then Gary Miles demanded a mistrial, saying that the district attorney had mentioned Patricia Cahill's grand jury testimony in his opening remarks. The judge denied the motion, but agreed to instruct the jury not to consider her grand jury testimony.

"Anything you want?" the judge asked Fitzpatrick.

"Yes, Judge. Can we have the testimony of Mrs. Cahill [left in]? You didn't let me cross-examine her. I tried six ways from Sunday. You stopped me every time. I didn't pursue it. I didn't blab out anything in an unethical manner, I followed the Court's ruling and sat down." Burke told him the answer was still no.

The trial had stirred such strong emotions locally that the Syracuse *Post-Standard* set up a hotline where callers could be kept up to date on the latest developments from the jury room. At 5:15 P.M. word flew around the courthouse that there was a verdict. Just over half an hour later, the jury filed somberly into the box. The usually affable forewoman was in a grim mood.

"Mrs. Terry, would you stand for me? You've reached a verdict here in *The People* versus *James Cahill*?" asked the judge.

"We have," she replied.

"And would you recite that verdict for me as to the first count, Assault in the First Degree?"

There was a brief delay while the court attendant went to find the verdict sheet, which had been left in the jury room.

The judge started again: "Mrs. Terry, may I ask you, what's your verdict on Assault in the First Degree?"

"We, the jury, find him guilty."

"And what's your verdict on the fourth count, Criminal Possession of a Weapon in the Fourth Degree?"

"Guilty."

"Now, and the second page of your jury sheet, Murder in the First Degree?" asked Burke, referring to the act of poisoning Jill in the hospital.

"Guilty."

"And your second count, Murder in the Second Degree and the second count, Murder in the First Degree?" in regard to Jeff 's having killed Jill to stop her testifying against him.

"Guilty."

"And then you went on following my instructions?"

"Yes."

"To the last count?" quizzed the judge.

"Yes."

"The sixth count, what's your verdict on the Criminal Possession of a Weapon in the Fourth Degree?"

"Guilty."

"You may be seated," said Burke.

He repeated the charges, then asked, "Is that your verdict, so say you all?"

"Yes," they chorused.

Cahill stared ahead, as if unable to comprehend the magnitude of the decision. He showed no emotion and never looked at the twelve men and women who had just convicted him in less than five hours of deliberations. He faced the verdict alone; his parents and brother, who had supported him throughout the trial, were absent. "I think there was an attitude that was there during the trial, that this is a nice, white, upper-middle-class college-educated chap who was not going to do hard time [for the assault] and then, when it became a murder case, he was certainly not going to be sentenced to death," said Bill Fitzpatrick.

In the spectator seats, Debbie, who had buried her face in her hands while the verdict was being read, burst into tears and collapsed into her husband's arms. Fred and Joan Russell clutched each other.

Priest jumped up and demanded the jurors be polled. It

made no difference. Twelve times the judge called out a name and twelve times came back the same answer: "Guilty, on all counts." The judge then set a date for the penalty phase of the trial, Tuesday, August 17, at 9:00 A.M.

After the jury left, Jeff's parents slipped into their seats. Like their son, they sat stonily composed, teeth clenched and arms folded, avoiding everyone's eyes. When Jeff was led from the courtroom, he didn't look at them; they didn't rise to touch or comfort him. They left hurriedly, avoiding the barrage of flashbulbs and TV cameras, while Bill Fitzpatrick, Dick Trunfio and Steve Dougherty shared smiles, handshakes and heartfelt hugs with the Russells.

15

Death Penalty

"When the verdict came down, we all burst out crying. We couldn't believe the guilty verdict. We cried with relief, it was such an ordeal," said Joan. "We turned the radio on in the car and there was a local talk show on and people were calling. And one man said he was all for the decision, but they should have done what they did in the old days, when they'd have strung [Jeff] up at the courthouse, or shot him. One woman called in and said she was a friend of the Cahills but she felt he'd deserved what he got. We were elated to think that these people were all from Skaneateles, and everybody that called was in favor of the outcome of the trial. We went to Morris's grill, where Jill used to work, to celebrate. We had a drink. The bartender bought us a drink. Then we just went home."

Seven days later the jury that had convicted Jeff reconvened to decide how he would pay for killing Jill. It was the first death penalty trial in Onondaga County since the State of New York had reinstated it in 1995, and if they so chose, this jury, who were in no doubt that Jeff was guilty, could make him the fifth man awaiting execution on New York's death row.

Before they were in the courtroom, Jeff's lawyers had submitted to Judge Burke a list of mitigating factors as to why he ought to be spared. They had put together twenty-five reasons why the twelve jurors should overcome their revulsion to the calculated murder of Jill Cahill; some of them, given the seriousness of the crime, were laughable.

At the top of the list were his friendships with people of all ages and walks of life. Jeff had been a loyal and dependable friend to his brothers; while employed at Merrill Lynch he had gotten along well with coworkers; he worked during summer vacations when he was at school. If sentenced to life without parole, he could make a "tangible contribution back to society by sharing his skills and talents."

Others were designed to tug at the heartstrings: Jeff was a respectful, dutiful and devoted son; he was a nurturing and supportive presence to children in his Little League and soccer teams; he'd had a loving relationship with the wife he nearly clubbed to death, then poisoned. When his children were born, he was a doting and devoted father and he had no prior history of violence. If he was sentenced to life without parole, Jeff would have to answer to his grown children, to his nieces and nephews. Priest and Miles trotted out that while awaiting trial Jeff had been a model prisoner; he'd tutored his fellow inmates; he had sought spiritual guidance in prison and was no danger to others.

But despite his attorneys' insistence that he was an upstanding guy seeking the Lord's help, being pious was far from Jeff Cahill's immediate thoughts. Just after the verdict he wrote to a jailhouse buddy, complaining about not having enough bodies for a decent basketball game and whining that he couldn't play cards or watch the Discovery Channel on TV. Life in his prison pod was "no fun," he wrote. He also voiced his anger that he was not isolated from the usual prison indignities.

He blamed his current predicament on Dick Priest (Gary Miles escaped his finger-pointing), the law, the jury, the prosecutor who'd brought up Jill's vicious assault at the trial—he even took issue with God's divine plan while telling his crack-addicted pal that he was confident the good Lord would forgive his "mistake," because he was different from the rest of the scum behind bars; he was caring, concerned, educated, thoughtful, responsible, outgoing, friendly and honest. The only reason he and his new friend were behind bars was that both of them had been whacked with an "interruption" in their lives.

Jeff was confident that he'd enjoy his inevitable transfer to the State Penitentiary at Dannemora—where, ironically, Jill's college sweetheart Steve Pfister's father worked—because there he would have access to a radio, books, magazines and the prison store. If he kept out of trouble for sixty-nine days, he would be allowed a TV set with up to twelve stations. He could have visits once a week from his family and a once-weekly ten-minute phone call. The downside would be only one shower per month, strip searches three times a day and not being allowed to stick pictures of his family up on the walls of his cell. He wrote he was hitting the law books with his kids in mind.

In a revelation that would hardly have seasoned correction officers shaking in their steel-capped boots, he boasted that he spent his days thinking up stinging barbs to sling at four prison guards he loathed. And in an unconscionable show of chutzpah, he devised the perfect excuse to justify stuffing poison down his wife's throat: it was a mercy killing. He maintained that Jill often talked about not wanting to go on if she had to live with severe deficiencies. Getting rid of her was just putting her out of her misery and he railed at Priest for failing to put him on the stand to explain this to the jury. Now he was being punished for doing the right thing and he told his junkie confidant that he fully expected to be out of jail in 15–20 years.

No one at the time, including Judge Burke, was aware of Jeff's views on his conviction. He quickly whittled down the list to nineteen mitigating factors. Priest objected contending that Mr. Cahill would be denied a fair sentencing and his eighth Amendment protection against cruel and unusual punishment would be violated. He then announced he would call twenty-one witnesses who would testify to Jeff's prior good character. Legally the prosecution could not produce any witnesses to challenge their testimony.

Jeff's younger brother John told the court he lived twenty miles north of Pittsburgh with his wife Darlene and their seven kids, Catherine, Maria, Elizabeth, Joseph, Christine, Jack and Anne. In a demonstration of family strength that outraged Zaney Haux, they brought the littlest Cahill to the trial. "John brought the baby. I thought, 'You've got to be kidding.'"

John said that his mother was their backbone. It was she who had stressed that the six of them must stick together through thick and thin. While he was talking, photographs were passed round the jury showing the towheaded Cahill boys, the family at the Cape, Jeff and Jill's first home together in Skaneateles, Tim at 3 years old, Jeff on a periwinkle hunt, Jeff with a flower in his ear, at a wedding and with his nephews. The recent snaps had all been taken by Jill.

John admitted that his mother had tried to interfere in his brother's love life, and on the day of Jeff and Jill's wedding, she was in Cape Cod. But Jeff was in no mood to listen. Jill was pregnant and he wanted to marry her.

He said he and his wife had often visited with Jeff and Jill. His children loved being around their bubbly aunt. The girls adored her, especially since she let them raid her closet and try on her clothes. He told the court that he intended taking them to visit Jeff in jail if his life was spared. It is a corporeal rule of mercy in the Catholic Church to visit people in prison, he explained. Looking at the jury he added, "I love my brother very much. I know he's done something particularly awful. And I have to communicate that to my kids." His youngsters were grappling with the tragedy and he hoped he could make them understand the possibility of redemption, forgiveness and the importance of praying for Jill's mother, who had suffered so much.

John was followed by Patty's brother, John Morrissey. He brought along a chart of the family tree to show the court how the Cahills and Morrisseys were connected. His daughter Lynn had been Jeff's soul mate growing up, and she was crushed by her favorite cousin's "activities." He reminisced over the pranks they'd played on vacation and showed snaps of the family at the Cape and of a lifeguard's chair that they had painted with polka dots and kept moving around the beach.

Next was Auntie Jane Sterling. She talked up idyllic summers when she and Patty would take the kids blueberry picking or to see the herring run. She remembered Jeff spending most of his vacation in the toolshed knocking pieces of wood together and produced photographs of Adirondack chairs he had made in all different sizes, of window boxes he'd installed at the summerhouses and the birdhouse he had given to her. They were both so artistic, she said. Jill had painted cranberries and "Sterling Steps" on a ladder for her, and "Jane's Joint" on a shelf. She showed a picture of a table with a cranberry design that the couple had made for his mother.

Skaneateles neighbor Margaret Major told of the home improvements Jeff had done for her when she inherited the rundown house next door. Sometimes he had brought Timmy to work with him and the kid seemed as happy as a lark puttering around with his father. When her son Michael moved into the restored property with his family, his 4-year-old daughter Victoria had peppered Jeff with questions for a whole day, and to her amazement, he had patiently answered them all.

Jeff's former roommate, real estate appraiser Mike Morrissey, who'd played soccer with him at Community College, described the grueling hours at Merrill Lynch. He recalled the night they had gone into the Syracuse bar and met Jill. He said Jeff was a terrific father. When asked by Gary Miles to rate him on a scale of 1 to 10, Morrissey gave him 11. That brought Fitzpatrick to his feet. "How would you rate him on the April twenty-first when he beat his wife with a bat with his children in the home, or on October twenty-seventh when he broke into the hospital and poisoned her?" he asked.

Navy vet Dr. Brewster Doust Jr., a swabbie in the Pacific during World War II, said he had worked with Jeff's grandfather and admired the young stockbroker for walking away from the rat race to work with his hands. He had replaced the windows in Doust's home, built a stairway to his dock and fixed his pier. Every summer Jeff would return to work on his property. The old man said he'd grown fond of him and had been charmed by the lovely Jill, who flattered him by telling him he grew the best corn she'd ever tasted. He recalled going over to their house just after Mary was born, picking her up and telling Jeff, "This is the fourth generation of Cahills that I've held."

"Jeff was a terrible businessman," he said. "I used to have to call his wife and say, 'Send me the bill.' He would never do this on time and I knew that he needed the money. I think there is good in Jeff. . . . I don't think he should be put to death."

Retired schoolteacher Jane Dove said she had taught all six Cahill boys at Skaneateles Middle School. They'd had a *Leave It to Beaver* childhood with wonderful churchgoing parents.

By this time, the Russells, forced to listen in silence to this litany of praise for the man who'd savagely murdered their daughter, were squirming in their seats with barely suppressed rage. "It was hard to sit and listen to all that garbage," said Joan. Whatever happened to the Sixth Commandment, Thou shall not kill?"

But the parade of Jeff supporters went on all that day and half of the next. Teacher Nancy Murray told the court that Jeff had installed windows for her and Jill had helped her with her garden and arranged her window boxes. She also said that Jeff had no head for business. "He'd leave notes around saying he'd enjoyed the cookies and cake and forget the bill."

Others trooped to the stand to talk about Jeff's love of his kids, how he would drop his tools as soon as the school bus arrived. Parents said he was a great coach. One said he never lost patience with the kids, another said that Jeff had coached his son in 1995 and 1996 and showed pictures of a team that went all the way to the finals. A weeping Marion Drastal and her husband Matthew agreed he had boosted their diffident son's self-esteem when he was on Jeff's baseball team in 1997. As she left the stand, she whispered to Jeff, "We miss you."

The Beckemans also brought their 12-year old daughter, Kimberly, to testify. "He [Jeff] taught Tim to catch a bird with a little net," she said and burst into tears. The memory still sticks in Joan Russell's gullet. "That was horrible, just awful, they brought the little girl up there, and she was crying. When [his lawyers] were done with her, Bill Fitzpatrick asked her, 'And how old were you when he was doing all these wonderful things?' and she said, 'Three and a half.' "

Deputy Robert Richardson from the Onondaga County Sheriff's Department's Custody Division told the court that Jeff was on his cleanup crew at the jail, and that he had done an "excellent" job of handing out meals and cleaning tables.

He posed no threat to other inmates, had even helped some of them with a G.E.D. test, and was "respectful" of the staff. Rolling his eyes, Bill Fitzpatrick sniped: "Just like kindergarten: tidy the room, keep it clean and play nice."

The deputy offered a clue as to where Jeff had picked up the janitorial skills he'd deployed to kill his wife. As a trusted inmate he was allowed out of his cell to clean the pod after everyone else was locked up, and became adept with a squeegee, a mop, a broom and a buffer. Father John Schopper, who said Sunday Masses at the Justice Center, had put Jeff in charge of selecting a reading from the Old Testament. He opined that Jeff was a "very, very good person."

George (Woody) Malone traveled from his home in South Carolina to testify. A USAF vet who'd served in Japan, he produced a sheaf of bills Jeff had submitted to an elderly lady for whom he'd worked. At Priest's invitation, he read them aloud. The first one came to $35.00, the next one amounted to $40.00, and Jeff had written on the bottom, "Just send this to me whenever." He lists replacing broken tiles, grouting a bathroom, removing tar from gutters, sealing joints, resetting corner tiles and countertop and regrouting a vanity top. The total was just over $150.

Priest asked Malone why he'd come. "I don't excuse what happened, but Jeff is a friend, and when I was in trouble somebody reached out and helped me and I just felt I had to do that."

Priest then read out a letter from the old lady, Maria Crouse, in which she said that although Jeff had committed this unspeakable crime, he was a trustworthy, helpful young man who never took advantage of an elderly person like herself. He was anything but a hardened criminal, she said, and asked that he be punished with life imprisonment.

Donna Adamo said that while Priest read the letter, snapshots of the windows he had put in Mrs. Crouse's house were shown and Jeff began to weep. "That's the only time I saw him cry throughout the whole trial, not when they showed the photographs of Jill with her head bashed or when they talked about his children, but over some windows he'd installed."

By then it seemed that even his attorneys had had their fill of Jeff Cahill's sugary goodness. "At this time, Judge, the defense is going to rest. I thank you." Priest sat down. Bill Fitzpatrick certainly had heard enough of Jeff's saintly ways. He walked over to the jury box and began: "I am here on behalf of the State of New York to ask you to impose a sentence of death, death by lethal injection, upon this defendant for a reason and for one reason only: because the aggravating factors of this dastardly murder so far outweigh the mitigating factors, that death is both the appropriate punishment and it is the just punishment.

"When you are asked to think about mercy, I want every one of you to think about this: for five months, one hundred and fifty days, while Jill Cahill was crawling back to humanity, this defendant was plotting her execution.

"And now he asks you for mercy? If the death penalty [is not appropriate] in this case, my God, then when? Was this some drug deal gone bad where shots were fired? Was this some longtime simmering feud between two hotheaded individuals where one reacted on the spur of the moment? Was this some poor kid going into a grocery store and shooting the store clerk in panic? No. This was a calculated, premeditated killing of a helpless woman.

"Jeff Cahill wants you to know he was a good soccer player, a good sportsman; wants you to know he did great work on construction jobs. Don't bother arguing about it. You don't have to look at forty photos of woodwork and the chairs and all this other stuff. Take it as given—he's a great construction guy. He was a good coach. Fine. . . .

"Consider all of the mitigating factors. One of them is going to say he was a good father prior to April of 1998.

What evidence is it they put in to show you he was a good father? That he took Tim to the park? That he coached Little League? He played basketball? You know, folks, where I come from, that's what a father is supposed to do. And this morning we learn he is a model prisoner. Big deal.

"Remember the words of Julie Labayewski, who said Jill was sleeping in her bed about ten o'clock at night. And then that dwelling was violated by the very man who put her there, the man who thirsted for five months for her death, who disturbed her slumber and, despite her best effort at resistance, forced open her mouth and filled her stomach with a hideous poison.

"In May of 1998 this defendant chose to scan the Internet. . . . He picks one of the most horrible poisons known to man, potassium cyanide. He chooses to order the cyanide, he chooses to steal the cyanide, he chooses to wear a disguise, he chooses to visit Jill on either the nineteenth or twentieth of October and she's spared an extra week of life by the intervention of Donna Holloway. And he chooses on October twenty-seventh to force this cyanide into her stomach. And then he chooses to go home and go to bed. And now he wants you to choose life without parole?"

Priest stood and faced the jury. "Folks, death is not needed in this case. You verdict assured that. Mr. Fitzpatrick tells you that we will ask for mercy and I don't deny that. Let me tell you something. It's a shallow mercy that condemns a human being to a six-by-nine cage for the rest of their life with no hope of ever being able to be heard in a plea to get out. . . .

Is there no justice for Jeff other than death? Is there nothing about this man's life, past, present or future, that you could find would justify a sentence to allow him to continue to exist in a cage until God calls him?

"You don't have to check your morality at the door," he told the jury, adding that they should not lower their moral standards to the same depths as Jeff Cahill's on October 27. "That's what they are asking you to do, to lower yourself to that depth. Your verdict has assured that Jeff Cahill will not be allowed to make even the simplest of personal decisions on his own ever again. Not when to go to sleep, not when to get up, not when to take a shower, not what or when to eat. He will never again experience total solitude or privacy; he assured that when he killed Jill and you assured that when you found him guilty. Is that not enough?

"You never, ever have to choose death. And if your conscience tells you that life is appropriate, don't be shoved off that position by someone who says, 'Look what he did to his wife, look what he did.' " Then Priest launched into a homily spouted by his 7-year-old daughter Elizabeth: " 'When I have to make a right choice, I close my eyes, I get real quiet and I ask Jesus, because I don't want to make a wrong choice that I'm going to be sad about later.' "

Judge Burke began his summation by reading all the mitigating factors, then instructed the jurors how to apply the law. Each of them had the power to decide whether the witnesses had told the truth and whether it mattered. "You alone are responsible for deciding whether this defendant will spend the rest of his life in prison or that he'll be executed by lethal injection. . . . Such a sentence must be unanimous," he cautioned them. If they couldn't agree, the law required him to impose a sentence of imprisonment with a maximum term of life and a minimum sentence between 20 and 25 years.

At 3:30 A.M. on August 19, deliberations began. The jurors wrestled with their decision until 7:00 P.M. when they took a first vote. It was 10–2 for death. One of the two people who opted for life without parole was the jury foreperson, Michelle Terry, who worked for Kmart. The tension in the room, coupled with worry about her sick mother and mother-in-law, began to overwhelm her. Half an hour later, a note was delivered to Judge Burke. One of the jurors had fainted.

Suddenly, the courthouse erupted in a flurry of activity as paramedics were called and Mrs. Terry, complaining of chest pains, was removed to University Hospital where she spent the night with a court deputy standing guard to make sure her husband, or any other members of her family who had rushed to her side, did not mention the case. The remaining eleven jurors were driven to a nearby hotel and sequestered for the night.

Before she had even left the building, the lawyers and the judge began to argue over the legal ramifications of this twist of events. Priest and Miles immediately called for a mistrial. Burke refused to grant it, telling them that Mrs. Terry would be under constant supervision, there would be no way she would see a newspaper, listen to a radio report or see coverage of the trial on television because he had ordered the deputy to be with her at all times.

The next morning, Friday, August 20, the legal wrangling continued in court while the jury remained at the hotel. Again the defense pressed for a mistrial; at the very least, they insisted, the judge should seat one of the alternates. Burke settled the matter by announcing that he would go to University Hospital himself to check on the forewoman's condition and then make a decision.

With a retinue of clerks and security trailing in his wake, the judge left. Half an hour later he was back saying, "I saw Mrs. Terry. Her physician was there at the time. I spoke to her about obtaining the release [of her medical records] and she was standing up, fully dressed and ready to come out. Her doctor came in and without any discussion from me, other than to introduce himself, he indicated that Mrs. Terry is in A-one shape. She needs iron tablets and some other things, medication that won't take effect for weeks. She's got maybe a vitamin deficiency. There's nothing wrong with her," he said, and deliberations would resume.

Miles had another problem. While the 39-year-old mother of two was being treated in the courtroom, he insisted he could hear what the paramedic was saying to her.

"There's no possibility that that woman overheard what we were saying," said Burke.

"The court cannot say that, Judge, when I can hear what the paramedic is saying to her," argued Miles.

"I know what you are saying and I am saying to you that there's no possibility that lady overheard what we were saying," replied Burke firmly.

"Judge, there is no statutory authorization for what occurred here, separating her from the rest of the jurors and bringing her back into the mix," complained Miles.

The judge said he would caution her not to discuss her absence.

Michelle Terry rejoined the jury at 11:30 A.M. Another vote was taken at noon and this time, she was the only holdout. Nobody pressured her to change her mind. "If you are still not sure, we'll go over it all again," the other jurors assured her. She thought of Jill, how beautiful she had been, how that beauty had been destroyed. She thought of Jill's kids and her family, how they had been robbed of their mother and daughter in a premeditated and cruelly painful way. She thought of other women trapped in a vicious cycle of domestic violence. And by 12:30 P.M. she was sure. She wrote "death" on her ballot.

A stir rippled through the courthouse when a note was sent to the judge. He warned everyone to keep quiet. At 12:37 P.M. the jurors filed in. "The jury is all present, all the lawyers are present, the defendant is present," began Burke. "Mrs. Terry, you've reached a decision here in the sentencing phase of the trial?"

"Yes," she whispered.

"You're going to hand me up your verdict sheet, is that right?"

"Yes."

"And on the first count of murder on Murder in the First Degree, what's your verdict, what's your sentencing determination?"

"Death."

Joan Russell let out an audible gasp and burst into tears. Jill's father looked stunned, and beside him, Debbie began to sob. Jeff stared straight ahead as if he was tuning it out. His parents, sitting with two of Jeff's brothers, never flinched, but the color drained out of Richard Priest's face and at his side Gary Miles sank his head into his hands.

"And on the second count on Murder in the First Degree. What's your verdict in that?"

"Death."

"OK, you be seated. Each of you individually has found unanimously that this defendant should be sentenced to death. Is that your verdict, so say you all?"

"Yes."

Priest asked for the jury to be polled. "Sure," said the judge. "Mrs. Terry, is that your verdict, death?"

"Yes."

"Mr. Terrine?"

"Yes."

"Mrs. Krauts?"

"Yes."

It went on until all twelve answered. "It was the only time I saw him react when they came back with the death penalty," said Donna Adamo, the Channel 5 reporter. "I remember watching his tie moving, underneath it his chest was pounding. Then he just walked away, never looked at his family or anyone. I thought, 'What kind of creature is this?'" As soon as their condemned son was removed, the

Cahills rushed from the courtroom with his attorneys, Patty covering her face with a newspaper. Escorted by court officials, the Russells quietly left to meet with the prosecution team. Shortly after, at the jury's request, they returned to the courthouse for an emotional meeting with the twelve people who had given them justice for their beloved Jill.

It was over, for now. Ahead lay years of court hearings and legal wrangling as an appeal, automatic in a capital case, would make its painstakingly slow progress through the system. But for now, justice was done. Jeff Cahill had taken a life, and for that he would forfeit his own.

16

Thou Shalt Not Kill

It was the indelible image of Jill's children frozen in fear and horror at what they had witnessed, too scared to move when she begged them to call 911, and of her desperate last moments of consciousness when she'd used every ounce of her depleted strength trying to fight him off that had persuaded Michelle Terry that her fellow jurors had it right. Jeff should explain himself to his Maker—sooner rather than later. She had been the last one prepared to spare him.

As she wrestled with her conscience, she'd thought of the thousands of battered and brutalized women who had suffered like Jill, and how she could send a message to the Jeffs of this world that they would be held accountable. For the final hour of deliberations she had prayed, and prayed some more. And then she knew what to do; let Jeff Cahill beg God for forgiveness and mercy, because this jury was going to show him none.

"I was shocked," said Debbie. "I thought it would be life without parole. I don't know if I could have made that decision. It was the saddest thing." Then her thoughts flew to the children: how on earth could they be expected to cope with having their father executed?

At his sentencing on October 5, Debbie talked to her brother-in-law for the first time since he'd taken a bat to her sister's head. "Why did you murder Jill?" she asked him. "What in the world did you think you'd accomplish by killing Jill? You turned our family's lives into a living nightmare. . . . The vicious, cowardly beating with Tim's baseball bat wasn't enough for you though, was it? Just when Jill was on her way back to us you had to finish the game. . . .

"Look what you've done to your family, your parents, brothers, uncles, nieces and nephews. The Cahill name will forever be associated with the cold-blooded murder you committed. Most importantly, what about Tim and Mary? They have to live with the haunting memories of April twenty-first; the sound of a baseball bat shattering their mother's skull, her pleas to them for help. Only they know the guilt they must feel because they couldn't help her. . . . Did you think of them at all? Did you, for one minute, stop thinking about yourself and think about how their lives would be changed forever? You have selfishly ripped apart their entire world."

What made it almost unbearable, if anything could have made this ordeal worse, was their conclusion that her husband's parents and brother had gone to the house and done nothing to help her. Someone had taken the time to try to wipe up the mess; the cops had found a bucket and blood smeared washcloths in the sink, but they had not picked up a phone. Fred, June, and Debbie were at a loss to explain how they could have watched her moaning in agony, the blood draining out of her, with no one dialing 911.

"To this day we don't know when it started, how long she lay there and nobody's been able to figure that out," said Debbie. "Did it start at midnight? How could you walk into that scene and not get help right away?" Something else rankled her. Two days after the assault Patty Cahill told her, "It's God's will."

"If Jim Cahill had not gone for Dr. Kelly, Jill would have died on that kitchen floor," said Fred. "When he arrived he was appalled at what he found, Jeff sitting in the living room with his mother holding his hand. And a few feet away was such a scene of savagery, blood literally running down the walls. After taking on board the incredulous fact that no one had called 911, Dr. Kelly called himself. He saved her life."

All this was raging through Debbie's mind as she addressed Jeff and his family across the courtroom.

"As difficult as this trial has been, it gave us the opportunity to learn so much. We have never seen such total disregard for human life as in those early hours of April twenty-first. To leave Jill, the mother of your children, a daughter-in-law, a sister-in-law, lying on the floor, bleeding to death; that no one called for an ambulance is absolutely despicable. On that morning, where were those Christian beliefs we've heard such righteous testimony to?

"Jill hid her pain from us for so long. Jill never had a bad word to say about you . . . . She felt terrible about hurting you, but she just could not live with the unhappiness any longer. She wanted her family to have a future. She ignored our advice to not go back to the house. . . . Jill truly believed you would never hurt her because you loved Tim and Mary too much. Even she was blind to your evil.

"We promised Jill . . . that we would take care of Tim and Mary. We were granted custody . . . as a result of evaluations of both families by the many professionals involved whose only concern is for their well-being. . . .

"When they came to us in July they were two hurt, angry, confused children. They still are in a lot of pain and have a difficult time dealing with what's happened because, as Tim says, 'It hurts too bad.' They are two courageous kids who are fighting as valiantly as their mother did. They smile, they laugh, they hug and they are making friends. They are no longer repressed little soldiers. Tim and Mary are being loved and protected by our entire family.

"We're not here to tell you we hate you, we're sure you couldn't care less. We would like you to take these thoughts with you when you leave today. While you're sitting in your seven-by-nine-foot cell, twenty-three hours a day, think about the trips you won't be taking to Austin Park or Cape Cod, think how you'll never kick another soccer ball with Tim or watch Mary blossom into a beautiful, talented woman like her mother. Justice will truly be served if you suffer every day for the rest of what's left of your life, the same excruciating pain you've given all of us who truly loved Jill."

Richard Priest had immediately wanted the sentence overturned, hanging his objection on the jury foreperson's overnight hospitalization and the morphine she was allegedly given while there. But without any affidavits from Michelle Terry or her doctors that proved she was given the drug and was unfit to serve, it was a waste of breath. Two days after Debbie had vented at her brother-in-law, Judge Burke sentenced Jeff to 12 1/2 to 25 years for the assault and two 1-year stretches on the weapons charges, and signed the warrant for his execution. Jeff was spirited away at dawn from the Onondaga County Justice Center and transferred to the Clinton Correctional Facility in Dannemora, to live out the remainder of his limited days on death row.

It must have been an unspeakable moment for the former Ivy Leaguer when he shuffled, his ankles shackled, into the Unit for Condemned Persons where he would live until he would be carted off to Death House, the Capital Punishment Unit at Green Haven State Prison, where he would be strapped to a gurney to await, fittingly, an infusion of deadly poison.

Compared to his new digs, the Justice Center in Syracuse was a luxury hotel. The rules here were very different. The operation of the C.P.U. was criticized by the American Bar Association as "unnecessarily harsh," in a 2002 report, "Dying Twice."

Each of the C.P.U.'s twelve cells contains a toilet, sink, bed, mattress and pillow, no air-conditioning or fans and, lights blaze for twenty-four hours a day. (This was modified a couple of years ago when infrared lamps were installed for night.) The white-painted cells are monitored around the clock by surveillance cameras and microphones. At the back of each there is a stainless-steel shower stall, the entrance to which is operated electronically by guards. Three meals a day are pushed through a slot in the door. No packages are allowed and death row occupants cannot have a job and therefore have no cash to spend at the commissary. Ten-minute calls to an immediate family member or religious adviser have to be approved and made on a mobile phone provided by the prison, and a staffer must dial the number. Visitors are prevented from any kind of physical contact by a thick Plexiglas shield that forces both prisoner and guest to shout to make themselves heard. Inmates are subjected to random checks and searches.

Here there would be no posse of basketball buddies for Jeff to organize into teams. Exercise is a solitary business, one hour a day in a 2000-square-foot "dog-run." Unlike members of the general prison population, condemned prisoners are not allowed to buy from the commissary. That their son-in-law was facing such deprivations was music to the Russells' ears.

POSTSCRIPT

At the beginning of November 1999, with the thirty-day deadline about to expire, Jeff's lawyers filed notice of appeal. Acknowledging that the process would take years, Bill Fitzpatrick pointed out that no matter the outcome, there was one thing not in dispute. Jeff Cahill murdered his wife. To date, his defense had cost New York taxpayers over $400,000 and the Capital Defender's Office had estimated that that total could go substantially higher.

On February 6, 2000, Jill's hometown held its own fundraiser for her children, featuring an auction, where bidders vied for items donated by local football and hockey teams, including a Buffalo Bills football jersey autographed by quarterback Jim Kelly, items signed by the Bills' Doug Flutie, hockey sticks autographed by the Buffalo Sabres and a weekend at Niagara-on-the-Lake. The event, dubbed "Open Your Heart," which took place at the American Legion Post on Main Street, Tonawanda, raised $40,000 to help the family defray education and legal costs.

In the years that followed, Jeff Cahill settled into his new surroundings and just how well he acclimatized dismayed Jill's family. "The fact that you can take a death row inmate," said Debbie, "and put him in an isolated room where nobody touches him, he doesn't have to deal with the rest of the prison population, he doesn't have to wake up every morning wondering what's going to happen—he had a very good life. I loved that he had adapted to it, he was very happy. The whole judicial system is ridiculous in New York State. He was going to Masses every Sunday, he was doing his penance."

For their part, Jill's family were consumed with raising her children and getting back some semblance of the anonymity they'd known before the whole nightmare erupted. There was one piece of business still to be taken care of. Just a week before a trial was due to start in New York Supreme Court, they settled the wrongful death suit. In January 2003, The Doyle Group, the company responsible for security at University Hospital, agreed to ante up $850,000. After costs, approximately $500,000 was invested in annuities on behalf of Mary and Tim to pay for college tuition and to give them an income for the rest of their lives.

But just when they thought it was finally over, there was one more shock to absorb. During the ongoing litigation with Doyle, the Russells' lawyer, Tom Shannon, disclosed that just a few days after the assault, Jeff's lawyer had arranged for him to see a psychiatrist at the hospital where he was barred from ever setting foot by restraining order. He made five scheduled visits to Dr. Wendy Armenta, whose office was two floors away from where his wife lay helpless, and popped in a number of other times to deliver cards and gifts to her. On the morning of the day he murdered Jill, he'd stopped by to give his shrink a birdhouse.

It was a gut-churning revelation that took even Bill Fitzpatrick by surprise. "I knew he was seeing a psychiatrist, but I did not know that he was in any way at the hospital," he said.

For the rest of that year an army of lawyers were busy haggling over what would be presented to the Court of Appeals in Albany. Although his office cooperated with the state's Capital Defender's Office attorneys, Fitzpatrick wasted no time in second-guessing his decision to seek the death penalty for Jeff Cahill. The terror Jill must have felt when she woke to find him bending over her, and the subsequent hell her family endured, never left him. He lost no sleep over her killer's pending execution.

As he had predicted on the courthouse steps after the sentencing phase of the trial, the process slowly ground through the system until it came before New York's highest court, the Court of Appeals, on September 22, 2003. In an 800-page brief, the defense scared up thirty-eight reasons for tossing the sentence, including Judge Burke's handling of Michelle Terry's collapse and the prosecution's stance that Jeff Cahill had unlawfully entered Jill's hospital room as a prelude to killing her. But the main issue was the New York statute that lets a convicted murderer eventually go free if a jury is torn between the death penalty and life without parole.

Jeff was represented by the CDO's Chief District Attorney and Syracuse University professor of constitutional law, James Maxwell; Bill Fitzpatrick and Rick Trunfio made the case for the People. Special interest factions like the New York Civil Liberties Union and anti–death penalty groups were also allowed a say. Ironically, on the panel was Chief Judge Judith Kaye, who, in tandem with Westchester District Attorney Jeanine Pirro, and with great fanfare, had set up the state's first Combined Felony and Misdemeanor Domestic Violence Court in White Plains, NY, in 2001.

The court came back with its decision on November 26, 2003, five years after Jill was murdered. In a 63-page ruling, it tore up the warrant of execution and ordered Jeff to be re-sentenced to 25 years to life with the possibility of parole. In explanation, the majority held that Jeff Cahill had meant to kill his wife, but dismissed the idea that silencing her was the underlying motive. They also took issue with the inclusion of one juror who had admitted to a domestic altercation of his own and the exclusion of another who said she could not vote for the death penalty.

Debbie learned of the ruling when Bill Fitzpatrick reached her while she was shopping for Christmas presents in T.J. Maxx. She called Fred and Joan. To all of them it was a heartbreaking, asinine decision. As far as they were concerned, the jurors in Syracuse had listened to days of testimony and had gotten it right. Now all their soul-searching was being thrown out the window by a clutch of judges who'd listened to just five hours of argument. Where was the fairness and legality in that? Everybody was so concerned about Jeff Cahill's rights. Didn't he trade those in when he murdered their daughter? Didn't these fools read what he had actually done to her?

It seemed to them that the Appeals Court didn't give a damn about Jill, her months of suffering, the loss of her children or even her painful and terrifying death. Although they had heard just a fraction of the evidence, they had bought the cheap soap opera line that he'd killed her because he couldn't bear his marriage being over, the baseball bat attack proved that, they said. The opinion flew in the face of Jeff Cahill's own submission that he'd performed a "mercy killing." It was both cruel and insulting.

To rub salt into the gaping wound, they had opened the door to let Jeff eventually resume his life. And the thought that this man would ever go free appalled not only Jill's family, but everyone in the Onondaga County District Attorney's

Office. "The decision was sickening," said Bill Fitzpatrick. "It was preordained, there was nothing we could have said that would have made a difference. It was a political decision foisted on us, replete with illogical assertions and inconsistencies, and relies for its foundation on some obscure case in Arkansas rather than the jurisprudence of the forty-eight other states."

The way he saw it, the court had no grounds for knocking back the verdict, since the trial had gone without a hitch. That left them two alternatives, one, to declare the death penalty unconstitutional—which they were not prepared to do, since it would have opened a can of political worms—or two, to decide that Cahill was guilty of a lesser charge. According to Fitzpatrick, they had literally made up the law.

"What they said was that if you have the intent to steal a pen from her hospital room and kill her, it's Murder One. If you have the intent to go in and kill her and then go in and kill her, that's not Murder One. So what the New York Court of Appeals did was make premeditated murder, which everyone thinks is a capital offense, not a capital offense." The bottom line was that Jeff would be eligible for parole in twenty-one years. The three dissenting judges were just as outspoken in their criticism of the decision.

Dick Priest broke the news to Jeff by phone. "He was relieved. He broke down a little," the attorney told the local paper, which also reported that many citizens of Skaneateles were angered by the court's ruling.

The Resentencing

Two days before her brother-in-law was resentenced, Debbie became the first private citizen to address a judicial confirmation in the state capital of Albany where she asked lawmakers to strengthen the death penalty law to avoid peremptory challenges like the one that had sent her family reeling.

The meeting was spurred by Dave Grant, her boss at Praxair where she has worked for 29 years. He had called her home outraged by the court's decision and arranged for her to meet with Senators Dale Volker, George Maziarz and Assemblywoman Robin Schimminger in the company's conference room. They agreed to help her change the law. Senator Maziarz told her that Senator John DeFrancisco, the head of the Judicial Committee, had invited her to speak at the confirmation hearing as a victim of the flawed Death Penalty Law.

On January 13, Debbie and Mallory went to Albany. The following day, their train back to Buffalo left five hours late and they didn't get home until 5:30 A.M. She just had time to shower and have breakfast before leaving for Syracuse that afternoon for Jeff's resentencing.

On January 14, 2004, nearly six years after he'd beaten their daughter senseless, Joan, Fred and Debbie had to face her killer one more time. "Well, James Francis Cahill the Third, here we are again. Just hearing your name sickens us," began Joan, trembling with pent-up fury as she began to read the letter she had composed to him. She recalled fearing for Jill's safety and being assured by her that Jeff loved his children too much to do anything so cruel, the call from Patty Cahill and the state troopers telling them to hurry because she wouldn't last five hours, and also directed her anger at his family. "Jill was under the name of Jane Doe in the hospital because nobody went with her to the E.R.," she said, nearly breaking down.

"What does God think of you now?" she asked, looking straight at him. "Thou shalt not kill, that's one of the Ten Commandments, isn't it? So much for your holier-than-thou Catholic upbringing. It certainly didn't do you any good, did it?" She wanted to set the record straight: Jill was not comatose in the last two months of her life, as some newspapers had reported. When one of the rehab staff had said to her, "Oh, Jilly, we've been so worried about you," she had replied: "I'm going to be OK."

"You do not deserve to ever see Tim and Mary. I wish we could keep you from writing to them, especially after your last birthday card to Mary. It was sick and pretty raunchy and totally inappropriate for a fourteen-year-old girl." With one last disgusted glance in her son-in-law's direction, she pleaded with the judge to throw the book at him.

Debbie told him that having his children with her and Bill was like having a part of Jill live on. "We celebrate their accomplishments and every smile from their beautiful faces is a little victory." She told him the kids never replied to his letters, not because of anything Jill's family said—they had resolved be as fair as was humanly possible—but because it was too hurtful. "If you haven't figured out in the last five years what they need from you as a father, I doubt you ever will," she said. "What they don't need to know is your favorite TV show, or their cousins are taking Irish step dancing or who is going to the Cape this summer. That's a sad reminder of the life you made them leave behind. The only thing Tim and Mary are looking for from you is to get on with their lives and forget the horror of what you did and to hear that you will never be a threat to them.

"And I want to set the record straight to those judges on the Appeals Court who bought the line that Jeff Cahill was a broken man. . . . It was a fact of the agreement that both Jeff and Jill signed, that he would get joint custody of the children and the family house. Jill was walking away from a marriage that was over, with joint custody and the loose change in her pockets. I don't know many divorced fathers who got as much after a divorce as Jeff Cahill."

She expressed her anger at the Court of Appeals' decision. This was the latest time her sister had been let down by a justice system that had allowed Jeff Cahill to walk around on bail, by the ineptitude of the DeWitt police who didn't follow up why Mark Cahill's car was picking up cyanide and by the people who'd let Jeff wander around University Hospital five days after he had nearly taken Jill's head off with a bat.

Debbie's only consolation was that Jeff would be moved into the general prison population. "I hope you wake up every morning in fear, just as Jill was for six months," she told him.

Bill Fitzpatrick's remarks were aimed not just at the judge, but at a future parole board who might be tempted to leniency. "Little things tell a lot about a man's character," he said. "When they hear you shoplifted, they might say, 'He was down on his luck, his business was not doing well, he stole to get food for his children. He stole lobster to sit down to a lobster dinner while his children were eating cereal.'" Fitzpatrick said he doubted Jeff Cahill would ever enlighten Jill's family as to why he murdered her. "He can't tell, that's why he killed Jill, to stop her telling a jury what they had argued over the night he beat her, the secret she took to her grave would have exposed him for what he is."

He'd beaten her so badly that the doctors were at a loss to decide how many times he'd hit her, Fitzpatrick said. "Her beautiful blonde hair was streaked with blood like a mop as he hauled her into his own kitchen, where the arc of blood hit the ceiling. And he'd done all this in front of his children, then had the gall to argue that he should not be put to death because he was a good father." He asked the parole board to look at the picture of Jill with the gouge marks on her chin and to know the last waking thing she saw on this earth was him prying open her mouth to force her to swallow cyanide. "Let him be carried out of prison in a pine box and let him confront his Maker. There will be no lawyers, no judges, no Appeals Court, just his God."

Fitzpatrick lashed out at the court that had decided what Jeff Cahill did was not heinous enough to warrant a lethal injection. "If no one is ever going to be put to death, we have a right to know as prosecutors in his state. I could have spared this family five years in addition to what they are going through." Then he threw in a heartfelt plea: "I beg that parole board not to let this Trojan Horse of evil to be allowed out of whatever prison he is in."

Despite the venom zinging his way, Jeff sat motionless, unmoved, an arrogant smirk occasionally flitting across his face, just as he had at his trial. Nor did he flex a muscle when Dick Priest rose and launched into a statement that brought tears of rage to replace the Russells' tears of anguish. He apologized for his client, who declined the judge's offer to speak on his own behalf. "I have brought great pain, suffering and loss to Jill's family. Nothing I can say or do will ever replace the sadness in their lives. Every day I share in that sadness." Then he quoted Jeff as feeling sorry for his kids and in a last skewer to Jill he claimed they were "the truly innocent victims of this tragedy."

But if Jeff was looking to Judge Aloi to cut him some slack and let him serve out his sentences concurrently, he was out of luck. His Honor was clearly livid at having to even contemplate the possibility that one day he would be freed.

"Mr. Cahill, when I look at you, I see a coward. You are an evil man, one who has committed a series of evil and unimaginable acts," the judge started. "I think it is ironic that you took Jill's life and now got away with yours. You deserve no mercy and you deserve never to be paroled. You, Mr. Cahill, turned that safe haven into her execution chamber. You imposed your own death sentence on the mother of your two children and now you have escaped that very death sentence." Without further ado, Aloi sentenced Jeff to 25 years to life for the murder and to 12 $\frac{1}{2}$ years for the assault. The sentences were to run consecutively. It was the maximum the law allowed, 37 $\frac{1}{2}$ years to life.

It went some way to comforting the Russells. "The judge got it right," said Debbie. "We don't have to deal with this man for thirty-seven years. In five years he has shown no remorse, all he talks about is what TV he's watching, music he likes, he's feeding a little bird outside his window."

To make sure Jill did not die in vain, Debbie and her parents have worked tirelessly with the district attorney's office to try to enact a law to mandate that spouses who brutally batter their partners "sit their butts in jail until they have their day in court." "We need a judge to be able to consider future actions when he's considering bail," she said. In May 2004, the New York State Senate passed Jilly's Law. It is currently with the Codes Committee, and if it makes it through it will go to the full assembly for ratification.

Jilly's Law allows a judge to take the following into account when issuing or denying bail:

- Is the defendant a danger to the alleged victim, anyone else or to him or herself?
- Has any order of protection ever been issued against him/her or has he/she made violent threats against the alleged victim or others?
- The nature of any criminal record.
- The nature of the act of violence against the alleged victim and the consequences of the crime to the victim.
- Any other relevant circumstance.

Six years have passed since Jill Cahill died. Jeff Cahill is now in Comstock Prison near Albany, New York. Kevin (Howdy) Cahill has moved out of his parents' home and Patty spends much of her time in Cape Cod. Halloween, which had always been one of Jill's favorite holidays, has become one where Joan and Fred Russell mask their grief and stifle their thoughts of what might have been, so as not to spoil the excitement of their grandchildren as they dress up for trick-or-treating. They are comforted only by their many happy memories of Jill, and by her children, who continue to do well with the unconditional love and support of Debbie and Bill. They are constant reminders of her.

Like Tom Tulloch, who moved to Texas to get away from the painful surroundings of Skaneateles and has since married, Dave Russell is still haunted by Jill's death. "Every day I think about it. How our life could have been. . . ." Her murder has aged the parents Jill loved and who would have crawled into bed and traded places with her in a heartbeat, if that had been in their power. Joan spends many days overcome with sadness. "I go over it every day since I walked into that hospital," says Fred. "There's no such thing as closure—it's a rotten word."